THE GLOBAL POWER OF TALK

THE GLOBAL POWER OF TALK

NEGOTIATING AMERICA'S INTERESTS

FEN OSLER HAMPSON AND
I. WILLIAM ZARTMAN

Paradigm Publishers
Boulder • London

Copyright © 2012 Paradigm Publishers

Published in the United States by Paradigm Publishers, 2845 Wilderness Place, Boulder, CO 80301 USA.

Paradigm Publishers is the trade name of Birkenkamp & Company, LLC, Dean Birkenkamp, President and Publisher.

Library of Congress Cataloging-in-Publication Data

Hampson, Fen Osler.
The global power of talk : negotiating America's interests / by Fen Osler Hampson and I. William Zartman.
    p. cm.
  Includes bibliographical references and index.
  ISBN 978-1-59451-942-0 (hardcover : alk. paper)—ISBN 978-1-59451-943-7 (pbk. : alk. paper)
  1. United States—Foreign relations. 2. United States—Foreign relations—1989–
3. Diplomatic negotiations in international disputes. I. Zartman, I. William. II. Title.
JZ1480.H36 2011
327.73—dc23

                                                                              2011021285

Printed and bound in the United States of America on acid-free paper that meets the standards of the American National Standard for Permanence of Paper for Printed Library Materials.

Designed and Typeset by Straight Creek Bookmakers.

16 15 14 13 12   1 2 3 4 5

CONTENTS

PREFACE

Talk Power is the power of negotiation when used skillfully and well. It is a vital but underutilized tool of statecraft in the post-9/11 world. It should be a key instrument for promoting global economic and political security in an era where there are obvious limits to the use of military power in dealing with the multiple problems of terrorism, rogue states, failed states, intractable conflicts, nuclear proliferation, and the continuing fallout from the global economic crisis of 2008–2009. How precisely should Talk Power be used? This book argues that an extraordinarily rich variety of Talk Power tools can be deployed to deal with the many global challenges that the United States now confronts. The challenge for US foreign policy is to make effective use of the different tools in its negotiation toolbox to advance its interests and promote global security.

Since the first Gulf War of 1991, the United States has relied heavily on *Gun Power* to advance its core national interests when the right mix of Talk Power tools and instruments could have sometimes achieved better results at vastly lower cost. Today, at a time when fiscal and debt pressures loom large and US capacities to project its military power abroad are increasingly constrained, diplomacy will take center stage and be central to US engagement in the world. Talk Power has a critical role to play here if US diplomacy is to be effective and ensure US primacy.

Understanding the key lessons of the successful application of Talk Power is a crucial first step in advancing US interests, power, and standing in the world. As we argue in this book, Talk Power is not an instrument for the weak, inept, or faint of heart. It offers a set of tools that, when used skillfully and nimbly as part of sustained and coherent diplomatic offensive, can make America strong. Throughout much of the Cold War and occasionally afterward, America's power and standing in the world derived from its adept and timely use of Talk Power to advance its national interests, thwart rivals, squash enemies, court allies, defuse regional and global tensions, and effectively manage a succession of international crises. In the second decade of the twenty-first century, America's challenge is to relearn from this legacy and deploy its full arsenal of Talk Power tools to deal with the many global challenges it now confronts.

In writing this book, we have tried to popularize some of the key concepts that come from more than forty-five years of systematic study and research on negotiation and international negotiation processes in the hope of making some of the key ideas about the "what, where, and how" of negotiation accessible to a wider audience. Much of this research has been led by the Processes of International Negotiation Program, founded by Howard Raiffa, which for many years resided at the International Institute of Applied Systems Analysis in Vienna and has now moved to Clingendael (the Netherlands Institute of International Affairs). We would like to express our thanks to our many friends and colleagues whose work and keen insights we have greatly benefited from in the course of writing this book.

We also would like to thank Isabelle Talpaing-Long and Simon Palamar, who provided invaluable research assistance and editorial guidance in preparing the manuscript.

As we were completing this book, we were dismayed to learn that the United States Institute of Peace, a nonpartisan, Congressionally funded "think" and "do" tank, which is America's premier institute committed to the study, research, and practice of diplomacy, might fall victim to budget cuts just after it had moved into its stunning new headquarters facing the State Department and Lincoln Memorial on the Washington Mall. This would be a tragedy of mammoth proportions and, to say the least, would damage America's standing and reputation in the world. The Institute has been blessed to have been led by some of America's leading diplomats and practitioners—individuals who have successfully advanced America's interests and standing in the world through the successful use of Talk Power. We are therefore pleased to dedicate this book to them: Sam Lewis, who served as the Institute's president until 1993; Richard Solomon, who succeeded him; and Chester Crocker, who until recently was a chair of the Institute's board of directors.

PART I
TALKING

CHAPTER I
TALK POWER FOR THE TOUGH-MINDED

Men nowadays are becoming more and more convinced that any
disputes which may arise between nations must be resolved by negotiation and agreement, and not by recourse to arms.
—John Paul II, *Pacem in Terris,* 1963, Para 126

You can do a lot with diplomacy, but of course you can do a lot
more with diplomacy backed up by firmness and force.
—Kofi Annan, *New York Times,* February 23, 1998

This book challenges two myths: that when America chooses the diplomatic
path and tries to negotiate with its enemies it does so out of weakness, and that
to stay the strong, sole-standing superpower, the United States has to rely above
all on its military might. It is negotiation or Talk Power, as we argue in this
book, that when wielded wisely is the most used and the most powerful tool
in America's arsenal. Negotiation is getting something by giving something,
and in international conflicts it is the search for solutions that meet the foreign
policy goals of one country while giving enough to another to motivate it to
keep its promises. It is a tool that can be used to advance America's interests,
amplify America's power and standing in the world, and win back old friends
who have lost faith in its leadership. It is a tool that can forge new alliances to
deal with today's new security threats. In short, it is a tool that can do, and on
occasion has done, much to advance America's global positions and the cause of
world peace. Talk Power is not the refuge of the weak. On the contrary, it is the

fine-honed instrument of the hard-headed and tough-minded who understand its uses, purpose, and limitations.

Military force may win wars; diplomacy ends them. These days, the use of military force usually ends in a stalemate, and when it does better than that, its result is not to eliminate conflict but rather to create a new conflict situation, sowing the wind and reaping the whirlwind. It takes large doses of diplomatic talk and negotiation to clean up afterwards. When violent confrontations end in deadlock, this often sets the table for negotiation. Sometimes deadlock is necessary. Terrorists and rebels need to feel it before they abandon unrealistic goals and work to meet their opponents in the middle. But when force has done its job, the diplomat moves in to end violence and return peoples' lives to normalcy. It takes diplomatic talk and negotiation to put a house in shambles back in order.

Cuba

No president understood this better than John F. Kennedy. Fifty years ago Kennedy faced the biggest crisis since World War II. On October 14, 1962, following a botched American attempt to land at the Bay of Pigs to overthrow the Communist regime of Fidel Castro, Kennedy received word that the Soviets were deploying nuclear-armed, offensive missiles on Cuban soil. Within weeks, the Soviets would be able to attack America's cities and military bases without warning. America would become Russia's hostage or worse unless the president acted fast and decisively.

In the days that followed, President Kennedy met with his advisors in the White House to consider his options. His top general, Curtis LeMay, head of the US Strategic Air Command, and others, argued emphatically that America should take swift and decisive military action. A knock-out punch by US air power would eliminate the threat and send a powerful message that the United States was not about to give in to the Soviet Union. But some of the president's other advisors, including Secretary of Defense Robert McNamara, were not so sure. They worried that a preemptive strike against Soviet missile installations in Cuba could lead to World War III and nuclear Armageddon if the Soviets decided to retaliate. At the very least, the Soviets might be emboldened to seize West Berlin, a British, French, and American enclave deep inside East Germany behind the iron curtain.

From October 16 to October 22, 1962, President Kennedy and his closest advisors thrashed out, in secret, the problem of how to deal with the missiles. During those deliberations, six basic options were put on the table: (1) doing nothing; (2) diplomatic pressure; (3) a secret approach to Cuban leader Fidel Castro; (4) invasion; (5) a surgical air strike; and (6) a naval blockade. Ultimately, Kennedy chose a mixed approach of blockade and diplomacy, negotiated within those limits, and achieved his goals of avoiding war.

On Monday, October 22, the president went on national television to break the news to the world and announce the immediate imposition of a naval "quarantine," to prevent the shipment of missiles to Cuba and pressure the Soviets to remove the ones already installed. At the same time, he launched a vigorous diplomatic offensive to deal with the crisis. He secured the formal support of the Americas' hemispheric organization, the Organization of American States (OAS), and then of the United Nations. He opened negotiating channels to probe Soviet intentions and show how their actions threatened their own vital interests. Working against the clock, he drew a proposal from Soviet leader Premier Nikita Khrushchev, and under the pressure of time the two were rapidly able to strike a face-saving agreement: The Soviets agreed to withdraw their missiles and nuclear warheads from Cuba in exchange for a US promise not to invade Cuba, and a side deal sweetener on the removal of US nuclear-armed Jupiter missiles from Turkey (already decided by the United States). Kennedy then praised Khrushchev for having avoided war. President Kennedy's superior negotiating skills clearly won the day, defusing a major crisis that could have become World War III.

It is worth stopping a moment here to consider the elements of the joint diplomatic victory. Each side gave diplomacy its "best effort" by being prepared to give something in order to get something to defuse the crisis. Coercive diplomacy or Tough Talk was complemented by reassurance and positive inducements, or Sweet Talk. However, President Kennedy offered inducements to the Soviets only after he had limited Soviet options through the naval blockade, making it clear as day to Khrushchev that his actions would lead to war if he did not comply with US demands. When he did, he was rewarded, in terms of his own interests. Tough Talk backed by US military power preceded Sweet Talk.

What is also important to note is that there was deep presidential engagement in these negotiations and a serious personal commitment to exploring with the Soviets what was possible and acceptable to both sides. Kennedy also worked the clock to his advantage. There was a finite bargaining period, a clear deadline, and a threat to resort to arms in the absence of a satisfactory response. International legitimacy for firm action was obtained through the support of international organizations, both regional and global. And, as a coda, the side that gained more thanked and congratulated the other.

Georgia

Fast forward forty years to the beginning of this century. On August 8, 2008, Russia invaded the neighboring break-away provinces of Abkhazia and South

Ossetia in the independent Republic of Georgia in the Caucasus. The boundary the Russian army crossed had been established by the Soviet Union before Georgian independence in 1990, but the Russian army did not stop at the provincial boundaries; it penetrated 40 kilometers into Georgia, occupied the crossroads city of Gori, and threatened the capital of Tbilisi and the strategic Baku-Tbilisi-Ceyhan pipeline running through it. The Georgian army was whipped, Russia lost respect before broad international condemnation, ethnic cleansing swept the two areas, and the specter of the Cold War overshadowed East-West relations. Careful negotiation could have done much to prevent the conflict, but it was used clumsily if at all.

The two decades after the collapse of the Soviet Union were filled with mixed policies and signals concerning the former republics of the USSR. By the beginning of the new millennium, Russian policy hardened into a goal of undoing the Soviet breakup wherever possible, but nowhere more pointedly than in Georgia, the home country of Josef Djugashvili (Stalin), where the seaside Abkhazia region was the summer resort for many Russians and the mountainous South Ossetia region was caught up in its own identity crisis. Some members of the post-Soviet Commonwealth of Independent States (CIS) viewed the collapse of the Soviet Union as a Russian defeat to be sealed by the extension of the Western alliance—North Atlantic Treaty Organization (NATO)—to the very doorstep of Russia. The republics of the former Soviet Union could not agree more; out from under the protection of the Soviet Union, they sought protection from the Western alliance and the United States. The result was that the republics next door to Russia joined NATO, and the candidatures of Ukraine and Georgia, also next door to Russia, were laid on the table for NATO membership. US ex–Cold Warriors were triumphant at the idea of carrying NATO to the doors of Russia, across the former satellites of Eastern Europe into the very republics that had constricted the USSR down to simply the Russian Federation.

The Republic of Georgia underwent a number of swings in its internal politics. Eduard Shevarnadze, Mikhail Gorbachev's foreign minister, acted as president until 2004, when Mikhail Saakashvili, a charismatic pro-Westerner, was elected president in a political revolt against Shevardnadze. He became the chosen ally of the democratic West and he denounced the Russian-backed secessionist movements in Abkhazia and South Ossetia, launching police operations to clean up both criminal and militant groups in the regions.

These actions were seen as a direct challenge to Russia and its interests in South Ossetia. In the early 1990s, Russia helped South Ossetia secure its de facto independence from Georgia and maintained close ties with the breakaway province ever since. In 1992, a four-member Joint Control Commission, made up of representatives from Russia, Georgia, and South and North Ossetia, was established to maintain a negotiated ceasefire in the region. A formal ceasefire agreement was concluded in Moscow on May 14, 1994. In accordance with the ceasefire agreement, Russia also established a "peacekeeping" force within South Ossetia. The truce, however, was an uneasy one. In June–August 2004, there were incursions by Georgian security forces into South Ossetia that Russia considered to be in violation of the earlier agreement. On November 5, a Russian-mediated meeting between Prime Minister of Georgia Zurab Zhvania and President of South Ossetia Eduard Kokoity was held in Sochi. Both parties agreed to a ceasefire and to withdraw all illegal armed formations from the conflict zone. However, in early 2005, President Saakashvili abandoned the Georgia–South Ossetia agreement. As relations deteriorated, Georgia launched police operations in the upper Kodori Valley of South Ossetia in attempt to restore "constitutional order" in the region.

Meanwhile, elsewhere on the international scene, events were evolving slowly in Kosovo, the breakaway province of Serbia in former Yugoslavia. Under NATO management since the breakdown of the Rambouillet negotiations and the bombing of Belgrade in 2000, Kosovo was handed to a conference presided by former Finnish President Martti Ahtisaari in 2007 for final disposition. Ahtisaari entered the negotiations with the conviction that independence was the only course available to avoid ethnic cleansing, ignoring other possibilities for autonomy of Kosovo's Serbian regions. When his mediation between Serbia and Kosovo failed, Kosovo declared its independence on February 17, 2008, (a unilateral action prohibited by the NATO mediation guidelines), and was promptly recognized by the United States and many other NATO members, to the stern warnings of Serbia's backer, Russia. Three days before US recognition, Russian President Vladimir Putin warned that recognition would bring increased Russian support for the separatists in Georgia.

A month later, President George W. Bush assured Saakashvili of his intent to press hard for Georgian entry into NATO, and a NATO meeting endorsed the proposal in principle, including Ukraine as well. As in the case of Kosovo, intermediate solutions, such as recognition of buffer status and special relationships short of full NATO membership in the Georgian case, were not considered. Before leaving the presidency to become prime minister, Putin established legal ties with the breakaway regimes in South Ossetia and Abkhazia. Russia violated Georgian airspace over the two regions in coming months, promising support against "aggression" for local populations and Russian citizens in the two regions and increased its "peacekeeping" force in Abkhazia; the Ossetian Georgians, in turn, geared up for more police action.

Despite the public US praise for Saakashvili, Secretary of State Condoleezza Rice in a visit in July warned Georgia privately not to provoke Russia, calling for a no-use-of-force pledge, and other high-level diplomatic officials continued to press for restraint in the following month. But the South Ossetians, encouraged by Russian support, stepped up the conflict, shelling Georgia proper from the shelter of the Russian peacekeepers and blowing up Georgian police traffic. On August 6, they fired again on Georgian villages; the next day Georgian troops moved into Tskhinvali to clear out the attackers, and the following day, Russian troops, tanks, and planes streamed into Georgia.

Diplomacy had failed and was seriously called into action only after the horse had been snatched from the stable. Thereafter, it took three days before French President Nicolas Sarkozy was able to broker a truce agreement, leaving large loopholes for the Russian troops to run through, and then another day before Secretary Rice was able to fill the breach and plug the holes with a revised agreement; always a difficult thing to accomplish when an initial accord has been reached. But it took another month before some of the Russians withdrew from Georgia proper back to Ossetia and Abkhazia, now recognized as independent states by Russia (and only two other countries in the world); Russian troops still remain years later despite the agreement to withdraw and leave only the "peacekeepers."

Where did negotiation go wrong? From the very beginning. The French saying, attributed to Talleyrand, *Pire qu'un crime, une faute* ("Worse than a crime, a blunder") captures the delicacy of diplomacy. At the turn of the millennium, the West began its blunder, stepping up its escalatory verbiage and challenging Russia at its doorstep with NATO membership offers for Georgia. Midway alternatives, such as special relationships within buffer zones, were blithely bypassed, and the bypass was repeated in dealing at the same time with Kosovo (the similarities were trumpeted by Moscow but vigorously denied in the West). Russia, of course, continued to blunder its way into the rebellious zones of a neighboring sovereign country, throwing down gauntlet after gauntlet. Filled with Western hype, the Georgian president picked them up; while in his right to try to quell rebellion in his northern provinces, he proceeded to blunder into direct military operations, thumbing Georgia's official nose against a neighboring army twenty-five times the size of his and ignoring repeated, if belated, calls for calm from Washington. An escalation of blunders produced their culmination in the brutal Russian aggression against a small sovereign neighbor.

Much of the negotiation until the point of invasion was public, with signals given on the airwaves, although they were repeated face to face between the Russian and American presidents in April. Thereafter, toning down the rhetoric on the Western side would have signaled to the East to tone down, too, as had previously been done on the contentious missile defense system in Poland and the Czech Republic. More concrete considerations of intermediate steps in negotiations over Kosovo and restraint in Georgia would have sent further signals. Direct Russian and American contacts over Georgia, as took place over Cuba, were not pursued.

From its position of strength, Russia bargained hard with top world leaders until a balanced but unimplemented agreement was reached. Western multilateral diplomacy worked at its best in ratcheting the agreement into acceptable shape, an unusual display of negotiation after the crime was committed and horse stolen.

Talk Power in the Twenty-First Century

This book is a study of the uses and purposes of negotiation and diplomacy in America's power projection capabilities in today's world. We argue that the power of negotiation, when used wisely, can transform difficult situations and further US interests, as President Kennedy showed in the Cuban missile crisis. When used badly or belatedly as the case of Georgia-Ossetia illustrates, problems can get a lot worse. We will highlight the conditions and consequences of the effective use of Talk Power in subsequent chapters of this book.

As we look to the many foreign policy and security challenges President Barack Obama and his advisors confront today we will explore the role that Talk Power can play to advance America's interests and promote global security. What kinds of diplomacy and bargaining strategies are appropriate for addressing current and future threats and security challenges? What can Americans and their president learn from past negotiations about how to deal with friends, enemies, and rivals? These are just some of the key questions we will take up.

Today, the United States confronts a wide assortment of different security challenges. They include the continuing threat of terrorism, renewed outbreaks of sectarian violence, the clash of cultures and religion, the ever-present danger of nuclear proliferation, the growth of transnational criminal networks, and so on. However, threat perceptions differ within the NATO alliance. For example, key European states have been at odds with the US about how to respond to civil unrest in the Middle East and North Africa and, as we saw earlier in this century, to US-led military interventions in Afghanistan and Iraq. The will and capacity for collective action have been diminished by these differences, along with a precipitous decline in defense spending as Western governments tighten their fiscal belts.

Although the terrorist attacks of September 11, 2001, were a watershed moment in history, many of the underlying causes of conflict in the twenty-first century have not changed. Consider, for example, the so-called clash of civilizations between the Islamic world and other cultures. While the members of al-Qaeda may be motivated by a common hatred of the United

States and the West, the societies that they spring from are struggling with much more basic issues: the tensions of modernization, including unequal wealth distribution and unmet expectations; suppressed democracy; internal ethnic divisions; and unstable neighborhoods. Anti-Western sentiments in an already explosive environment further underscore the complexity of current security challenges.

There are other developments that also pose a threat to political stability. A wave of democratic protest and civil unrest is sweeping through the Middle East and North Africa from Tunisia, to Egypt, to Libya, Yemen, Algeria, Jordan, Bahrain, Syria, and even Saudi Arabia. Some of the region's leaders have been toppled and more may follow with uncertain consequences for political stability in the region as a whole. Negotiations within these societies to set up a new order, as well as negotiations with key neighbors and allies, will be essential to ensure political stability and secure the pace of democratic reform.

In many parts of the world, state institutions lack political legitimacy. Public goods that Westerners take for granted, such as clean water, roads, and a security environment where citizens feel safe, are non-existent, localized, or in general short supply. Such structural weaknesses are the tinderbox for internal conflicts that draw in neighbors and call for protective external intervention. The "failed state index," developed by Fund for Peace and *Foreign Policy* magazine, finds that some sixty countries in the world are dysfunctional because the government does not effectively control its territory, provide basic services to its citizens, or protect against internal unrest.

Regional stability also continues to be compromised by those long-standing conflicts that fester and that largely remain "intractable"—interstate conflicts such as Israel-Palestine, Ethiopia-Eritrea, India-Pakistan, China-Taiwan, Morocco-Algeria, and the Korean peninsula, but also internal conflicts in places such as Euskadi, Sri Lanka, Sudan, Kurdistan, Pashtunistan, Somalia, the Kivus, or sectarian conflict in the Muslim world, to name just a few. Many of these conflicts have refused to succumb to repeated rounds of mediation or third-party efforts to broker some kind of lasting political settlement. They are breeding grounds for terrorism and a major source of international instability because of the obvious risks that these conflicts pose to their neighbors.

Great power rivalries are also coming back into fashion. Russia finds national cohesion in attempts to play its former Soviet role as a great power rival, now based on its oil resources. Rising global powers like China and India are beginning to flex their military and economic muscles. Neither directly challenges the primacy of US power as yet. Chinese security policy—even judged by the usual realist specifications—is remarkably phlegmatic; China is both an inwardly preoccupied, status-quo power with regional standing and a rising power that exhibits global ambitions. India, except for the continuing dispute with Pakistan over the future of Jammu-Kashmir, is almost entirely focused on its radical economic transformations and always-noisy democracy. But bigger mischief-makers are regional powers like Iran, North Korea, Pakistan, and Venezuela, who are playing power politics in ways that threaten to undermine regional and global stability.

What role does Talk Power play in dealing with these challenges? Our answer in this book is that it has the potential to do much, based on the evidence of past negotiations. This assessment stems from successful stories of state-building, peacemaking, and security management late in the last century that have yet to be fully told. It is a story of many different negotiations—some of which were effective, some not—aimed at transforming the global security environment in both good and bad ways. It is a story that has many acts, and many players and institutions in its cast.

In many of the world's conflicts over the past two decades, outside actors, including the United States, held the ring for negotiations, probed intentions, prodded combatants to resolve their differences, and played peacemaker when called upon. Recall the key role played by President Bill Clinton's envoy Richard Holbrooke who knocked heads and brought warring Muslims, Croatians, and Serbians together at the peace table to end the murderous wars in Bosnia and Croatia. Emissaries sent by presidents Ronald Reagan and George H. W. Bush also helped negotiate peace settlements that ended decades of conflict in Southern Africa, Cambodia, and elsewhere, and others sent by President George W. Bush helped reduce conflicts in Sudan and Korea. The United Nations, small countries like Norway, and even non-official organizations have also been important peacemakers and negotiators, working alongside and sometimes directly with the United States.

The bad news is that this enviable record of peacemaking in the late 1980s and 1990s was left to wither in several major lapses in US diplomacy, and in some regions established peace processes have been allowed to wilt. Nowhere was this failure more apparent than in the Middle East where, as we argue in the next chapter of this book, a series of diplomatic blunders laid the foundations for the uninhibited use of Gun Power with catastrophic results. In what is now an all but forgotten, yet sorry, episode the United States made a series of irreversible errors in its diplomatic dealings with Iraq prior to the onset of the first Gulf War in 1991—errors that represented a major missed opportunity to nip Saddam Hussein's imperial ambitions in the bud. Had the United States properly conveyed its interests and position to Saddam Hussein in negotiations, Iraq could have been deterred from invading Kuwait and the world would not have unfolded as it did.

America's handling of the Israeli-Palestinian conflict in the 1990s also represented a major missed opportunity to transform relations not just between Arabs and Israelis, but also America's relations with much of the Islamic world. The Israeli-Palestinian conflict fell victim to the "on-again, off-again" whims of US diplomacy as the interest (and attention) of different presidents in this conflict wavered. One of the biggest failures of diplomacy and negotiation, as we discuss in the next chapter, was the United States' failure to muster its mediation and muscle to maintain the momentum generated by the Madrid conference and the Oslo agreements in the early 1990s and then again to seize the initiative from al-Qaeda in the same theater of operations in the early 2000s. The United States did not push the peace process that it had invented.

This book explores the uses and limits of the power of negotiation and diplomacy in US foreign policy at a critical—if not decisive—juncture in the nation's history. America's friends, allies, rivals, and adversaries will all be influenced in some measure by the choices that the United States makes to secure its own future. It matters whether—working with its partners and key security institutions such as NATO and the United Nations—the United States has the energy, purpose, and constructive optimism to deal with its security challenges and to sustain its long-standing engagement in the search for a more peaceful and less threatening world. An alternative scenario in which US policies come to be viewed as exacerbating regional tensions and undercutting US influence could trigger an opposing mood of isolation, retrenchment, and reduced focus on a narrower, defensive agenda that tolerates or ignores foreign conflicts until they become direct threats. Rather than marching together, the world would fall apart. Events of the past decade have shown that military force alone cannot deal with the myriad problems of failed and failing states in the international system or the malaise that grows out of continued conflict in far parts of the globe. But the same is true for weak, confused, or ham-fisted diplomacy, which can also make problems worse and undermine US power and influence.

This book points to the need to resuscitate a key set of tools in America's strategic arsenal: the tools of negotiation, statecraft, and diplomacy. In the chapters that follow, we discuss how the United States can make more effective use of the different tools of Talk Power to restore its reputation and promote a safer and more secure world.

᛭

CHAPTER 2
HOW AMERICA LOST ITS WAY

IRAQ AND PALESTINE, AND THE FAILURE TO USE TALK POWER

> My fellow citizens, at this hour, American and coalition forces are in
> the early stages of military operations to disarm Iraq, to free its peo-
> ple and to defend the world from grave danger.... Now that conflict
> has come, the only way to limit its duration is to apply decisive force.
> And I assure you, this will not be a campaign of half measures, and
> we will accept no outcome but victory.
> —US President George W. Bush addresses the nation
> on the eve of the Iraq war, March 19, 2003

In late 2002 and early 2003 the United States sought remedy to what was
seen as an ongoing "Iraq question." Fears about weapons of mass destruction
(WMD) and about the potential for Iraqi President Saddam Hussein's desire to
reassert his role as the leading anti-US agitator in the post-9/11 world gripped
the attention of the George W. Bush administration. Flushed with a seemingly
speedy victory in toppling and replacing the Taliban regime in Afghanistan, the
foreign policy approach of regime change and sponsored democratization had
an increasingly vocal core of supporters in Washington. Vice President Dick
Cheney and Secretary of Defense Donald Rumsfeld argued emphatically that
America should take swift and decisive military action, along with several of
Bush's other advisors. It was believed that a massive display of US military power
would eliminate the threat posed by Hussein and send a powerful message that

the United States was on the path to install democracy in the Middle East—a cure-all that would restore stability in the region and eliminate the growing terrorist threat from Islamic fundamentalist groups. This view rode on the belief in the superiority of Gun Power, particularly as an approach to foreign policy concerns in the Middle East region.

For its part, diplomacy had been used in the UN Security Council (UNSC) for the previous ten years, in fact since the first Gulf War, to try to get a clear and unambiguous indication from Hussein that he did not possess the WMD capabilities he had once claimed. The UNSC had passed seventeen resolutions calling for a conclusive Iraqi response but had received only evasive answers.

In opting for Gun Power, some argue that the Bush administration rejected the pursuit of the negotiation option in ways that damaged US interests. In the UNSC, the United States rebuffed successive attempts by other Security Council members to secure another negotiated compromise that would have given Iraq still more time to meet its disarmament obligations while building support for the US position to take military action if Iraq continued to be noncompliant. The United States and its key ally in the invasion, the United Kingdom, sidelined the United Nations, embarking on a course of action that many deemed illegal under international law.[1] Perhaps more important than its legality, however, was the fact that ineffective diplomacy resulted in the United States losing the support of key allies and participants in both the invasion and the subsequent reconstruction of Iraq.

Many authors have sought to better understand the rationale for going to war in the first place. Arguments have varied widely in this regard.[2] For some, the Iraq war was an effort to remove an aggressive dictator and open the polity to democracy that got bogged down in implementation. For others, it represented a failure of government and the exercise of presidential leadership—whether in terms of communication between sectors of government (executive branch, intelligence, military, etc.) or in terms of proper policy analysis and ultimate execution. Still others have argued that the war was inspired by a misguided policy approach using military power as a way to deal with terrorists and to promote democracy by overthrowing autocratic regimes. Some have also seen economic imperialism as a key motivation—a US-liberated Iraq might better be able to provide the United States with immediate oil contracts and long-term resources needed for continued US economic growth.

This chapter, however, will take a somewhat different position: The roots of the Bush administration's policy decision can more accurately be found in previous failures of diplomacy and negotiation in the region. Why use Gun Power in March of 2003? We argue that an evolution of US policy in the Middle East that was never fully or even sufficiently committed to Talk Power solutions made Gun

Power approaches unavoidable. Furthermore, the ineffectiveness of ill-practiced Talk Power resulted in a misperceived sense that Talk Power could not and would not work and therefore a misguided faith in the supremacy of Gun Power. The approach of the United States in dealing with both the Iraq file before the first Gulf War and the Middle East Peace Process that followed is indicative of our argument that the use of Talk Power has long been shortchanged in US foreign policy in the Middle East.

While it may sound incredible to maintain that Talk Power could have stopped Saddam Hussein's invasion of Kuwait in 1990, the well-documented failures in coordinating and presenting clear diplomatic signals arguably led Hussein to underestimate US intent and resolve. Mixed messages from administrators, congressmen, and diplomats alike; ambiguous statements of praise and condemnation of Iraq; and weak, ephemeral statements in support of Kuwait all served to undermine the direction of the US position in the months leading up to war, dooming its ability to rely on Talk Power. Senators and ambassadors alike assured Hussein, personally, that inter-Arab relations were not the business of the United States. Had the opposite message been clearly expressed, Saddam Hussein might well not have carried out the invasion.

The response of the US-led international coalition to the Iraqi invasion of Kuwait has been touted as a significant move to counter aggression and protect states in the new world order. The massive projection of military power, and with absolutely minimal loss of life on the part of the interveners, seemed to demonstrate a new source of strength and opportunity for those seeking to maintain the status quo in international order. Such results, however, must be seen for what they truly were, a thin veneer of hubris covering over a monumental diplomatic failure. The first Gulf War was an enormously costly move, in budgetary and general economic terms; in terms of the lasting damage to Kuwaiti and Iraqi life and infrastructure; and, perhaps most seriously, in terms of its impact in setting up the subsequent decades as an era of Gun Power instead of Talk Power in the Middle East.

The Middle East saw another neglect of Talk Power in the last two decades of sporadic and lackadaisical pursuit of the Middle East Peace Process. After a splendid beginning, in the Madrid Phase (1991), which the United States engineered with major skill and effort, and the subsequent Oslo meetings (1993), wherein the United States had no direct role, a change in the principal political actors—in the United States, Israel, and Palestine—brought the Peace Process to a silent halt. The silence was broken at the last minute by Bill Clinton's theatrical but insufficient engagement into crisis diplomacy at Camp David. The silence returned under the new Bush administration, which waited for a year to distance itself from the process at Camp David before planning a new Mideast policy demarche. These plans, however, were cut short by the attacks of 9/11. Instead of moving ahead with its plans, recalling to the world that the United States was the inventor of the Peace Process, the Bush administration fell back into silence on the Middle East Peace Process, and moved ahead with an explosion of Gun Power in Afghanistan and Iraq.

The failure to pursue an actively engaged policy of Talk Power in the Middle East was not the cause of al-Qaeda's terrorism. The fanatics who hijacked the Muslim religion and lashed out against US-led globalization and their own corrupt and authoritarian regimes were and are largely beyond the reach of Talk Power either in their cause or in their control. But the revival of an active US diplomacy, both long before and after 9/11, would have put the United States in a far stronger position to combat the popularization of fanaticism and would have reclaimed the initiative from Osama Bin Laden and associates in the struggle for the hearts and minds of the Muslim Middle East.

The first Gulf War and the post–Cold War experience in the Middle East Peace Process are cases that illustrate two types of Talk Power that will be explored further in this book. One involves the use of diplomacy in dealing directly with an opponent. This use requires efforts to understand the other party and its fears and motives, clear messages of one's own intentions, and the use of both threats and promises to indicate the dangers of current courses and the benefits of changing directions. This is all standard stuff, the ingredients of normal engagement with an opponent.

The other type of Talk Power, however, involves an active role as an interested third party or Triple Talk. Most conflicts between two parties do not call for the involvement of a third; there is not enough interest or danger at stake to merit an outsider's interference in others' affairs. But when others' conflicts pose a real danger to the interests of a third-party bystander—especially when that bystander is a neighbor or a great or superpower—engagement finds its justification. Mediation can take one (or more) of three forms, depending on the obstacles that keep the conflicting parties from resolving their own conflict. If the barrier is an inability to communicate with each other, the intervener is needed as a facilitator or communicator, urging them on, carrying messages, holding meetings, but not putting itself or its ideas on the line. If the barrier is an inability to conceive of solutions, the mediator is needed as a formulator, bringing new ideas to the table, suggesting messages, playing a part in the solutions. If the barrier lies in the size of the outcome needed to attract both sides and overcome their risks, then the mediator is needed as a manipulator to sweeten the pot and provide guarantees and controls, a vital if risky role. An important implication is that a facilitator/communicator is not enough when the conflict is deep and the mediator's interests are wide. Committed engagement is needed, or else the involvement will fall through and the conflict will continue unabated or perhaps even escalate.

The two highly significant occasions of failure of the United States to appropriately use Talk Power in the Middle East at the end of the Cold War provided the foreign policy preconditions that culminated in the current troubles in that region. The failure to take a clear and active diplomatic position in regard to Iraq in 1990, as well as to the Middle East Peace Process from the second half of the 1990s onward, wrongly elevated the palatability of Gun Power as the only way to conduct foreign policy in the region.

Talk Power Versus Gun Power in Iraq, 1990–91

In the Iran-Iraq war (1980–88), the United States and several of the Arab states supported Iraq, viewing it as a bulwark against the more radical ideology of Ayatollah Khomeini's Iran. This support came in the form of weapons and weapon systems, access to low-cost loans and other financial assistance, access to US intelligence reports, and agricultural credits. When the war ended in August of 1988, the United States continued to pursue its good relations with Iraq, a state that it felt was crucial to the stability of the region.

Throughout these attempts at good relations, however, it is possible to see examples of the United States hedging its diplomatic bets as well as responding to political necessity in ways that undermined US-Iraqi relations. During the course of the Iran-Iraq war, the United States, while overtly supporting Iraqi war aims, was also covertly selling arms to Iran in what was to become known as the Iran Contra scandal. Following the end of the war, relations continued to strain as US investigators alleged that Iraq had been using funds granted for food aid to seek out sensitive nuclear technologies. Former Iraqi Foreign Minister Tariq Aziz also raised the issue of political interference on the part of the CIA, who Aziz claimed was attempting to incite Iraqis into overthrowing the Hussein regime. Public condemnations of Iraq's use of poison gas and torture against its own Kurds (with no mention of the use of the same weapons against the Iranians in the war) added to increasing tensions between the two states. This sort of diplomatic mixed-messaging was to become the norm of US relations with Iraq.

While diplomatic dealings had become somewhat strained in the months following the Iran-Iraq war, the US-Iraqi relationship remained one of importance to the US government. In recognition of this fact, and perhaps in response to increasing tensions, Assistant Secretary of State John Kelly paid a visit to Baghdad on February 12, 1990, bearing the message to Saddam Hussein that the United States wanted better relations with Iraq, encouraging it to be a "force of moderation" in the region. Indeed, while an argument can be made that the relationship had already become strained prior to Kelly's visit, it is in the subsequent months—following the tacit recognition by the United States that a rift was widening—that relations rapidly disintegrated.

For its part, Iraq had emerged from the war drained and depleted, having spent in excess of $500 billion on the war effort. Iraq owed Western lenders some $40 billion and Arab governments roughly the same amount. With a state budget based on an $18 barrel of oil, the rapid drop in the price of this commodity from $20.50 to $13 a barrel between January and June 1990 further tightened the fiscal crunch. Iraq was being regarded by banks as the world's worst credit risk, facing bankruptcy. Its debt to Arab states was held principally by its neighbors, Kuwait and Saudi Arabia, whom Saddam Hussein approached for debt forgiveness and a further $30 billion loan. When both requests were met with resistance, Iraq responded as a state not only wounded but also offended, believing that it had fought the war on behalf of all Arab states opposed to the Shi'ite fundamentalism advocated by the revolutionary Khomeini. Adding to Iraq's displeasure, Kuwait was slant-drilling into the Iraqi portion of the shared Rumaila oilfield, an affront for which Iraq eventually demanded $2.4 billion in compensation. Furthermore, Kuwait and the United Arab Emirates had exceeded their Organization of Petroleum Exporting Countries (OPEC) oil quotas, flooding the markets and thus driving down Iraq's revenues from its own oil. It was estimated that the depressed price of oil was costing Iraq roughly $1 billion a month—a considerable sum given Iraq's fiscal state. Probably the crowning insult was that Kuwait was an obnoxious, arrogant neighbor.

It was in this context that Iraq, or perhaps more accurately Saddam Hussein, began to follow a two-pronged strategic approach that ultimately led to the first Gulf War. On the one hand Hussein took aggressive stances toward his Arab neighbors in an attempt to compel from them the compensation he felt Iraq was owed for both the struggle with Iran as well as for the oil revenues lost to these states' questionable practices. On the other hand, Hussein sought to advance himself as a pan-Arab populist through anti-US and anti-Israeli rhetoric. This two-pronged strategy broke from the closer relations Iraq had enjoyed both with its neighbors and with the United States during the course of the Iran-Iraq war and represents a point when Talk Power could have been used effectively by the United States to remedy a growing rupture in the region. Hussein figured—correctly, in the short term—that the United States would not react and that his rhetoric would get him some Arab sympathies.

When faced with Arab neighbors who were resistant to his calls for leniency in the midst of a financial crisis, Hussein's response was typically bombastic and belligerent. His demands escalated with time and as Iraq's fiscal crisis deepened.

Leniency and loans gave way to demands for compensation for revenues lost. "Let the Gulf regimes know that if they do not give this money to me, I will know how to get it,"[3] he threatened in February 1990. As a result of Kuwait's deaf ear to his demands, he revived his claim on the neighboring emirate and his demand to at least be able to use or lease two Kuwaiti islands that effectively blocked the entry into Iraq's sole oil port, Umm Qasr. For the next six months his verbal attacks on Kuwait became more pointed and more vitriolic. In May, he denounced the Gulf States for waging economic warfare against Iraq, and in mid-July he harshly outlined his grievances and military threats against Kuwait.

In addition to crumbling relations between Iraq and its neighbors, similar tensions were escalating between Iraq and the United States. In order to attract greater support in the Arab world Hussein wrapped himself in an increasingly strident anti-American and anti-Israeli message. On February 24, he had demanded the withdrawal of US naval forces from the Gulf at an Arab Cooperation Council summit and called on all Arabs to resist "the imperialist-Zionist conspiracy."[4] He further drew the ire of the United States and the West in March with the execution of British journalist Farzad Barzoft on charges of spying for Israel. Hussein himself had assured British diplomats and politicians that Barzoft would receive a fair hearing. When closed-door proceedings took less than a day to determine Barzoft's guilt, British diplomats were recalled and several high-profile visits were canceled. Iraq also enflamed tensions with Israel when it installed permanent missile launchers that could strike targets in Israeli territory. In so doing, Hussein was taking steps to purposefully weaken Western relations in order to build up his image as an anti-Israeli populist Arab leader. On the first of April he furthered these actions by claiming to hold binary chemical weapons for use against Israel and threatened that "we will make the fire eat up half of Israel, if it tries to do anything against Iraq."[5] Finally, in May he attempted to find political action to match his rhetoric, calling for Arab states to take back Jerusalem.

Throughout the course of these collapsing relations US reaction was mixed and mealy. In the absence of a carefully studied policy, the US government was torn between those in the bureaucracy who supported Saddam's regime and those who did not. In this context, policy became a battle between opposing forces rather than a strategic instrument in a time of crisis. While it is clear that this period saw a transition in relations between the United States and Iraq that can perhaps excuse some of the murkiness in US approach, there were nonetheless clear indications of a potentially hostile escalation of tensions. The US response not only missed an opportunity to deter Hussein's increasingly aggressive demands, but, in its murkiness, signaled to Hussein that the United States was complacent toward events unfolding in the Middle East.

Confusing the US position toward Iraq was a series of tough stances followed up by apologies or backpedaling by other officials. An example came on February 15 when Iraq's human rights crimes were highlighted in the Voice of America (VOA) broadcast and human rights report. The US ambassador in Baghdad, April Glaspie, later apologized stating that the VOA did not represent administration policy. As diplomatic tensions continued to escalate, some in the US government began working for a tougher policy toward Iraq. Against administration opposition, Assistant Secretary Kelly and Dennis Ross in the State Department's Policy Planning Staff started preparing a proposal for sanctions against Iraq in early April. Ultimately this included discontinuing the Commodity Credit Corporation (CCC) agricultural credits and dual-use commercial exports. These proposals met resistance inside the US government and were repeatedly stalled by procedural challenges. Eventually, nearly two months later, the CCC program was suspended but the export program of dual-use materials (including some military goods) continued until the war broke out. Instead of the United States' employing Talk Power and punitive measures in response to Hussein's efforts at purposefully escalating tensions, Iraq faced only half-hearted sanctions that lacked the teeth to deter its choice of strategy. Tough Talk was being insufficiently employed and as a result the situation continued to disintegrate.

Successful diplomatic deterrence using Talk Power would have involved a carefully conceived policy aimed at delivering an appropriate message, something that should not have been an unreasonable expectation for a superpower. The appropriate message likely would have conveyed a mixture of understanding and even support for Iraq's economic needs, coupled with a sharp warning against its impending military adventure against any country in the Middle East. Instead of this, the United States attempted to project continued normalized relations with Iraq, repeatedly stating that it had no security agreements with Gulf States, including Kuwait. The appropriate message should have begun in February, with Kelly's visit to Baghdad, and culminated two months later, in mid-April, with the senatorial visit to Baghdad and the interview with Ambassador Glaspie. According to testimony from some within Hussein's inner circle, it was at this time that a decision on a Kuwaiti invasion was made, some four months before it eventually took place. Later would have been too late, but a strong and clear message in the first quarter of the year had enough time to be effective. While it was in early May that the CIA began warning of an imminent attack on Kuwait and the Emirates, such a warning did not come out of the blue. As we have shown, indications of collapsing diplomatic relations and impending aggression had begun months before, signaling a need for different policy approaches.

Talk Power would have been sufficient. Saddam repeatedly sought a clear statement of intentions in the face of confused signals from the United States, from February to the final ill-fated meeting with Ambassador Glaspie on July 25.[6] A statement that the United States was prepared to do what it eventually did would have had to be credible, but would not have had to be tested. The fact that the administration could make such a clear policy announcement despite the existence of domestic opponents would have increased its credibility. Instead of insisting that it had no security agreements with the Gulf States as Glaspie told Hussein, the United States could have referenced the commitments it (and Iraq) had taken against aggression under the UN charter.

In these events, the United States was a direct participant diplomatically, as it was to be militarily, but it could also have better employed Talk Power in a mediating role between Iraq and other countries in the region, notably Kuwait, in order to forestall the need for military action. The US decision instead to stand outside the region, claiming no formal commitments but simply urging moderation, was disingenuous given the constant and rallying attacks to which it was subject and the deep and long interests it held in the region. It was insufficient to simply engage in the burgeoning crisis sporadically and urge moderation, particularly given that it was prepared to step in eight months later and use military intervention. Between the two extremes is a wide area of diplomatic action to which the United States seemed content to make reference, but which it ultimately left insufficiently tested.

There were other exercises of Talk Power besides warnings that would have been complementary and helpful. Addressing both Saddam's legitimate grievances and the appeals of his supporters in Congress, the administration could have endorsed his call for a debt moratorium and even consorted with Western creditors to lead the way. A tough message and discussion with Kuwait, calling for a more responsive financial policy toward Iraq but assuring support in case of attack, would have been a complementary measure. It would have also been possible to broker Iraqi-Kuwaiti negotiations, working toward a deal on the two islands and economic aid for Iraq in exchange for recognition of the Kuwaiti border. The United States could also have urged the OPEC secretary general to mediate the Rumaila dispute, as Kuwait had agreed, and to enforce the oil quotas, as he finally did just before the invasion—too late.

Of course military displays to back up the words would have been helpful, but would have been as a form of coercive diplomacy rather than the principal thrust of foreign policy. Increased naval presence in the Gulf did not require an entire navy; a simple increase would have underscored the message of Talk Power. Standing security treaties with the Gulf States, which the administration wished to avoid, would not have been necessary, as mere assurances referring to this particular case would have sufficed.

There are many reasons, good and bad, why such a message was not issued. The disagreement over the appropriateness of a hard-line policy toward Iraq within the US government and the administration has been mentioned. The Arab states themselves were confused about the unfolding events, chary of military cooperation with the United States, and dithering in their reactions to Saddam's needs and threats. But these problems would have been surmountable on the background of clear and resolute US policy statements. Such statements would have had to be explicitly two-handed, both promising support for Iraq's grievances and clearly warning it against military adventures. Instead, however, US policy was diplomatically toothless and did little more than feed into Hussein's pan-Arab and anti-American populist tirades.

There is in fact a precedent for this sort of clear messaging that makes an effective use of Talk Power coming from previous dealings with Iraq itself. Thirty years earlier, in June 1961, the Iraqi dictator, General Abdul Karim Qassim, threatened to invade and annex Kuwait as soon as it became independent. In response, Great Britain, the departing colonial power, made it clear to Baghdad that it would not tolerate such aggression, and the invasion was forestalled. Of course, the era and context were different, but the broader lesson remains relevant—that effective Talk Power rallied Kuwaiti and Arab League support and stopped the threatened invasion. In addition, Qassim was overthrown within two years by Saddam Hussein, and Iraq recognized Kuwait, as part of a broader regionally brokered package including financial incentives.

Unlike this previous experience however, the United States missed the window of opportunity for Talk Power. Instead its hesitation allowed a crisis to build and Hussein to grow emboldened. Ultimately the United States was left with little choice but to employ Gun Power following Iraq's occupation of Kuwait in August. In so doing the United States made a major contribution to its subsequent foreign policy misadventures in the region. The inability of the United States to successfully implement Talk Power in the lead up to the first Gulf War introduced the use of Gun Power in the Gulf, where the United States had never used it before. Furthermore, it established a new standard for dealings with the Hussein regime that retreated irreversibly from normalized international relations. Subsequent UN inspections in Iraq were marked by difficulties of access and by evasiveness on the part of the Iraqi government. Gun Power had altered the calculus of affairs and proved incredibly difficult to roll back once employed.

Talk Power, used before Hussein's decision had been finalized, would have made a difference. The United States had intelligence reports delineating Hussein's character and was well aware of his grievances. He was known to be a blusterer and a bully, but passing to action only when he calculated that he could get away with it. The United States confirmed his calculation: US diplomatic signals leading up to the August invasion of Kuwait had not dissuaded such an aggressive undertaking. Since the United States still had credibility in its words, following its policy toward the breakup of the Soviet Union, German reunification, and South Africa, Talk Power would have had a good chance of being effective. By remaining uncommitted to Talk Power, the United States was left with little option other than to reply to the Iraqi invasion of Kuwait with Gun Power, and in so doing, established a dangerous precedent in the region for years to come.

The Middle East Peace Process, 1991–2003

With President Bill Clinton taking over the office of the president from George H. W. Bush in 1993, America's diplomatic activities in the Israeli-Arab dispute effectively came to an end. Earlier breakthroughs in the Peace Process—the negotiated military disengagements between Israel and Egypt in the Sinai under Secretary Henry Kissinger and President Richard Nixon in 1973–75, Camp David and the Washington Treaty under President Jimmy Carter in 1978–79 (which concluded in a formal peace treaty and Egypt's recognition of Israel), and then the Madrid process itself under President Bush in 1991–92—can be seen as the result of direct engagement by the president and secretary of state in a formulator and even manipulator role. After Madrid, however, the US government downgraded its activist intermediary role to one of passive "go-between" or messenger (and even only occasionally facilitator). The United States was content to back the parties in subsequent contacts, especially Israel, but not to step out in front and take the lead or even to push from behind. The change in US presidential administrations in January 2001 continued that inactivity, although planning for a new demarche was underway, only to be brought up short by the attacks on the World Trade Centers on September 11, 2001. The United States second-guessed its desired approach, changed its newly prepared diplomatic garb for a military uniform, and instead fell back on Gun Power as the preferred foreign policy instrument.

Along with most of the rest of the world, the United States was absent from the two most important diplomatic sets of advances in the Middle East since the end of the Cold War: first, the process begun by the Oslo Agreement between Israel and the Palestine Liberation Organization (PLO) of September 13, 1993 (including the timetable Cairo Agreement of May 1994), and then the implementation of the Oslo II Agreement of September 28, 1995, the Beilin-Abbas Plan of October 1995, and the Israel-Jordan Peace Treaty of October 26, 1994. In these, President Clinton was the star witness but not the matchmaker, a pattern that was to become the norm during his administration. To some, including many members of his administration, the Oslo agreements proved that negotiations could be left to the parties and that the United States need only involve itself as an occasional communicator/facilitator. The results, however, belied that insight and the process that began so well unraveled in the absence of a much-needed formulator/manipulator. Instead of taking such a stance, Clinton stood by passively on the sidelines, ultimately choosing to assign blame for any and all failures elsewhere, a decision that proved procedurally and substantively ill-advised. Once, when he did step in actively, as his term was running out, he relied on his personality instead of knowledge, and his brief presence attained no purchase on the process.

After formal peace on the Egyptian and Jordanian fronts, the post-Oslo decade was dominated by US indecision on both of the remaining two fronts that concerned the overall Middle East Peace Process—an Israeli-Syrian track to a peace treaty and an Israeli-Palestinian track in pursuit of the Oslo process. Neither track benefited from the active engagement and support from the United States that was required. The Oslo process needed further negotiations to deal with the issues of timing and territory. Egypt had some success as the mediator in creating the Cairo Agreement over the Oslo calendar, whereas Israeli Prime Minister Yitzhak Rabin and the PLO's Chairman Yasser Arafat made efforts to find agreement over the status of different zones of the occupied territories, which culminated in Oslo II.

At the same time as the Oslo talks were attempting to advance the Israeli-Palestine track, there was significant normalization in the relations between Israel and its Arab neighbors. Prime Minister Rabin had repeated public meetings with the leaders of Morocco, Jordan, and Egypt, leading to the participation of all Arab states except Algeria, Iraq, and Libya in the Peace Process. Forward momentum carried over into June of 1994 when plans were announced for considerable joint infrastructure investments that would create a Red Sea–Dead Sea canal, as well as other integrated electricity and telephone networks. While progress with many of its Arab neighbors advanced smoothly, relations with Syria continued to prove much stickier. At the same time as the Oslo talks, Secretary of State Warren Christopher delivered the basics of an Israeli-proposed normalization strategy to Damascus. When the proposal received a tepid response, the Israelis were less than satisfied and withdrew the offer. Fearing for the broader implications of a setback, the United States retreated even from its role as a communicator between Israel and Syria and seemed content with the hope that regional successes would ultimately lead to a breakthrough. Small initiatives were attempted throughout 1994, and continued irregularly through 1995 until these were cut off as a result of the Hamas suicide bombings of early 1996 and the subsequent election of Binyamin Netanyahu.

Forward progress in both tracks of the Middle East Peace Process was halted when Rabin and Israeli President Shimon Peres were removed from the scene, by assassination on November 4, 1995, and electoral defeat in May 1996, respectively. Both the Israeli-Syrian efforts and the final status talks on Oslo II, scheduled to begin in the month of the elections, were abandoned. The US government, while shocked by both events, continued to assume proceedings were on track and made no move to increase its involvement in an increasingly unstable situation. Clinton had supported the engagements of the parties; however, he had done little to lead the way to the next stage, in spite of mounting evidence that the path was poorly marked and potholed and that the players were rapidly stalling in their forward progress.

William Quandt observes that the United States in this period "was unable to close a deal that seemed ripe for the making.... [O]ne sees little sign of an American effort to persuade either Syrian President Hafez Assad or Prime Minister Rabin to cast aside their normal caution and go for broke. Nothing happened in Clinton's first term comparable to the Kissinger shuttles, Camp David I, or Baker's organization of the Madrid conference."[7] Secretary of State Christopher traveled frequently to the region but did not pressure outcomes or seek closure on even small matters. For his part, Clinton shied away from wading in personally, which is the sort of action that this window of opportunity would have required. As events and diplomacy between the parties had produced movement and signs of promise, the stage was set for the United States, as the principal mediator, to move beyond a simple communicator role and take on the job of a formulator, as Carter had done earlier, or even a positive manipulator, as did Kissinger.

Clinton's second term began with activity on the Israel-Palestine track of the Middle East Peace Process. The Hebron Agreement was reached on January 15, 1997, the first piece of negotiation with the new Netanyahu government and the last of Secretary Christopher. The agreement sought to work out the application of Oslo to the difficult situation of Hebron, a flashpoint between Palestinians and Israeli settlers. Attached to the agreement, however, were a "Note for the Record" by Middle East Coordinator Ross and letters from Christopher to the parties that were subsequently viewed as partial to the Israeli side, watering down the Oslo II commitment. As a result of this perceived partiality, any favor gained by the United States from the negotiations was lost. Soon after, in March, the United States vetoed a UNSC resolution condemning Israel for building large housing units for Israeli settlers on Arab land in East Jerusalem. The veto served no practical purpose but rather negatively impacted the broader movement toward resolution, particularly when coupled with the complaints regarding the Hebron Agreement. The administration, however, defended its stance on the vote by arguing that the situation was not ripe for negotiation, ignoring the fact that "ripeness doctrine" tells us that such situations call for a policy of *making* things ripe or "ripening" through active engagement. The impact of policies leaning toward Israeli positions was foreseeable, and when coupled with an absence of broader action on the peace process, undermined the ability of the Clinton administration to take the sort of action required of a manipulator of Talk Power.

After a year of little activity, the United States unveiled a new plan to return to Oslo II, an agreement viewed as defunct in the region. When Arafat accepted it but Netanyahu did not, Secretary of State Madeline Albright indicated that if Israel did not follow through the United States would "examine its approach to the peace process." But then when Israel did not follow through, the United States did nothing either. The mere whiff of a threat did little to advance the parties closer to the objective and Oslo II was not returned to the table. In fact, by backing down from an attempt at coercing an outcome diplomatically, the United States weakened its future abilities to make like-leveled threats credibly, undermining its own Talk Power.

Subsequently, President Clinton decided to abandon mere facilitation and finally step personally into the fray, in Triple Talks. He called Netanyahu and Arafat to the Wye River Plantation in Maryland to break the two-year deadlock. Clinton did not remain on site throughout the proceedings, however, departing on occasion to attend fundraisers for the Democratic Party. In his absence, disagreements multiplied rapidly and tensions rose at the plantation. When called back, Clinton proceeded to play an intense endgame with Netanyahu over the release of an American naval officer held in an American jail for divulging intelligence to Israel. Tensions were reined in and ultimately the three leaders signed the Wye Agreement of October 23, 1998, which revived the Oslo commitments. Unfortunately, however, there was no follow-through pressure by the mediator on either party, and implementation stalled within a month and was then officially suspended by Israel the month thereafter. Once again, this experience demonstrates the lack of direction with which the United States approached potential Talk Power solutions in the Middle East. After a prolonged stay on the sidelines, Clinton's first real foray into proceedings could have been used to a tremendous advantage. Unfortunately the opportunity was not seized to its maximum and the US Talk Power position in the Middle East crumbled further.

Despite appearances, the election of Prime Minister Ehud Barak in May 1999 reinforced the passive role played by the United States in the peace process. Barak actually found the United States to be too actively involved in Wye, and as a result Clinton indicated his desire to once again be a mere facilitator/communicator and nothing more. Secretary Albright brokered an agreement by Arafat and Barak at Sharm el-Sheikh in Egypt to revive the Wye accord in September and Clinton hosted Syrian-Israeli talks in Washington and Shepherdstown, West Virginia, in December 1999 and January 2000. When he subsequently met with President Hafez al-Assad in Geneva in March he came away empty-handed, merely communicating new conditions from Prime Minister Barak, having thrown no weight behind the Syrian demand for a return to the 1967 boundaries. The communicator role once again demonstrated its limits as insufficient pressure was put on either party. As a result, the Syrian track died, as did Assad two months later.

President Clinton then returned to the Palestine track, with facilitating calls and visits to both sides. When these seemed insufficient or the moment seemed to be getting riper—it is not clear which—Clinton invited the parties to emulate Carter's success at Camp David, on July 11, 2000. In this instance he played a much more active role, moving from facilitator/communicator to formulator, entering his own ideas and cajoling the parties to accept them or put forward constructive ideas of their own. Unlike Carter, however, Clinton came relatively unprepared in comparison to the massive study and documentation developed by the former president, and he relied more on his charm and quick study than on in-depth strategizing. Carter had played his role with studied evenhandedness, and had made up a single negotiating text from the proposals and used it to clarify divergences, whereas Clinton put nothing on paper and cleared his proposals with Barak before communicating them on to Arafat. While Carter had stuck with the meeting through thick and thin, Clinton departed for a G8 summit in Japan partway through the proceedings, indicating how quick he thought success would be, and leaving the plate in the hands of Albright, who could ultimately offer little by way of either carrots or sticks.

The United States had in fact put forward a number of proposals of its own at the Camp David Summit, in addition to pressuring the parties. In spite of the effort advanced, however, results were meager. Barak was losing his parliamentary majority by the hour and saw his proposals—some significant and deserving of extended dialogue—as absolute take it or leave it items. Arafat protested that he was not ready for a summit at all. Clinton, having now invested himself in earnest, was nonetheless at the end of his term limits. In examining the record, the most he could seemingly do, after two weeks of meetings, was to blame Arafat for his failure, something he had specifically promised not to do before proceedings began. While the Camp David Summit did see a more prominent role for Clinton, he was ill-prepared for the responsibilities required of a formulator, and as a result, the potential for forward momentum was lost.

Despite the fact that both Barak and Clinton were now lame ducks without a mandate and Arafat was blindsided by the second intifada, Clinton called another summit at Sharm el-Sheikh in October and still another at the White House in December. At this latter summit he tabled his own plan, going down to the details on all the major issues. He then continued to press the parties until he produced reluctant, conditional agreement from both. Ultimately, however, it was too late. Both Barak and Al Gore, candidate for Clinton's succession, lost their elections, and Arafat passed away. The Peace Process, such as it was, was dead and was to remain so for seven years, although the "Clinton parameters" remained irremovably on the table.

Over nearly a decade, the United States had hung around on the sidelines as a facilitator, well-intentioned but careful not to get into the water. It helped establish appropriate goals and outcomes, and then stepped back to watch the parties figure out how to reach them. It had even brokered a few small agreements, before pulling back to see if the parties would implement them. Ultimately, however, such a strategy proved insufficient and these initiatives fell apart.

The new administration under President George W. Bush began with the time-honored practice of distinguishing itself from the predecessor's legacy, even if it meant missing opportunities. Despite the absence of the United States, the parties to the Israeli-Palestinian track continued to discuss, moving from formula to details at Taba in 2001 and then returning to renew the Peace Process itself in the Nusseibeh-Ayalon initiative of 2002. Absent, however, was a third party to keep them at it and tie down the agreements (as President Carter had done between Camp David and the Washington Treaty). The parties themselves came close to concluding a deal, but committed engagement by a great power patron was needed to nail down and then implement it.

By the fall of its first year, the Bush administration was ready to launch into a Mideast program of its own, but the plan was cut short by the attacks of September 11, 2001. President Bush openly stressed the deep impact the terrorists' attack made on his mind and soul, and he launched into the "war on terror" with passion and commitment. The Mitchell Report, which was a US government attempt to get the Israel-Palestine Peace Process back on track, was dropped silently. Increasingly, anti-terrorist rhetoric became the norm. This turn of events represents a missed opportunity to remind the world that the Peace Process was in fact a US creation that had resulted in the return of Israeli-occupied territory to Arab neighbors, not the reverse. The United States could have said that, al-Qaeda or not, Washington was determined to continue its long-standing policy to complete the Process. Instead, Israeli Prime Minister Ariel Sharon was able to ramp up his own anti-terrorist rhetoric, further deepening his bond with Bush in the war on terror. He immediately offered a common identity as warriors against terrorism and the Peace Process was buried in the ruins of the Twin Towers. Again, Talk Power received short shrift in US foreign policy in the Middle East as the emerging war on terror elevated the place of Gun Power in responding to crises.

In spite of the emerging war on terror and the spike in counterproductive rhetoric in the Middle East, Secretary of State Colin Powell remained convinced of the need for US demarche. The initiative he proposed in 2002 was not supported by Washington, however, and withered on the vine. Bush demanded an Israeli withdrawal from the newly reoccupied cities but then subsequently withdrew the demand, instead calling Sharon a "man of peace." Within half a year, the Arab League adopted the Arab Peace Initiative (Saudi Prince Abdullah's plan), which offered normal relations in exchange for full Israeli withdrawal from the occupied territories; the Arab Peace Initiative represents a historic repudiation after a quarter century of the Arab League's Khartoum conference in 1967 that declared "no to negotiations, no to recognition, no to peace." The United States took no note.

Ultimately a reluctant participant in the Roadmap proposal for steps or pre-conditions to a settlement announced by the Quartet (United States, United Nations, European Union, and Russia), the United States convened summits in Sharm el-Sheikh and Aqaba in 2003 and promised to monitor progress on the Roadmap, but backed away from these promises as the parties defected. Indeed, the United States seemed to want to dump the Roadmap quicker than did the parties themselves. It was not until Bush's second term that then Secretary of State Condoleezza Rice was able to argue for and then assemble a new summit of Mideast leaders at Annapolis, a notable feat but without follow-through. Once again the parties were allowed to follow their own instincts without any US help; they talked to the wind and went home.

Current efforts to promote conclusive talk have followed a similar pattern. President Barack Obama made striking speeches in Istanbul and Cairo seeking to restore relations with the Muslim world and repeating his predecessor's reiter-ated assurance that "we are not at war with Islam."[8] The move confirmed the Israeli public's fears and was not balanced by a similar assurance in Jerusalem. A special representative, George Mitchell, was dispatched to mediate the revival of a step-by-step Process between the old spoiler, Prime Minister Netanyahu, now returned to power, and the Palestinian Authority of Mahmoud Abbas, now speaking for only half of the occupied territories and under attack from the other spoiler, Hamas, in charge of Gaza. Pressure to return to direct talks, interrupted for a decade, finally produced a series of meetings beginning in September 2010. But the parties fell to arguing about Israeli West Bank settlements, derailing on an issue President Obama raised a year before, rather than putting their noses to the grindstone on the 1967 borders, a topic that would incidentally have solved the settlements issue. By posing a halt in settlement building as a precondition unacceptable to Israel, the United States gave Israel all the time in the world to build more. This long list of failures to engage and failures to implement that marked the US involvement in the Middle East Peace Process post-Madrid testifies to the absence of the sustained attention that was required of a diplomatic effort using Talk Power. The efforts that remained were doomed to underwhelm and ultimately served only to create a misperception of the inability of the superpower's use of Talk Power to move the Process forward. As a result, the notion emerged that Gun Power—by the superpower and by local spoilers—was the sole remedy for the difficulties in the Middle East, built upon a series of disappointing results born of half measures. The experiences of the Middle East Peace Process compounded those of the earlier, first Gulf War and culminated in a US approach to Middle East foreign policy that was leery about muscled Triple Talk and continued diplomatic overtures.

The use of Gun Power in the invasion of Iraq in March of 2003 can therefore be seen not solely as an isolated incident of US foreign policy in the Middle East, but rather the result of more than a decade of diplomatic half measures. In both the case of the first Gulf War and in the two tracks of the Middle East Peace Process, US foreign policy was never fully or even sufficiently committed to Talk Power solutions, and as a result, Gun Power solutions were ultimately unavoidable. The ineffectiveness of ill-practiced Talk Power damaged US reputation at the diplomatic table and diminished the appeal of subsequent diplomatic efforts to the actors involved. As a result, the Talk Power solutions available in the months leading up to the second Gulf War were limited and their advocates much less convincing, and then sporadic returns to talks thereafter were weakened and weak.

The "Arab Spring" of 2011 made any early revival of a productive mediating effort most unlikely, as Arab governments old and new turned their attention inward and hardened their outward attentions toward Israel. For want of some tough and timely Triple Talk, years of opportunity were squandered and future opportunities were postponed perhaps for years.

Powerless Talk

The Middle East is one of the most important parts of the world in terms of US interest and presence. When things go bad there, while all suffer, it is America that pays acutely in terms of reputation, in oil and gas prices, and even in blood. At the very least, the region merits careful, coordinated observation and responses, so that positive and negative trends and attitudes can be noted and distinguished from each other, and moments of opportunity can be identified, encouraged, and acted upon. Diplomatic offensives are not required at all times, even for relations in a region as important as the Middle East. But when the time is ripe, they demand intense engagement and prolonged follow-through. Consultations, advice, encouragement, and cameo appearances without at minimum the appearance of engagement and resolve will not do the trick. When the time is not ripe, it needs ripening, not timidity, for the objective elements of present and impending pain are often glaringly present, unfelt by the parties themselves without an active councilor to open their eyes. Kissinger, Carter, and Baker provide the example, as chapter four will detail.

The parties in a conflict as deeply rooted as that of the Mideast have well-developed stereotypes of each other, are well insulated against the discovery of subtle changes and opportunities, and have made the conflict a central part of their own self-justifying myths. If they are to get out of their conflict intact, they need help. They cannot do it alone. That help can only come through Triple Talk from strong world powers and it requires their full attention. That attention demands the cultivation of trust with both sides, the skillful use of the art of persuasion, and the deployment of material assistance to underscore the dangers of the present and assure the promises of an alternative future—in brief, Talk Power. The alternative is as fearful for the timid bystander as it is for the parties themselves.

CHAPTER 3
THE TOOLS OF TALK POWER

The term "negotiation" means the art of handling the affairs of
state.... However negotiation is not limited to international affairs.
It takes place everywhere where there are differences to conciliate,
interests to placate, men to persuade, and purpose to accomplish.
Thus, all life could be regarded as a continual negotiation. We always
need to win friends, overcome enemies, correct unfortunate impres-
sions, convince others of our views, and use all appropriate means to
further our projects.

—Fortune Barthélemy de Felice, 1778[1]

Aesop tells of the wager between the Sun and the Wind as to who can make
the man remove his coat. When the Wind blustered, the man only drew it more
tightly around him. But when the Sun shone brightly, the man took it off. Negotiators have many ways of exercising Talk Power, tough and blustery, sweet
and sunny.

Power is resources plus will and skill. Resources stand behind their expression,
but the way they are wielded is what makes the effect, and that way is through
words. Talk Power needs reality behind it, but the reality of resources is brutish
and dumb. The world is what it seems, not what it is, and Talk Power shapes
that perception. If that were not evident throughout history, it hits us between
the eyes in the twenty-first century as we watch the stock market, where fear,
joy, and the whole gamut of perceptions in between is what makes the market
tremble or leap.

Words can be used in many ways, but because they are words and not the resources on which words sit, they should not be taken as something soft and flabby, opposed to the iron men who prove their mettle with their muscles. Talk is the way words are loaded and fired, and it can come out as smoke, as buckshot, or as a rifle bullet, among other forms. These forms can be named and discussed, so as to identify the ways and times they can be used effectively and the traps to avoid.

In this chapter we describe the different tools of Talk Power and the different ways that America's leaders and foreign policy decision-makers can negotiate with others in the pursuit of global security and peace. We argue that there is more than one way to negotiate and that effective diplomacy begins with a proper understanding of the different tools that are in the Talk Power toolkit. In describing these different tools, it is important to emphasize at the outset that good negotiation strategy does not rely exclusively on just one set of tools. One does not use a lathe to hammer a nail or a screwdriver to loosen a rusty pipe fitting. Good diplomacy, like good construction, means using the right tools for the right task at the right moment. It also means having a well-conceived plan of action before work starts.

There are a baker's dozen different ways that a country can negotiate with the world. **Tough Talk** expresses firm position, threats, and sanctions. It is talk that is usually backed by military firepower or economic clout and muscle and is often necessary to make clear what is important. **Straight Talk** means telling things as they are, particularly in regard to real alternatives. Straight Talk is sober and honest discussion about what the present course bodes and what must be done to rectify a bad situation. **Sweet Talk** contains a vast array of inducements, from reference to higher values (flattery), to promises of solid inducements (bribery), to soothing words that ease feelings of hurt and damaged pride. **Happy Talk** focuses on a better future, building castles on the horizon for the parties to share. It is the kind of talk that tries to get the parties to see the possibilities of working together and building a better world for themselves and their constituents. **Small Talk** focuses on the details of getting to a better place—the proverbial "who does what, when, where, and how" under a set of negotiated commitments, principles, and formulas—where the devil is said to reside and whose neglect has led many good dreams to be drowned. **Right Talk** is wordsmithing, editorial diplomacy, choosing that special right word to convey an idea when apparent synonyms do not express quite the same thing. **Trash Talk** is a put down, effective at times if used at the right moment in the right way. Humiliating or denigrating rivals is sometimes a necessary tool of diplomacy—especially if they misbehave or are way out of line—but Trash Talk is generally something to be saved sparingly for those rare occasions when friendly negotiation is not an option.

These kinds of talk are the major substantive tools of diplomacy. They are the "cutting" or "moving" tools of negotiation, which push, coax, or seduce parties from their entrenched positions. They are tools that have to be used as part of a long-term plan of action to achieve a definable set of political goals. But there are also other kinds of negotiation tools of a procedural nature, which can be used to bind, shape, and fasten the parties to a negotiation process much like the welding iron or rivet gun. And any negotiator, like the construction worker, sometimes has to don protective gear on an extremely hazardous work site.

Sticky Talk makes the negotiating encounter part of a process, and is often needed to keep the conflicting parties at the job of making peace and away from the alternative of making war. Like the welding iron or rivet gun, Sticky Talk binds the parties to a series of talks and agreements that makes it difficult for them to break free or walk away from the negotiating table when the discussion gets tough and concessions become costly. **Safe Talk** is protective gear that takes a negotiation out of the harsh glare of a damaging media spotlight. Safe Talk is critical when the secrecy of a private conversation is the key to building trust and getting agreement. It is the operative part of "open covenants, secretly arrived at," to paraphrase Woodrow Wilson. Safe talk is useful where even being seen in the company of sworn enemies or recognizing their claims can blow up a peace process, but it is also necessary in order to arrive at a balanced conclusion where each move would be judged by itself if it were to be opened to the media's scrutiny every moment. **Timely Talk** is talk that takes place before the parties have started to throw bricks at each other. It is talk that is directed at getting the parties to commit to a political as opposed to a violent solution to settle their differences. It is also talk that seizes the ripe moment in the conflict itself, or that makes the moment ripe when necessary. **Street Talk** is a way to generate public support for a peace process before formal negotiations begin or when they are stalled. It can also be used after a formal political settlement is concluded to get buy in from the public. **Twitter Talk** is a newcomer to modern electronified exchanges, a vehicle of instant mass communication that shrinks the time dimension out of diplomacy and mobilizes mass information but makes focused, binding agreement more difficult.

Just as clear, effective, and timely communication between workers is important on any construction site, any diplomatic venture requires the establishment of proper and effective channels of communications. **Triple Talk** is mediated negotiation, where direct two-party talks have become impossible for various reasons that the mediator must overcome. It includes shuttle diplomacy, for example, where the mediator becomes the telephone creatively carrying messages between the conflicting parties.

Most construction jobs usually require more than one kind of tradesman. On any construction site one will find surveyors, heavy equipment operators, framers, bricklayers, roofers, electricians, and carpenters, all of whom have to work together as a team to get the job done. Likewise, modern diplomacy requires different kinds of "tradesmen" who bring different capabilities and resources to the negotiating table. Some are equipped to do the heavy lifting in negotiations because they are well endowed with reward or coercive power. That is to say, they can back up Sweet Talk by offering positive inducements to the parties and when they resort to Tough Talk they are credible because they have the military or sanctioning capacity to act. Others are better for Straight Talk or Happy Talk roles because they are extremely knowledgeable about the issues and/or have good relations with the parties, so when they speak the truth or paint a rosy picture of the future they are credible interlocutors. Still others are better at playing a go-between, ferrying messages between the parties because they can be trusted to keep secrets, not distort the message or play fast with the truth. Most diplomatic undertakings require more than one kind of negotiator or interlocutor. **Team Talk** is the process of bringing different parties—sometimes even rivals—together in a shared enterprise so that they work effectively as a team and do not undermine a negotiation by freelancing or talking at cross purposes. **Stop Talk** is the threat of bringing diplomacy to a halt, by turning off the power switch, and letting the parties stew in their own juice.

There are many ways to handle the substance of a political dispute or a problem. Some of them emphasize how bad the current situation is and therefore the need to get out of it; others emphasize how good the future could be and ways to get into it. **Tough, Straight, Trash,** and **Stop Talk** fall into the first category, **Sweet, Street,** and **Happy Talk** into the second, and **Small** and **Timely Talk** bridge the two. Each deserves a fuller, illustrated discussion.

Tough Talk

Richard Holbrooke, America's negotiator who helped bring an end to the brutal wars on Europe's doorstep in the Balkans in the early to mid-1990s, was known as a tough talker, which is why he was chosen to talk to Serbia's leader Slobodan Milosevic, Bosnia's Muslim leader Alija Izetbegovic, and Croatia's Franjo Tudjman about the status of Bosnia in the mid-1990s, and then again to Milosevic about the status of Kosovo in the late 1990s. His assignment came after previous envoys, including former Foreign Minister Richard Owens of England and former US Secretary of State Cyrus Vance, were not able to talk sweetly enough in selling a plan for peace and government in Bosnia to the same antagonists.

President Jimmy Carter was also known to be a tough talker if the moment required. He leveled with Egyptian President Anwar al-Sadat and Israeli Prime Minister Menachem Begin on the basis of his deep study of the region's problems at the Camp David Mideast Peace Summit in 1978. Secretary of State James Baker was also legendary for his directness and toughness. He posed "serious conditions" and "unforeseen consequences"[2] to Prime Minister Yitzhak Shamir to force him to attend the Madrid Conference in 1991—something Shamir was loathe to do because Arafat was going to be there. President Bill Clinton was occasionally a tough talker, but his problem was that he didn't always get his timing right. He only talked tough to Chairman Yasser Arafat after the Camp David meetings broke down in 2000. Not a good move and one where Tough Talk during the actual negotiations could have made a real difference by keeping Arafat, who allegedly "never missed an opportunity to miss an opportunity,"[3] properly engaged. President George W. Bush shied away from Tough Talk altogether in his various visits to the Middle East in 2008 because he did not want to offend Israel. But Tough Talk by an American president to both sides, Israelis and Palestinians, would have helped bring them to their senses and accelerated the Peace Process.

Tough Talk need not be hostile, although sometimes hostility is needed to make the point. "Never get angry, except on purpose,"[4] said the late Harland Cleveland. But it does take persistence, insistence, repetition, and rephrasing. One's own needs and views are frequently not obvious to other parties nor are they always in harmony with their interests, needs, and views. "The secret of negotiation is to reconcile the interests of the parties," wrote François de Callières to the young French King Louis XV three hundred years ago. "The two principle purposes of a negotiator are to do the business of his master and to discover that of the other."[5]

Tough Talk serves as the bookends of any negotiation. If tough and clear words are appropriate at the beginning of negotiations, as the parties make their needs and interests known, they are also called for at the end, as the parties move closer to agreement. The endgame of any negotiation is no time to go soft but instead the moment to press toward a goal in sight, with insistence on the principles and details that make an outcome solid. In between, a party can relax the sharpness of the tone in order to give the other party leeway to think creatively of a way out of the conflict or impasse. Similarly, content has a relation to its bearer; when the other side is talking tough, it is sometimes necessary to call its bluff by retorting in kind, lest it begin to feel it can bully its way through. The United States does this regularly to North Korea, alone and in concert. Often bullies are stopped only by momentary counter-bullying, to be relaxed when the other party changes its tone.

Straight Talk

Negotiation begins with a clear exposé of one's positions and, behind them, one's interests—that is to say, what "really" matters. This diagnosis phase of negotiation is the time when a party has to make sure the other side understands what the stakes are. It is also the time to use Straight Talk to communicate one's own interests, ensuring that the other side understands them properly. During ongoing—and protracted—diplomatic exchanges it may be necessary to wield Straight Talk to make one's interests and aims clear. The need to talk straight therefore never really disappears.

Clearing the way to frank exchanges in search of a remedy to a problem frequently requires letting the other "know how much I hurt and how much you are the cause of my hurting." In effect, one is saying that "if this situation continues, we will never resolve our problems." As Jan Egeland, the Norwegian foreign state secretary who helped facilitate the Oslo Peace Process recalls, "The two teams were determined to break away from the tradition set by earlier Israeli-Palestinian talks and most Jewish-Arab discussions and agreed not to dwell on the past. I remember both sides saying during the very first meetings: 'If we are to quarrel about the historic rights to these holy lands, about who was there first, or about who betrayed whom and when, we will sit here quarreling forever. We must agree to look to the future.'"[6]

Straight Talk is also a way to expose a lie and show a cheater to be what he is. An ambassador used to be known as someone sent abroad to lie for his country. But as François de Callières observed more correctly, "the use of deceit in diplomacy is of necessity restricted, for there is no curse which comes quicker to roost than a lie which has been found out."[7] In the Strategic Arms Reduction Talks (START), the US negotiators gained an edge and surprised the Soviets by revealing information about the Soviet arsenal that some of the Soviet negotiators did not know. In July 1983, the United States went public with the revelation that US intelligence had detected a large early warning radar system that was being constructed near the city of Krasnoyarsk in the Soviet Union. Because the installation was more than 800 kilometers away from the nearest Soviet border, it was deemed to be in violation of the Anti-ballistic Missile Treaty the two countries had signed in 1972 which mandated that radars had to be located on the national periphery of each country and be oriented outward.

One of the boldest uses of Straight Talk came during the Cuban Missile Crisis when US Ambassador to the United Nations Adlai Stevenson, waiving the aerial photos, gained an enormous point before a world audience by telling the Soviet ambassador during the Cuban Missile Crisis that "I will wait till hell freezes over for you to admit that you lied about missiles in Cuba."[8] Straight Talk does not necessarily mean telling *all* the truth, but it does mean being truthful in what one tells.

Straight Talk is more than not lying, however. It is making the parties face unpleasant facts in a search for a solution. It is a cool look at the conflict as a painful mess in which the parties have caught themselves and which threatens to get worse. Sometimes negotiating parties need to be brought up against the hard facts of the situation, so that they can focus on real solutions to real problems instead of hiding in fantasy. In 1997 when the Carter Center's negotiating team was working to develop a deal among the three "presidents" of Congo-Brazzaville, two of whom were in exile but thought themselves still rightly in office, at one point in London one of the mediators took the risk of offending Pascal Lissouba by saying, "Mr. President, Let me remind you: you are no longer in office nor in Brazzaville, but Sasso Nguesso is!" Lissouba's tone suddenly changed and he began to turn to the problem at hand.[9]

Straight Talk is particularly useful in bringing out real alternatives to a negotiated solution, known as security points or BATNAs (Best Alternatives to a Negotiated Agreement). "If you don't like what we're doing, and you think you can get the Golan back in any other way, then go ahead and get it back," Secretary Baker snapped at President Hafez al-Assad as he worked to set up the 1991 Madrid Conference. "Assad and I made eye contact," Baker recalls; "he seemed to sense that we had reached a certain unhealthy threshold,"[10] and gave in. Alternatives are perhaps the major source of power in negotiation: If one's security point is high (close to a potential negotiated outcome), the negotiator is strong and can be tough, but if it is low (much worse than a possible negotiated solution) the negotiator is in a weaker position. Negotiations actually often take place between alternatives rather than between positions; parties try to weaken each other's alternatives to strengthen their own. This means telling it like it is, pointing out to the other party that its alternative is really not as good as it appears, using Straight Talk.

When to talk straight? The content should decide: When the point to be made is firm and important, it is necessary to say so. And when the position of the other side is fixed and unrewarding, it is time to say so, too. Negotiation, as has been noted, is giving something to get something; parties too often tend to think of the getting without considering the giving, and Tough Talk is often necessary to make them think about the compensation that is required to get the rewards they want from an agreement.

Sweet Talk

"I think that you and I, with our heavy responsibilities for the maintenance of peace, were aware that developments were approaching a point where events could have become unmanageable. So I welcome this message and consider it an important contribution to peace," wrote President John F. Kennedy to Chairman Nikita Khrushchev, after the Soviet Union had just embroiled that same world in a fast-moving crisis by installing atomic missiles in Cuba off the shores of Florida and had been dissuaded by careful, deliberate, restrained US diplomacy. Recognizing the other side's constructive contribution to securing an agreement, even if undeserved, is an important ingredient of sound diplomacy.

Looking ahead to other kinds of cooperative endeavors is important, too, especially if relationships are to be put on a sounder footing. Kennedy went on to discuss in his letter how the United States and Soviet Union could work more closely together toward the common goal of global disarmament: "Mr. Chairman, both of our countries have great unfinished tasks and I know that your people as well as those of the United States can ask for nothing better than to pursue them free from the fear of war.... I agree with you that we must devote urgent attention to the problem of disarmament, as it relates to the whole world and also to critical areas. Perhaps now, as we step back from danger, we can together make real progress in this vital field."[11]

"Don't crow!" is another key piece of advice that diplomats give to each other, and particularly to politicians. However, Kennedy needed no such instructions. As his brother Robert Kennedy recounts:

> After it [the Cuban Missile Crisis] was finished, he made no statement attempting to take credit for himself or for the Administration for what had occurred. He instructed all members of the ExComm and government that no interview should be given, no statement made, which would claim any kind of victory. He respected Khrushchev for properly determining what was in his own country's interest and what was in the interest of mankind. If it was a triumph, it was a triumph for the next generation and not for any particular government or people.[12]

Agreements have to be bought: If you can't take it, you have to buy it, and negotiation is the means of setting the price. Hagglers in a bazaar know that. In the more sophisticated world of diplomacy, the method is known as compensation, that is, promising the other party items that he or she values in exchange for items the first party values. In the Cuban Missile Crisis, as we now know, the agreement with the Soviets was "bought" with the promise that the United States would remove its nuclear-armed Jupiter missiles from Turkey in a secret deal that was worked out between Robert Kennedy and Soviet ambassador Anatoly Dobrynin.[13] However, diplomats and politicians often forget the need for exchange, because they fix on the items they value, forgetting that the other party is looking for items it values in order to clinch the deal. It is fair game, and sometimes necessary, to bring additional items into the discussion in order to make for a mutually satisfactory deal.

In the late 1970s, President Carter launched an initiative to win independence for South West Africa, telling South Africa, the colonial occupier, that it had a moral obligation to leave and would get nothing (not even praise, since it would remain the apartheid state) in exchange. The attempt failed. Under President Ronald Reagan, Assistant Secretary of State Chester Crocker assured South Africa of positive treatment if it would withdraw its troops from South West Africa (and also from neighboring Angola) and at the same time arrange that Cuba would also withdraw its troops from Angola (whose presence was South Africa's excuse for having its own troops there). Sweet Talk was backed by rewarding action.

When President Carter, Senator Sam Nunn, and General Colin Powell came to Haiti to talk General Raoul Cedras's military junta into relinquishing power before US troops landed to remove them, it was almost all Sweet Talk that did it, capped with a safe retirement spot for Cedras in Panama and protection for Mrs. Cedras's apartment in Haiti.

Happy Talk

"What we are trying to do is to show North Korea that there is a better way to achieve security than excessive armament, and that is to join the security arrangements of the international community,"[14] was the way that US Assistant Secretary of State Christopher Hill laid out the alternatives to Pyongyang, showing a better way to achieving its goals. Happy Talk is the complement of Straight Talk. The purpose of negotiation is to work out a more pleasant future to replace the unpleasant present. No negotiation will succeed if the parties do not feel that they are better off when it is over. Better off is a comparative statement. Parties have to be aware of the alternative that the other party has in mind. A party that may be hurting now may have an eye on a glorious day in the future when all will be golden again: "Next year in Jerusalem." Or it may be focusing on its current condition, seeking a way out of present pain. Obviously an agreement will have to be more promising in the first case than in the second. But whatever the reference point, the agreement must be presented as attractive to the other side, not just to one's own side.

As Ambassador Hill's quote indicates, positive outcomes need to be couched in terms defined by the other side as attractive, but they can come in several forms. This can be done only in one of three ways: concession, compensation, or construction. The first is riskiest, since it is essentially zero-sum—"what you get I lose"—and means that each gives up a bit of the contested item as they move toward some midpoint. A stark example is found in the intense debates at Camp David (2000) and elsewhere between Palestinians and Israelis over the percentage of the West Bank and Jerusalem that would constitute (along with Gaza) the Palestinian State. The second means giving something else to get something, and is based on the premise that the stakes can be divided into those that matter more to one side and less to the other, and that a satisfying exchange or compensation can take place. A happy example is the case of South West Africa/Namibia between Angola and South Africa, mentioned above. The third is by redefining the issues so as to construct a common goal that can benefit both sides. Under the assistance of hemispheric mediators, Peru and Ecuador overcame the zero-sum legal boundary dispute by turning to the goal of development of the border region, which required the cooperation of both parties. The same idea was offered by Shimon Peres in his plan for "The New Middle East," but the idea was stillborn and failed to shake the parties from their zero-sum view of the conflict. Compensation and construction are the two win-win alternatives to win-lose concessions that Happy Talk provides to make an agreement.

Small Talk

The devil is in the details, as every negotiator knows. After the parties have agreed on a formula outlining the terms of trade or the basic principles of justice or the identification of the problems and their solutions, they then turn to fleshing out this general agreement with its application in fine print. This is where the fat hits the fan. Each must make sure that the specific distribution of outcomes fits the general formula and then that each detail is satisfying in itself. Which 93 percent or 96 percent of the West Bank will constitute the Palestinian state, which settlements will remain where, and what additional 7 percent or 4 percent will come out of Israel's hide? Israel's talks with Syria broke down over a piece of Galilean shoreline, and almost broke down in 1974 over three small hills around Quneitra. All this, even though the general principles underlying the agreements were already accepted.

Right Talk

Right Talk touches a special corner of negotiation. Often agreement hangs on just the right word, none other will do, and the negotiator becomes a wordsmith. The right word symbolizes some particular idea or formula in the parties' minds, and synonyms will not do. Finnish President Martti Ahtisaari picked up the Aceh negotiations in 2005 and devised the term *self government* for the new status, which worked when the previous concept, "special autonomy," had failed. The difference between the two terms was almost indistinguishable but crucial. In the 1995 negotiations in Chiapas, the stalemate-buster was the suggestion of "free determination" in the place of "self-determination," which acceptably filled the space between independence and autonomy. Tatarstan signed an agreement with Russia in 1994 defining its status as a state "united with" but not "within" the Russian Federation, and the dangers of a Chechnyan-type conflict were dissolved. When UN Secretary-General Kofi Annan went to Baghdad in search of an agreement on terms of inspection, Saddam Hussein refused to have an "ambassador" accompany the inspectors; Annan came up with the term "senior diplomats," which was accepted. Sometimes Right Talk is quite the opposite: many words instead of one, to muddy things appropriately. Saddam Hussein objected to "inspections" and wanted "visits," as more respectful of Iraqi state dignity; Annan suggested "initial and subsequent entries for the performance of tasks mandated."[15] All these are examples of wordsmith diplomacy, where agreement hung completely on Right Talk.

Trash Talk

Trash Talk is another way of taking aim at an adversary by dragging their name through the mud and letting them know how one really feels about them. It is talk that can express a wide range of emotions from barely concealed contempt to outright anger and rage. Such talk may be a prelude to a declaration of war. It is talk that is typically directed at strengthening public resolve when dealing with foreign despots and dictators. It is also the kind of talk that is not tempered by the usual nuances and niceties of everyday diplomacy. "If Hitler invaded hell I would make at least a favorable reference to the devil in the House of Commons,"[16] Churchill famously said of Britain and America's alliance with Soviet dictator Joseph Stalin after the Nazis invaded the Soviet Union. When President George W. Bush lumped together Iran, Iraq, and North Korea in an "axis of evil" in his 2002 State of the Union speech he was, in effect, saying that the United States had reached a crisis point in its relations with all three countries.

Trash Talk does have its uses as Churchill knew. And he used it skillfully to attack Hitler and bolster the resolve of the British people in their mortal hour of peril in the fight. Reagan identified the USSR as an "evil empire," but at the same time offered inducements to repent. Stepping on the plane to attend the opening ceremonies of the 2008 Olympics in Beijing, George W. Bush chided the Chinese over their human rights policies: "America stands in firm opposition to China's detention of political dissidents and human rights advocates and religious activists," he stormed. This was careful Trash Talk tempered by the subsequent actions of the speaker. By attending the opening ceremonies America's president was sending a strong message that the United States was not only willing to do business with China but recognized its entry onto the world stage as host of the games. Beijing, in return, was deeply appreciative of the president's attendance over the objections of many members of Congress. A Chinese foreign ministry spokesman rejoindered with the usual mantra that China strongly opposed "using human rights and other issues to interfere in the other countries' internal affairs," but went out of his way to say that Sino-American relations "have kept a sound momentum of development over the past years" as a result of "effective dialogue, exchanges and cooperation in extensive bilateral fields and major international and regional issues."[17]

Such talk can be used to rally support in a diplomatic face-off. In a keynote speech he delivered in Abu Dhabi on January 15, 2008, while touring some of the states in the Persian Gulf, President Bush accused Iran of being "the world's leading state sponsor of terror" because "it sends hundreds of millions of dollars to extremists around the world while its own people face repression and economic hardship at home." The president also alleged that "Iran's actions threaten the security of nations everywhere. So the United States is strengthening our long-standing security commitments with our friends in the Gulf and rallying friends around the world to confront this danger before it is too late."[18]

Iran's leaders are no strangers to the use of Trash Talk, beginning with branding the United States as "the Great Satan" after Iran took the US diplomatic mission prisoner in 1979. On June 11, 2008, just prior to a meeting between the American president and German Chancellor Angela Merkel, President Mahmoud Ahmadinejad told thousands of supporters in central Iran that America was powerless to strike Iran and that Mr. Bush's "era has ended." "This wicked man [Bush] desires to harm the Iranian nation," Ahmadinejad sneered, as his audience chanted "Death to America."[19]

But if used clumsily, Trash Talk can be counterproductive. In the aftermath of Bush's State of the Union speech, US allies worried openly that the United States was opening up a new front in its war against terrorism. Such fears were warranted. The United States attacked Iraq a little more than a year later, leading to speculation about whether or not Iran or North Korea was next. Governments term a variety of rebel movements "terrorists," whether they fit the official UN and US definition as parties attacking civilians to influence their governments. The PLO, IRA, and Taliban fit the definition at times but the African National Congress (ANC) in South Africa did not, even though all four were so labeled. In so doing, governments limit their own possibilities of action, since negotiation with "terrorists" is officially proscribed. The Israelis who opened negotiations with the PLO in Oslo risked imprisonment on their return as a result. Trash Talk can rebound on the user.

As the Wikileaks diplomatic revelations indicate, diplomats in "private communication" sometimes resort to Trash Talk in reporting to their superiors about the wayward behavior of leaders and officials in other countries. Such communications are the normal stuff of diplomacy. Although the revelations have been embarrassing in some instances to US interests, they are not part of a deliberate strategy of negotiation that is intended to discredit the other party. In fact, the revelations have prompted a great deal of Safe Talk by American officials to smooth a lot of ruffled feathers and limit the political fallout.

There are also different procedures for talking, beyond simple two-party, face-to-face communication. Getting the other party's attention, to focus on a search for ways out of the dispute or problem, may be the biggest challenge of all. Sticky, Safe, Timely, Street, Twitter, Triple, Team, and Stop Talk are some of the most important procedural devices.

Sticky Talk

This is the kind of talking that simply will not let go. When Secretary Richard Holbrooke wanted to get an agreement on Bosnia out of the three leaders of the Yugoslav republic, he locked them in Wright Air Force Base at Dayton and would not let them out. When President Carter wanted to get a peace agreement out of Begin and Sadat, he holed them up in the wooded hills of Camp David and would not let them out. There were special circumstances in all these cases: The issue was a major violent conflict, and the mediator with the key was a (or the) superpower. Yet, in any negotiation, the conflicting or problem-ridden parties need to be kept at the job or the job will not be done, even though they often would like to go home and leave things for another day.

When the door cannot be physically locked, Sticky Talk needs to be imposed from the inside or outside: The problem will not go away and so the parties must be convinced to face it. Patience, persuasion, and persistence are the marrow of negotiation, the soft core that carries the blood and nerves of the communication. Too often conflicting parties get together, by themselves or through the work of a mediator, agree on what they can agree on, and go home to live with their problem or continue their conflict, perhaps in a slightly altered form. The list is endless, from the fifteen incomplete peace agreements signed among the warring factions in Liberia between 1990 and 1997 to the hurriedly signed peace agreements in Angola in 1991, 1992, and 1994 that failed to end hostilities between the government led by the Popular Movement for the Liberation of Angola (MPLA) and the opposition forces of the National Union for the Total Independence of Angola (UNITA), to the impatiently aborted negotiations between Moscow and Chechen terrorists in a succession of incidents that took place at the Ministry of Interior armory in the Dubrovka Theater in October 2002 and Nazran, Ingushetia in June 2004. The former incident prompted Russia's President Vladimir Putin to forego potentially lengthy negotiations and resort to the use of force in response to the Chechen terrorist assault on a primary school in Beslan, North Ossetia, in September 2004—a decision that led to the deaths of more than 300 people including 186 children.

The counter-list contains impressive cases of successful Sticky Talk negotiations. It took six years of painstaking prompting and cajoling and preparing for a ripe moment by Assistant Secretary of State Crocker, meanwhile fending off domestic criticism, before he was able to extract an agreement that put an end to the war in South West Africa, brought independence to Namibia in 1988, and paved the way to the end of the apartheid regime in South Africa. It also took many months of hard slogging and endless rounds of diplomacy to end the civil and regional conflict in Cambodia in the early 1990s as we see in chapter seven. The Good Friday Agreement in 1998, which provided the blueprint for the Peace Process in Northern Ireland, was only reached through years of talks that arguably began some seven years earlier with the launch of the multiparty talks in Belfast in 1991. The Middle East disengagement agreements of 1974–75, as seen, were designed to be unstable and "fall forward" toward a final Israeli-Egyptian peace treaty, marking the nature of the step-by-step Process.

Safe Talk

Safe Talk is the diplomacy of the corridors and cafes, the woods and wharves, or the bar at the hotel or conference center where negotiations are taking place. We now know that President Woodrow Wilson was lost in his idealism when he said just prior to the peace conference at the end of World War I, "Open covenants openly arrived at."[20] The delicate exchanges of negotiation require closed doors, and also some breaks away from the table where people can talk as people, not as formal delegations. These breaks have been some of the most productive moments in important negotiations.

The so-called June 1982 "walk in the woods" is a famous episode during the Cold War when the United States and the Soviet Union almost clinched an agreement to stop the nuclear arms race in Europe. For almost two years, the United States had negotiated with the Soviets to reduce intermediate-range nuclear forces (INF) on both sides to the lowest equal levels, ideally zero. Both sides came close to an agreement when the chief US negotiator, Paul Nitze, and his Soviet counterpart, Yuli Kvitsinsky, secretly decided to take a long walk in the woods on an outing near Geneva, Switzerland, where the talks were being held. During their walk, they agreed to a formula that would limit each side to a specified number of missile launchers and long-range aircraft. Both the White House and the Kremlin initially rejected the gambit because neither side felt the need to make concessions. However, some years later on December 8, 1987, President Reagan and General Secretary Mikhail Gorbachev did sign the INF Treaty banning intermediate-range and shorter-range missiles from Europe.

The "walk on the wharf" is a less well known example of the value of Safe Talk. In January 1988, the United States and Soviet Union launched the Stockholm Conference to begin a negotiation that would lead to the adoption of a comprehensive, mutual set of confidence-building measures that would cover the entire continent of Europe by opening military activities to greater levels of transparency by sharing information and strengthening communications. The negotiations had to deal with thorny issues of asymmetry in geography and differences in the structure and training of NATO and Warsaw Pact forces. A little publicized "walk on the wharf" by US delegation head Ambassador James Goodby and Soviet delegation head Ambassador Oleg Grinevsky along Stockholm's magnificent harbor front led to a productive exchange of views between the US and Soviet delegation heads. During their walk they came up with the idea of a new and complementary principle of equivalence—Soviet agreement to confidence- and security-building measures in exchange for US commitment to a "non-use of force" (NUF) declaration. The suggestion was conveyed to President Reagan who included it in a speech he delivered to the Irish parliament in June 1984, which not only broke the impasse but quickened the pace for the rest of the negotiations.

Finally, whole sessions in secrecy and informality provide the best example of the opportunity offered by Safe Talk. The groundbreaking agreements between

Israelis and Palestinians, known as the Oslo Accords, were the direct result of secret and informal negotiations that took place over an eight-month period in 1993 in a Norwegian farmhouse with the assistance of a handful of Norwegian facilitators. The Norwegians were able to open up a confidential back channel to the ongoing formal and public Washington-led negotiations that involved high-level, direct face-to-face negotiations between Israeli and Palestinian officials. The nongovernmental partner in these negotiations provided academic camouflage that gave the parties much-needed deniability, and the Norwegians' ability to deflect media attention allowed parties to take some risks without fear of exposure. A small country like Norway was able to play the role of third-party facilitator precisely because it was perceived by the parties as neutral and impartial. In this instance, Safe Talk under Norwegian cover helped change the entire political architecture of the Middle East in the 1990s by bringing together bitter enemies who became, in the words of one of the Norwegian facilitators, Jan Egeland, "each other's legitimate counterpart in peaceful negotiations."[21]

Of course, the first part of Wilson's proposition still holds true: Safe Talk results must be made public so that parties do not find themselves tied down later on by privately given commitments. Such secret agreements were correctly seen by Wilson as a major cause of World War I. While whole secret agreements have generally been avoided because of the World War I experience, lesser secret commitments still occur; they are often the necessary payment to lock in an agreement but they can cause problems later. Henry Kissinger promised the Israelis that the United States would not talk to the Palestinians without prior notification, which was not too bad, but Carter unfortunately changed the promise from notification to prior permission. Secret or open, the commitment would have caused a problem, but secret at the time it was made, it had a double negative effect—its limitation and its revelation. Secret negotiations have their downsides, but when properly used as a breather during more formal talks, they allow for trial balloons and explorations without commitment and let negotiators use their most productive approach: "What if...?"

Timely Talk

Negotiations, especially when led by a third party, can sometimes prevent the outbreak of violence or a further escalation of a conflict. Before violence occurs and positions have hardened, parties may be able to handle disputes on their own or consider negotiated interventions by mediators. Such mediated or Triple Talk interventions are often directed at lengthening the "shadow of the future" by dramatizing the long-term costs of violence to the parties if negotiations fail.

Once a conflict is underway, such interventions typically become more difficult and harder to sustain because conflicting parties' attitudes and perceptions have usually hardened and they are not prepared seriously to explore the negotiation option. The low-key manner in which the High Commissioner on National Minorities (HCNM) in the Organization for Security and Cooperation in Europe (OSCE) has tackled the problem of national minorities in Central and Eastern Europe and areas of the former Soviet Union in the 1990s underscores the value of Timely Talk. By maintaining an arm's length relationship with the OSCE, and ironically by eschewing the formal language of mediation, the commissioner at the time, Max van der Stöel, was able to gain entry into conflicts in ways that a formal mediation approach could not have because it would have raised the political stakes and limited the flexibility of the parties to make concessions.

When the conflict is not prevented, Timely Talk means sensing when to mediate and seizing the moment. To recognize that the parties need to feel themselves locked in a painful impasse from which they cannot escalate their way out does not guarantee that they will do so. Ripe moments need to be seized, for they are only subjective perceptions and necessary only (though insufficient) to opening negotiations. If the parties cannot feel the moment (which may indeed be fleeting), Triple Talk must come into play to help them, as discussed below. When the moment is simply not present, Timely Talk is needed to ripen it for negotiations to take place, again a job for Triple Talk.

Street Talk

One of the key challenges in a peace process is to build support for negotiations within the society-at-large and to address the needs of local communities who bear the deepest scars of the conflict. Peacemaking is a multifaceted enterprise and in today's world must actively involve citizens themselves if the enterprise is to succeed. Track Two and its multiple variations use unofficial discussions for problem solving, at best in coordination with official efforts. As former Assistant Secretary of State for the Middle East during Camp David I, Hal Saunders, who has been one of the pioneers of engaging citizens in sustained dialogues in public peace processes around the globe, argues, "There are some things that only governments can do, such as negotiating binding agreements; there are other things that citizens can do, such as change human relationships."[22] Street Talk is a form of dialogue which in Saunders's own words, "engages representative citizens from the conflict parties in designing steps to be taken in the political arena to change perceptions, stereotypes, to a create a sense that peace may be possible and to involve more and more of their compatriots." One of the most famous instances of Street Talk comes from the Cold War era. The Soviet-US Dartmouth Conference was the longest continuous bilateral exchange between leading US and Soviet citizens, which began in 1960 at the behest of US President Dwight Eisenhower and Soviet leader Nikita Khrushchev. After the Cold War, the Kettering Foundation, which supported Dartmouth, put its efforts into the Inter-Tajik Dialogue under Saunders. The Dialogue provided a second track to conflict resolution parallel to official discussions, leading to the end of five years of conflict (1993–97) in the former Soviet Republic.

The Peace Process in Guatemala, which began with a meeting in Oslo organized by the Lutheran Church, continued until the Contadora Declaration of August 1995 and concluded with a settlement in 1996 that was negotiated under UN auspices. This is another illustration of a Street Talk initiative that engaged civil society and public participation. The Civil Society Assembly, which was launched with the assistance of the United Nations, contributed to national dialogue and provided important input into the negotiations and subsequent terms of the peace settlement that ended one of Central America's most brutal civil wars. However, the political situation more than fifteen years later remains fractured and tenuous, largely because of continued fragmentation of civil society, a lack of accountability to the country's populace by the country's leaders and political institutions, and a weak and biased media that has made it difficult to debate issues and criticize the government.

Twitter Talk

In a world where power is shifting from governments to individuals and groups who can communicate through new technologies such as Facebook and Twitter, "people power" matters more than ever as protests in Egypt, Tunisia, Libya, Yemen, Bahrain, and elsewhere underscore. Twitter Talk refers to the unreconstructed conversations that take place over the Internet and through a variety of different social media. It is the kind of Talk that leads to social and political mobilization, and brings people into the streets to voice their demands. Twitter Talk, when unleashed in its full, unbridled form, can unseat unpopular authoritarian regimes and topple despots. But when those despots resist, as we have seen in Libya, it can also precipitate the onset of civil war and protracted social unrest.

As we look to the future of peace processes in the Middle East and North Africa in an increasingly volatile and unstable political environment, it will be important for political authorities and those from the outside who wish to support peaceful change to engage citizens in the formation of new social networks and initiatives that are supportive of political reforms and democracy. More "struc-tured" varieties of Street Talk will be a necessary accompaniment to this process of political change as will negotiations and varieties of Talk Power that engage political elites, including the military, who hold the levers of power and are in a position to decide whether or not their societies are going to move forward.

Triple Talk

The progressive moments in the Middle East Peace Process were made possible by the active participation of a mediator. When there was no progress in the Process, there was either no committed involvement of a third party or an involvement that was poorly targeted on the problem, such as Reagan in his 1983 plan or Clinton in Camp David II. The correlation is one to one. There are some Middle East hands who maintain that the United States should stay out of the area's conflicts and let them handle them themselves, but they are somehow not considering both the one-to-one correlation and the cost that the Middle East conflict imposes on the outside world. The closest things to participant solutions to Middle East conflicts are Oslo and the Jordanian-Israeli Peace Treaty; Oslo (delicately facilitated by the Norwegians) reverted back to the conflict-ridden status quo, and the Jordanian Treaty made peace where there was already little conflict.

Negotiation is an exchange of contingent agreements: "I will do this if you do that." As such, it is a very delicate job of making sure that both contingencies are kept, and parties—and particularly enemy parties seeking to overcome their enmity—are very wary of being caught in even a semblance of a commitment before the other side has made a similar and balancing commitment. Even direct meetings (or even intimations that negotiations are going on) may be the first step toward entrapment. For this reason, parties often can only talk without looking like they are talking, and frequently that can only be done only by talk-ing to someone else—a mediator.

A mediator (by any other name—facilitator, good offices, third party, etc.) is often required to get parties talking. Triple Talk is necessary. Conflicting parties may need and hope for a negotiated solution to their conflict but they do not trust the opponent; that is part of the conflict. They need a surrogate for trust, a third party whom they each can rely upon. That third-party mediator may be needed simply to carry trustworthy messages, or to bring new ideas, or even to sweeten the pot of the agreement to make it attractive. In whatever form, parties in conflict need help, and that help has to respond to the particular obstacle that keeps them from seeking and finding an agreement. But it is not the solutions that are lacking; it is first of all the need for a vehicle of trust between the two parties, a crutch to help them walk, a way out of their Prisoners' Dilemma, in game theory terms.

In its simplest role, when the parties simply cannot talk to each other, the mediator acts like a secure telephone, carrying messages from one party to the other when direct contacts would be deemed compromising. The job is simply to get a clear and accurate message across. This is the minimal role of communicator or facilitator, guaranteeing the bona fides of the communication but nothing more. It is often done at arm's length, by shuttling between the parties who never meet. The facilitator uses no pressure, adds no content, and lets the momentum of the mediated exchanges carry the negotiations forward. This is what presidents Clinton and Bush did for most of their tenures in office, mainly what the Norwegians did at Oslo, and what Kissinger did before moving on to the next step. Sometimes, it is not enough.

When facilitating or communicating alone is not enough, the mediator must put some of him- or herself into the exchange, notably some ideas and pressures toward an agreement. The third party must help formulate some new ways out of the conflict, either some concessions to be made, some compensation to balance a one-sided concession, or some construction of a new way of framing the dispute, or even just some Right Talk. Disputes that are impervious to facilitation because the parties cannot think creatively beyond their fixed position need greater mediator involvement as a formulator.

But maybe ideas are not enough, either; the obstacle may simply be that the stakes of peace are not enough to draw the parties out of their conflict. The mediator needs to act as a manipulator, a term that emphasizes the deep involvement and risks that the role carries. And if that exposes the mediator to greater involvement than he or she wants, then the mediator simply has to decide whether hanging back and letting the conflict fester meets his or her interests. Kissinger, often a formulator, became a manipulator as the Peace Process went on, and it brought success.

Mediators can be found all over the world. In many cases, what is necessary is not muscle but simply clever thinking, careful massaging, dignified authority, trustful relations, and no visible interest involved, all operating under propitious circumstances—in many cases where the parties themselves want to end their conflict under acceptable terms but just can't do it by themselves. Former Finnish President Ahtisaari pulled the rabbit of an agreement out of the hat in the Aceh conflict in Indonesia, a civil war that had proved remarkably resilient to any kind of negotiated settlement. He did so right after the 2007 tsunami had done its damage to Aceh and there was a sudden willingness on the part of all sides to bury the hatchet. The office of the Vatican mediated a bitterly fought dispute over the bitterly cold Beagle Channel in 1984, after the December 1983 revolt had removed the bellicose Argentine junta. The Catholic lay organization, Sant'Egidio, mediated an end to the Mozambican civil war in 1990–92 after a terrible drought had weakened both sides. The United Nations mediated an end to the Soviet Afghan occupation in 1986–88 as the Soviet Union was heading for a change of leadership and collapse.

Syria and Israel have been at war for sixty years, openly fighting on a half dozen occasions, and negotiating peace only a few times. They have never arrived at their proclaimed goal, and conflict remains their fallback position. In 2007, a neighboring country, Turkey, with special ties to both parties, launched a mediation process after ascertaining from both parties their interest in the try. What has gone on is secret—Safe Talk—and has been conducted by shuttle diplomacy with the mediator filling the message space between the two sides—Triple Talk. The conflicting parties trusted the mediator; the mediator had no interest in a particular outcome, only an outcome acceptable to the parties; and the parties were in a weakened position and would benefit from an end to their conflict. Turkey did the detail work, but both parties wanted the United States to sanctify (and maybe contribute) to the agreement itself. Although the parties' positions were brought closer together, Syria made it known that it would not close the gap and the deal until after the 2008 US (and Israeli) elections. But the Israeli elections brought in a team that vigorously wandered off course. Triple Talk went far, but it could not bring the parties close enough together to shake hands.

So when it comes to long-standing, intractable disputes of a serious nature not involving superpowers directly, the United States is perhaps the only capable mediator and it must become deeply involved. Without the United States and the resources, leverage, and sheer clout it brings to the table, no settlement is possible. Facilitation and communication are not enough; the United States cannot just carry messages and let the process flow forward on its own momentum. The momentum will only turn into a boxing match. The world's hegemon needs to be involved up to its elbows, if not up to its waist, carrying ideas and alternatives back and forth between the parties as a formulator or carrying incentives and inducements as a manipulator. There is no alternative, and anything short will fail, as the historical record has shown. "The US has the vocation to mediate," wrote Ambassador Stephen Low in 1985.[23] That is no less true now that the United States is the last remaining superpower than it was when there were two.

Team Talk

"In negotiation," wrote Jean Monnet, the leading architect of the European Coal and Steel (and eventually European Economic) Community, "the parties should not sit across the table facing each other but should sit on the same side facing the common problem."[24] Much longer than Syria and Israel, France and Germany had been in a deadly boxing match for centuries, repeatedly doing mortal damage to each other, most recently twice in the first half of the twentieth century. They emerged from World War II with the same attitudes until, a decade after its end, the same two leaders who had continued to carry the hatred, said, "Let's stop doing each other—and ourselves in the bargain—harm, and let's do something together larger than ourselves, like building a Europe." Their conversion took place in a remarkably short time, a few years.

The story is well known. But similar stories come from other times and places around the world. Equally well known is the South Africa version, where Blacks and Whites (and Coloreds and Asians in between) had been fighting each other since the mid-1800s, and the victory of any one side (in this case, the Whites) was inconclusive and exacerbating. At the end of the 1980s, the White leader, Frederik Willem de Klerk, realized that victory entailed an unsustainable cost and was unstable at that, and the Black leader, Nelson Mandela, realized that giving the minority certain assurances about their way of life and standard of living would allow the whole population to team together to face the problem of social enmity and economic growth together and cooperate to overcome it.

The point of all the stories is that when conflicting parties have the wisdom to realize the costs of the conflict and the ability to identify a common problem or project that they can attack as a team, they have benefited mightily. There are two lessons in this realization. One is, as stated, the enormous advantage the new creation brings to the parties, even when reduced by the cost involved in getting there. But the other is that this type of negotiated process and outcome does not automatically fit just any problem or conflict. Not all conflicts are replaceable by a common project, and even when they are, the project is often not easily identifiable. It takes work, creativity, imagination, and inventiveness to find an appropriate subject for teamwork to overcome historic enmity. Parties often hold incompatible positions because they themselves are incompatible, and it takes long and assiduous efforts to overcome images of irreconcilable differences that underlie differences in policies. The two communities of Northern Ireland arrived at an impossible compromise in 1998 to manage their conflict but they still are not fully reconciled. Ethiopia and Eritrea agreed to a divorce in 1993, but their mutual dislike is sharper than ever, as their murderous war in 1998–2000 all too tragically underscored. The repeated failure of Israeli-Palestinian negotiations has convinced many on both sides of the bad faith of the other and the impossibility of an agreement. Teamwork is a rare prize, worth seeking, but not always available.

Building negotiating teams is not simply confined to the warring parties themselves. Deliberate efforts to widen the coalition of mediators or interlocutors by bringing influential parties into the club can multiply the impact of the third-party collective effort. Here it is important to remember that leverage may or may not consist of material means to induce the parties to the dispute to change their behavior or attitudes. The four countries—Argentina, Brazil, Chile, and the United States—that served as guarantors of the 1942 Rio Protocol between Peru and Ecuador were able to work together to help resolve the boundary dispute that escalated into full-scale warfare between the two countries in 1995. The guarantors were the only channel of communications between the two countries, and no negotiation would have been possible without them. But their material investment—their role as manipulating mediators—was minimal.

Stop Talk

If negotiations are getting nowhere, it sometimes helps to let the parties know that you are ready to leave. Parties can negotiate for a number of reasons other than finding solutions, including delaying resolution or preparing for more conflict, and if they are using negotiations merely as a cover for something else, it is best to call the game and go home. Or parties can be simply unwilling to move to a point where problem solving and conflict resolution are possible, and they need to be faced with the choice of compromise or failure. Former Secretary of State Baker, while trying to get the Mideast parties to the Madrid Conference in 1991, has said that the most helpful tactic in the process was the "dead cat effect."[25] No one wanted the "dead cat" of responsibility for conference failure on its doorstep. A threat to leave is sometimes a powerful goad. It may take Stop Talk to make for Sticky Talk.

The qualifier "sometimes" relates to a particular condition: The third party must not want to leave more than the parties do and the parties being threatened must not want the third party to leave. In general, a threat to do something the threatened party wants done anyhow is not much of a threat. A common problem arises when sanctions are threatened, only to be withdrawn when the party imposing sanctions feels more hurt by them than the party being sanctioned. The same is true when a mediator that the parties would rather not have around threatens to leave, or a negotiator threatens to cut off negotiations that the other party would not like to happen anyhow. Such threats are not likely to galvanize the other party into action. When the United States and the Western Contact Group (composed of the United States, the Federal Republic of Germany, France, Canada, and the United Kingdom) were trying to get South Africa out of its

South West African territory, they threatened in 1978 to end their mediation and apply sanctions if South Africa did not agree to liberating terms. The threat to cut off negotiations was quite acceptable to South Africa, and the threat of sanctions was withdrawn by Secretary of State Vance as more harmful to the United States and allies than to South Africa.

However, when Senator George Mitchell threatened to leave his mediation and chairing of the peace talks in Northern Ireland in early 1998 if the parties did not get serious and move toward agreement among themselves, i.e., that the moment was now or never, the parties capitulated. They recognized that Mitchell's principled leadership was necessary to get there, and so they went back to work and brought him with them. The Good Friday Agreement was the result. And at Dayton in 1994, Secretary Warren Christopher and Assistant Secretary Holbrooke packed their bags and were ready to call the negotiations a failure, but for an agreement of the three parties to continue their efforts toward an agreeable solution. Earlier, at Camp David in 1975, the parties also packed their bags, ready to leave and out of ideas; President Carter, the mediator, pleaded with them to think of the consequences, and so they returned to draw up the Camp David Agreements.

Threats by one of the parties to call off the mediation or negotiation, or to focus heightened conflict on the parties, are the ultimate tactics of Talk Power, inducing a return to negotiation by a threat to stop it.

Finding the Right Tools

In this chapter we have discussed the different tools of Talk Power, which, in essence, are different ways to negotiate with friends, enemies, and strategic rivals as well as with the parties in a conflict who are incapable of raising their sights beyond the battlefield to consider an alternative vision of the future. There is an enormous richness and variety in these different tools of statecraft as our discussion illustrates. However, the challenge for American diplomacy is not simply to make use of these tools, but to use them adroitly and skillfully and in ways that advance America's interests. In the chapters that follow, we argue that effective diplomacy depends not just on grabbing the right tools out of the negotiation toolbox, but crucially on timing, coordination, calibration, careful planning, and leadership. Effective negotiation also depends on having a diplomatic strategy that is informed by a clear sense of one's own strategic interests. As different kinds of problems are encountered along the road to securing a political settlement or diplomatic solution, negotiators also have to make use of more than one set of negotiation tools.

In the next chapter, we look to some of the positive lessons of successful peacemaking in the Middle East and the factors that led to the successful use of Talk Power by American presidents in earlier phases of the Middle East Peace Process, picking up on the discussion in chapter two. Specifically, the chapter will explore President Carter's adroit use of different negotiation tools—Tough Talk, Sweet Talk, Straight Talk, Timely Talk, Right Talk, and Sticky Talk—in mediating the Camp David Accords between Israel and Egypt in 1978, which led directly to the 1979 Israel-Egypt Peace Treaty. We will also examine President Richard Nixon and Henry Kissinger's earlier successes in helping to negotiate the Sinai accords between Egypt and Israel and the Golan Agreement with Syria. The chapter will conclude with a discussion about how the United States can effectively promote Middle East peace by drawing on lessons from an earlier era when US diplomacy in the Middle East was successful because the right tools and negotiation strategies were used and the US was prepared to play a key leadership role.

⊖

CHAPTER 4

THE PROVEN SUCCESS OF TALK POWER

LESSONS FROM THE MIDDLE EAST

> What the Porte can never attain by force of arms, it can achieve by
> negotiation.... You want Egypt, I understand. But France never
> intended to take her away from you.... Everything can be settled in
> a couple hours' talk.
> —Napoleon Bonaparte, August 17, 1799, *Correspondence* V, 565

Whenever we look at the mess in the Middle East, we must recall that the Peace
Process, launched after the October War in 1973, is an American invention. It
has reduced the territorial extent of the Arab-Israeli conflict to the confines of
the Palestine mandate (plus the Golan Heights), returned large areas of Egyptian and Syrian land to their legal owners, and achieved peace agreements with
recognized boundaries to the east and south of Israel. It was all done with the
tools of Talk Power.

The other American preoccupation for the area—scarcely an invention, despite occasional claims—has been democratization, in a region that has fewer
democracies than any other region in the world. The second decade of the new
millennium began with an epidemic of spontaneous, secular uprisings—intifadas
of sorts driven by Twitter Talk—that overthrew the old arrogant, repressive order
and aspired to bring in a new era of dialogue and debate. But between the initial
uprising and the awaited elections, and afterward, is a disorganized but decisive
period of Talk, as the insurgents negotiate out their plans and programs and then

turn to what is left of the government to negotiate the conditions of transition. In a nonviolent revolution, the power of Talk is paramount.

The Background in Failure

The story is well known but it bears retelling. It actually begins before 1973, going back to the UN sessions that gave birth to Israel in 1947, but the June or Six-Day War twenty years later—the war that happened by gross miscommunication and miscalculation—is a good place to begin some contrasting background analysis. The six-year period between the June and the October wars was filled with lots of "alarums and excursions," in Shakespeare's phrase. On the human level, the problem involved personal relations between the secretary of state (William Rogers) and the president's national security advisor (Henry Kissinger). In addition, on the policy level, Kissinger felt that it was necessary to deal with Egypt directly rather than through the Soviet Union, and that withholding arms would not soften Israel, two differences with the State Department; time proved him right. At the institutional level, the plate was full. The State Department pursued routine relations in the region, but initiatives requiring higher-level attention were crowded out by the Nixon administration's priority focus on Cold War relations—China, Vietnam, and the Soviet Union. Dangerous as it might have been, the Middle East was subordinate to these, and Kissinger felt the time was not ripe: The stalemate was not particularly hurtful to both sides.

Israel was cocky over its six-day victory in 1967 and convinced that there was no need for negotiation, contacts, or concessions on their side. They underscored their victory with a continuing air war across the Suez, until the Soviets sent in planes and pilots, which the Israelis also shot down before accepting a ceasefire, in mid-1970. The Egyptians needed to restore their honor and erase the humiliation of 1967 as a precondition to any negotiation, recognition, or peace with Israel, all forbidden by the three "NOs" of Khartoum on August 31, 1967. Nasser was too stuck on his defeat, and when he died in 1970, his successor Anwar Sadat was seen as weak and unreliable. When he made a striking bid for attention, in 1972, by sending home the Soviet advisors, scarcely a year after he signed a friendship treaty with the USSR, the United States paid little attention. Much of the period, until 1971, was peppered by initiatives from the UN Special Representative of the Secretary-General Gunnar Jarring, who could not get conclusive attention from the superpowers.

Yet the period had a number of positive moments. Most important was UN Security Council Resolution 242, which set up the formula for all successive negotiations as "security for territory," just three months after the destructive

Three "NOs" of Khartoum. Another was the idea of partial withdrawal of forces along the canal as a beginning of movement in negotiation, launched in the fall of 1970 by Israeli Defense Minister Moshe Dayan. But by mid-1972, Sadat saw the need for "one more war," as his widow Jehan Sadat put it, to equalize relations and advance to his more loudly declared goal, "No more war!"[1]

The Peace Process

The result was the October 1973 War. It is important to note the salutary and galvanizing effect it had on the hitherto inconclusive search for progress toward peace. But without a dynamic, creative initiative, it would have led to the same unstable impasse as before. "I believe that only a battlefield stalemate would provide the foundation on which fruitful negotiations might begin,"[2] later stated President Richard Nixon.

The war ended in a striking instance of a mutually hurting stalemate: the Egyptian and Israeli armies in a mutual encirclement at Kilometer 101, that distance from Cairo on the Egyptian side of the Suez Canal. When negotiations began to extract the armies from their headlock, Secretary of State Kissinger decided not to just settle for an agreement to separate forces along the ceasefire line but to work for a larger disengagement agreement along the canal. "From the outset I was determined to use the war to start a peace process,"[3] he stated. The Peace Process had begun.

The first step, after having aborted the military separation of forces talks at Kilometer 101, was to convene a peace conference under the auspices of the UN secretary-general with the US and USSR foreign ministers in the chair, which the US Tough Talked the Israelis into attending. The conference adjourned after opening speeches, but it provided a base for subsequent negotiations under US mediation and it defused calls for a large international peace conference, an unwieldy venture.

In less than a month, the first positive step of the Peace Treaty Process was accomplished with the signature of the first Disengagement. The Israel Defense Forces (IDF) pulled back last from the Suez Canal, limited Egyptian forces moved to the west, and between the two was a UN buffer zone. Several elements in the talks that produced this initial achievement are significant. On the US side, Washington was both enabled and obliged to play a decisive role, without the Soviet, European, or UN interference that had characterized the past decades' diplomacy. On one hand, the Nixon administration had freed itself of the many constraints and challenges under which it had labored; détente with the Soviets had been launched, relations with China had been opened, and disengagement from

Vietnam had begun. On the other hand, the Arab oil embargo weighed heavily on the United States and Europe and gave impetus to speedy action, and the Arab initiative in the October War had attracted European, Third World, Soviet, and UN attention. Kissinger, with close backing from the president, took over and began his hallmark shuttle diplomacy, bearing messages and inserting ideas as a mediator in a formulator role. Finally, the agreement reached was manifestly unstable, with the Israelis still in sight of the Canal and the Egyptians backed up against it, although the Canal was restored to Egyptian control but opened to Israeli ships: The disengagement had to move forward, lest it fall back. Sticky Talk was written into the text: The agreement stated specifically that it was "not a final peace agreement" but "a first step toward a final, just and durable peace."

The next step was to turn to the other front, where the IDF had made significant advances toward Damascus beyond the 1967 ceasefire lines. The situation was more difficult than on the Egyptian front; the Syrians were in a strong position, holding an undisclosed number of Israeli POWs, and Syrian President Hafez al-Assad was not the moderate Sadat. Triple Talk diplomacy shuttled back and forth for three months, from February to May 1974, and Sweet Talk and Tough Talk shuttled with it. The United States increased its aid to Israel, then warned or even threatened reexamination of relations in the absence of progress. There were few incentives to wave at Assad other than an Israeli withdrawal, so Kissinger used the mediator's ultimate threat of termination (Stop Talk), before finally reaching an agreement that had hung on a few hundred meters of territory. The formula was the same as in Sinai: boundary in depth toward final settlement, and it proclaimed that it was "not a Peace Agreement" but "a step toward a just and durable peace on the basis of Security Council resolution 338 [that had updated UNSCR 242]."[4] But close to the old ceasefire line and centered on the key town of Quneitra, now moved from Israeli control to the UN buffer zone, the "boundary in depth" was less unstable than the Sinai disengagement zone and has lasted ever since.

With movement on two borders, the Peace Process turned to the third, with Jordan. But here the situation was very different. Barely two months after the Golan agreement, Nixon was replaced by Gerald Ford as president; two months later the Arab Summit withdrew Jordanian responsibility for Palestine and handed it to the Palestine Liberation Organization (PLO); there were no forces to disengage, since Jordan had not entered the war; the West Bank was not Jordanian territory, except by adoption, and the Jordan River was a very stable boundary. No amount of talk could create movement on that front.

So the Process returned to the Egyptian front, where Timely Talk had promised a second disengagement. But each step was now getting more difficult. If the Golan disengagement had almost gotten stuck on the town of Quneitra and its three strategic hills, the Sinai passes were to prove a more troublesome stumbling block. Like the Jordan River, they were a salient point for both sides: Both sides wanted them, to prevent the other from crossing into strategic territory. In addition, Egyptian oilfields along the Red Sea, which Israel had tapped for eight years, were also a zone of contention. Nearly half a year of shuttling produced no movement.

At that point, the United States raised the notion of a "massive reassessment" of its relations with Israel—another version of Stop Talk. The threat shook loose some of the obduracy on both sides; more important was the permanent commitment made to both Egypt and Israel for substantial aid. The pot had not been big enough to attract agreement, so it needed sweetening, and the mediator turned from a formulator to manipulator, exercising an involvement beyond words. A second Sinai Disengagement Agreement was finally signed over a year after Ford came into office, again providing a boundary in depth, unstable and "leaning forward," the passes in the UN buffer zone surrounded by Egyptian and Israeli surveillance stations and US civilian-manned electronic sensor fields. Kissinger left the Peace Process as a vigorous heritage for his successor, having shown enormous skill in communicating and formulating ideas through the creative use of Talk Power.

The Carter administration took up that inheritance and ran with it. Less than two months into his term President Jimmy Carter was in action with Timely Talk. The thrust was toward a full peace treaty within the framework of a Geneva conference, but conflicting positions of the Mideast parties parried the thrust effectively. To break the deadlock, President Sadat decided to enter the lions' den and address the Knesset in Jerusalem, before the end of Carter's first year. With a dramatic use of Straight Talk, he took the peace initiative out of the Americans' hands and put it back in the Middle East for the first time. In reaction to both the successes and failure of the bilateral disengagement agreements, Arab states were united in holding that all must be involved in a peace agreement; yet Sadat's initiative was resolutely unilateral. To go further than a declaration of intentions and a call for "No more war!" the Mideast parties needed a mediator to conduct Triple Talks. From Sadat's Jerusalem visit in November 1977 until September 1978, when the autumn leaves became colorful in the Catoctin Mountains, the United States worked between Egypt and Israel to set up a face-to-face meeting between Sadat and Prime Minister Menachem Begin to replace step-by-step shuttle diplomacy with a directly negotiated Egyptian—and by extension Arab—Israeli peace agreement.

Preparations for the Camp David meeting were conducted with enormous diligence by President Carter. Although the meeting began direct three-party negotiations, it soon became clear that shuttle diplomacy (although at a shorter distance than under Kissinger) was again needed and that direct negotiations would be conducted by subordinates. They were mismatched: Begin's representatives were more flexible than Sadat's, but Sadat was more flexible than Begin. Begin was a real stickler for detail, while Sadat looked to the big picture. The United States took an active role in preparing drafts, as a mediator/formulator. Tenacity and creativity produced two agreements, with a glitch: The framework for an Israeli-Egyptian peace treaty was linked to a looser framework for Palestinian autonomy (interpreted differently) in a faulty use of Right Talk, but Begin welshed on a promise to halt the construction of settlements in occupied Palestine. Another key to success was the secrecy of the meeting, a Safe Talk in the woods, carrying with it the challenge of selling results at home. Begin had let it be known that he was willing to go home empty-handed whereas Carter and Sadat were not, putting Begin in a stronger position where failure would mean success.

Coming home was the challenge. On his return, Sadat faced a split in the Arab world, with the radical wing forming a disruptive Rejectionist Front that expelled Egypt from the Arab League and Arab leadership. Begin turned tougher on remaining details. The American mediator continued shuttling, collecting comments on a developing draft for the Israeli-Egyptian peace treaty and preparing a single negotiating text. The following year reflected the difficulties of turning the frameworks into legal obligations, both on the steps of Egyptian and Israeli reconciliation and, more problematically, on the linkage between the Egyptian peace treaty and Palestinian autonomy. As Israel gradually diluted its commitments, Egypt hardened its positions. President Carter and Secretary Cyrus Vance pushed hard, to the point finally of traveling to Jerusalem and then, with agreement on a separate peace finally in hand, to Cairo. The treaty was signed in Washington on March 27, 1979, after over five years of slogging talks since the first Sinai Disengagement Agreement. Although attempts to pursue talks on Palestinian autonomy failed and remained dead for over a decade, the Washington Treaty was a crowning success of dogged, skillful talk that has endured the tests of time for over three decades.

The Process in Suspense and Revival

In contrast, the subsequent decade illustrates the importance of talk in the negative. It began with an ambiguous "yellow light" given by Secretary of State Al Haig to Israeli Defense Minister Ariel Sharon that was taken to be a "green light" for an invasion of Lebanon. As a result, President Ronald Reagan fired

Haig and leveled with Israel, in clear use of Tough Talk all around. He then went on to call for withdrawal of Israeli forces from Lebanon and to offer a plan for full autonomy for the West Bank and Gaza and phased Israeli withdrawal from the occupied territories. However, the plan had nothing in it for Israel. Secretary George Shultz then shuttled to Lebanon to mediate a peace treaty with Israel, weaning it away from its protector, Syria, but with Israeli withdrawal dependent on Syrian withdrawal. Needless to say, none of the conditions was fulfilled; the Lebanese president was assassinated, the Lebanese parliament rescinded the treaty, the US embassy and then the marine barracks were bombed with 241 deaths. The only withdrawal accomplished was the United States from Lebanon.

Without dynamic, presidentially led and diplomatically accomplished US leadership and mediation, the region took control of its own affairs, as in the Israeli invasion, the Sabra and Shatila massacres, the destruction of the US marine barracks, and the intifada (Palestinian youth-led uprising). The United States could only respond lamely. Secretary Shultz was disillusioned with the possibility of talking with Arab leaders, and particularly with Yasser Arafat and the PLO, now seen as necessary elements in any pursuit of autonomy talks. Despite a certain amount of activity after the withdrawal from Lebanon, effective talk was on hold until the very end of the Reagan administration, when attention over the year turned to securing an adequate statement from the PLO to make dialogue with the Palestinians possible.

The new president, George H. W. Bush, and his secretary of state, James Baker, soon picked up the trail and began discreet talks with the PLO in Tunis. Disruptive events in the region again troubled the waters and pulled the two parties apart. When the Iraqis invaded Kuwait and the US-led coalition invaded Iraq, Arafat and Jordan's King Hussein backed Saddam Hussein. But with the coalition's swift victory, Baker swung into action, shuttling around the region for the remainder of 1991 with the idea of holding an ongoing conference to deal with comprehensive peace issues, including multilateral committees on specific issues such as water, arms, development, the environment, and refugees. But in the aftermath of the first Gulf War there were two rather remarkable diplomatic demarches: the US-sponsored Madrid Conference of 1991 and the Norway-facilitated Oslo meetings of 1993. Whereas the latter had little participation from the United States, the Madrid Process requires attention here as a major turning point in US involvement in the Middle East Peace Process—a historic opportunity that was seized but then dropped.

The slow pace of the decades-long Arab-Israeli Peace Process quickened with the end of the Cold War and the victory of the US-led coalition in the first Gulf War. As Secretary Baker, who led US negotiations in the run up to Madrid, notes,

Iraq's defeat in the Gulf War had a dramatic effect on the region's balance of power.... The destruction of Saddam's offensive capability enhanced Israel's security and strengthened the hand of moderate Arab states, such as Egypt and Saudi Arabia. In liberating Kuwait, and promptly withdrawing from Iraq, as we had promised, the United States earned the respect and gratitude of all the Gulf Arab states. Additionally, the Soviet Union, long a force for trouble in the area, was now a partner of American diplomacy—and no longer a source of patronage for Arab rejectionists. American credibility in the region and internationally was higher at any time since the end of World War II. I believed it was a historic opportunity.[5]

And so it was. In successive rounds of intensive shuttle diplomacy Baker alternately applied pressure and engaged in confidence-building measures in order to establish a dialogue between Israel and Palestinians, on the one hand, and between Israel and the Arab states, on the other. Steadfast US diplomacy coupled with a willingness to act as a "neutral broker" and "tell difficult truths to both sides" finally brought the relevant actors on board. Facing Triple Talk laced with Straight and Tough Talk, all sides were offered compromise propositions but were also threatened with being publicly blamed should their inflexibility derail the peace process.

These tactics ultimately led to a historic peace conference in Madrid, Spain, cosponsored by the United States and the Soviet Union. For the first time, all key actors in the region—Palestinians, Israel, Syria, the United States, Saudi Arabia, Jordan, Egypt, the United Nations, Russia—agreed to get together and to meet and talk with one another. The principal outcome of Madrid was that it broke the long-standing taboo on direct talks between Palestinians and Israelis and launched a two-track approach to negotiations with parallel reciprocal confidence-building measures that gave "both sides political cover to modify long-standing policy." And, as Baker further notes, "like a phoenix, the Middle East peace process was reborn in Madrid out of the ashes of the collapse of communism and of Saddam's ill-conceived invasion of Kuwait."[6]

The question of Israeli and Palestinian participation was the thorniest: Israel was induced to slow settlement construction and to attend when Bush held up loan guarantees, and the Palestinians were represented by leading figures from the occupied territories (and Jordan) not directly attached to the PLO. The conference opened in Madrid on October 30, 1991, and proceeded in Washington through eight rounds into the following year, making small progress despite a less active American role than in previous initiatives. It was dogged by the very opposite of the Camp David meetings—too much publicity—but also by the absence of authoritative Palestinians and by the impending US elections.

From the beginning, Bush and Baker had worked to bring representatives of the parties in the conflict together and had used their initial misjudgment of Saddam Hussein to carry off an impressive and galvanizing military victory and a path-opening assembly of the Mideast parties to continue the Peace Process.

Although President Bill Clinton inherited a promising chance for productive Team Talk at the Madrid Conference, now moved to Washington, little was done to address the major communications obstacle, the absence of official PLO representation. Instead, the United States helped Israel in its talks with Syria, which also bogged down in mid-1993. But at the same time, Israel under its new Prime Minister Yitzhak Rabin was doing talking on its own with an official PLO delegation out of sight in Oslo. At the end of the summer, to US surprise, Safe Talk brought an agreement of mutual recognition (as a state and as an official spokesman for a people, an unequal status), implementation of the autonomy principle in a Palestinian Authority with a territory of its own, and a commitment to pursue negotiations on other issues to a final peace agreement. The barrier to talking was broken, leading to further agreement in Cairo with Egyptian assistance on the procedures of implementation and the timetable, to bring final agreement by mid-1999, and then to further implementation in the Oslo II Agreement (although, like Oslo I, signed in Washington) in September 1995, two years after its predecessor. The Oslo Agreement also opened the way for direct and less contentious negotiation of a peace treaty between Jordan and Israel in October 1994.

The Process in Pieces

The Oslo talks, a creative and committed exercise, fell victim to the key of its success: secrecy, just like Camp David. Neither side worked to sell the agreement to its home audience, nor even more so, to help the other side sell the agreement. Terrorism continued, culminating in the assassination of Rabin by a Jewish fundamentalist. The loss was tremendous but talks continued, to provide the shape of a final agreement on a two-state solution. But the spoiler who had united Israel and the PLO in a preemptive effort at Oslo continued to strike hard. In the May 1996 elections, Netanyahu the hardliner was narrowly elected prime minister. Oslo had killed Rabin and Hamas had elected Netanyahu.

The United States was notably absent through the entire period, simply following the jagged ups and downs of relations among the parties themselves. Fundamentalist spoilers on either side were an active threat, and the parties needed pressure, support, and encouragement in their talks. They had shown spurts of creativity when left alone, but they needed above all engagement to keep at it when obstacles arose and that could only come from above or below. The public was wary and unengaged; meaningful assistance could only come from above, from great power involvement, to keep talks on track. The following summits at Wye Plantation in October 1998 and Camp David in December saw the end of the Peace Process. Many good ideas were broached at Camp David, including a proposal by new Prime Minister Ehud Barak to divide Jerusalem, but presented on a nonnegotiable basis. Since no single negotiating text was used, the ideas simply floated or sank but were never pulled together. It was Team Talk at its worst, under unsustainable deadlines.

Talking Points from the Middle East

There are many lessons on how to talk successfully from twenty years of experience in the Mideast. *The first is that the parties in conflict need help.* Conflict is overwhelmingly engrossing, and it is against nature to expect that the parties can turn from conflict to reconciliation without assistance, even if they proclaim they want to. Mediators, as they can be called generically, are needed to overcome various types of obstacles. The United States was a communicator or facilitator carrying messages, as in some of the instances of shuttle diplomacy and at Oslo. But this minimal role is generally not sufficient, as in subsequent situations leading up to Annapolis. More frequently, it needed to act as a formulator, inserting itself into the process with ideas of its own. Kissinger in the disengagements, Carter at Camp David, but also Shultz in Lebanon and Clinton at Camp David II, played this kind of key role. But when ideas are not enough and direct involvement through warnings and threats, predictions, and promises is required, then the mediator must act as a manipulator, the most involved. Kissinger in Sinai II and Baker at Madrid are key, instructive examples. Talking does not come naturally while fighting, so a persuasive, intrusive, compelling third party is required, leading Triple Talk.

So what makes the difference between the successful and unsuccessful exercise of Triple Talk Power is recognition that *mediation is a risky business that calls for deep engagement, long preparation, and serious commitment.* Talks that worked began with detailed study and brainstorming, and took persistence and patience in the process. The mediator had to roll up his sleeves and push, travel, call in high-level support, plead and cajole, warn, and even threaten. An enormous investment of time and personal—and even national—prestige is required. In the American system, it has to begin early in the presidential term and not be saved for a last-minute rabbit-hat trick.

Mediators and negotiators need to be willing to draw realistic deadlines, not immediately, but when talk drags on inconclusively. Talks on the withdrawals, at Camp David I and on the Washington Treaty, seemed to reach the end of the road, but the mediator pushed once more and brought negotiations to a successful conclusion. The threat to walk away (Stop Talk) is effective only when talks have made progress but gotten bogged down; at other times, it may actually be welcomed by the warring parties. Since a mediator is ultimately a meddler, disturbing the parties' pursuit and enjoyment of their conflict, the threat to leave is no threat at all unless a better alternative is not already in sight.

Ripe moments should be seized but more frequently unripe moments need to be ripened. If the parties are already in a mutually hurting stalemate with a sense that the other also sees talk as the path to a way out, as they did at Kilometer 101 in 1974 or in the fruitless Madrid/Washington talks in 1993, the mediator's job is cut out for him or her. But if those perceptions are not present, the mediator must first create them, sometimes even by creating the objective facts on the ground but other times by simply encouraging a subjective appreciation of the objective facts. When no one but the mediator feels the pain, negotiations are not likely to get very far. Ripening often means seizing new turns in events, as Baker did after the 1991 Gulf War or as Kissinger before him used the October War, or even as a pair of Israeli academics used the election of a new prime minister in Israel.

Secrecy or Safe Talk is important for a successful conclusion but the results must be sold publicly afterward. The process of making peace is delicate enough that a gaggle of reporters looking in the windows is of no help. The closed conditions of Camp David I and Oslo and the controlled communications of Kissinger on his shuttles were important to the achievement of results. But the challenge thereafter is to sell the results back home, building public support for the agreements. The successful negotiator has to convey the constructive atmosphere and positive results for his country that prevailed at the talks, overcoming what is termed the "reentry problem." The work is facilitated when the other party joins in selling the agreement to the opposite constituency, with Sadat's Jerusalem speech as a salient example. Oslo particularly was a victim of the reentry problem, as was Camp David II for even the limited progress made.

Not only is it important to gain immediate support for the agreement but also to put continuing efforts into its implementation. It is a normal human tendency to rejoice over the results of successful talks and turn to other pressing problems that have been neglected in the interim. Instead, the negotiators need to be told, "Take the weekend off to celebrate, but report to work on Monday." Camp David I died in part and Camp David II almost entirely over the challenge of implementation, and Oslo withered on the vine—or was cut off at the roots—within three years.

The aim of talk is persuasion, and persuasion is the essence of negotiation. It is impressive how much concrete progress was accomplished by creative talk using all the standard tools of Talk Power—Tough, Straight, Sweet, Happy, Timely, Sticky, and Safe Talk, and even Stop Talk when necessary. Heads of state and their aides met to exchange and debate ideas and to open them up to change. The process begins with careful exposition and listening; parties and mediators have to understand what each feels it needs and how the other side has hurt it (a significant first act in the Oslo process). It then turns to verbal efforts to bring these views and narratives together until common results are achieved. Creativity is the name of the game. Often this means editorial creativity or Right Talk, to find the proper wording for something the parties know or hope is there but do not immediately know how to say it. Other times it means new ideas, new visions, even new constructions of interests.

Part of persuasion is the ability to leap over current animosities and direct attention to future benefits. As important as meeting present needs is the ability to make sure it doesn't happen again, that the past is put away, and that parties have created a better future for themselves. Forward-looking talk to create shared guarantees and projects is more constructive than backward-looking efforts to ease past pains. When the parties at Oslo ended their opening statements of pain and the other's responsibility for it and decided to put it all aside, they opened the way to a joint search for a positive agreement.

Tough conflicts like the Middle East require the mediator to act as a formulator, inserting his or her ideas into the debate rather than just facilitating and carrying messages. New ideas are needed, but they must not be imposed on the parties. At times, the initiative need be ascribed to the mediator, to lift the responsibility from the initiating party, but in the end ownership belongs to the parties. Even by the parties themselves, take-it-or-leave-it proposals and ultimatums, such as Barak offered at Camp David II, no matter how good, leave no room for a sense of ownership by both parties that is necessary to clinch a deal.

Mediators and parties are people, and as such have their own cultural nests, national clothing, and personal styles. Part of the mediator's challenge is to be the hyphen between these differences, so that his or her mediation is not just about addressing technicalities or being a good wordsmith. Personal liaison qualities and cultural sensitivity are vitally important, too. Sadat's focus on general principles against Begin's on Talmudic details required a skillful mediator to make the translation.

All this can produce some very positive talk that overcomes conflict and moves a process forward toward peace. *Often the parties know where they are going; the problem is how to get there, and then to make it last.* Creative talking can find the way, and the record of the Mideast Peace Process in its better moments provides wonderful examples of how. That record is also littered with missed opportunities, as identified in chapter two, which also carry their lessons, lessons to be identified so that they may not be repeated. To be sure, the track becomes more and more challenging as it nears its conclusion, and the missed opportunities have left their grievances to be added to the original conflict. That is why it is better to talk sooner than later, or even later rather than not at all.

During 2011, the Middle East was in the throes of wrestling with the major change that the United States had been urging on it—democracy. It was as Arab masses and intellectuals wanted it: The possibility for democracy had been created at home, not imposed from the outside (although, ironically, the cry then turned to the outside for support). With internal politics in the process of evolution and rearrangement for some unforeseeable time, it is even more difficult to focus attentions creatively on the politics of neighborly relations. Yet, more than ever, such changes cannot be done merely from the inside; they need outside help. Ripening, persuasion, and salesmanship become more important than ever.

PART II

MANAGING

CHAPTER 5
TIMELY TALK TO PREVENT VIOLENT CONFLICT

In almost every case, the most difficult step was to obtain agreement as to when the negotiation should commence and who was to be included.... All sides must be convinced there is a problem, that they can only resolve it together, and that the others are willing to bargain in good faith.... Those who desire to begin negotiations (including an interested third party) can sometimes take action—either in the form of reward or punishment—to create these necessary factors.

—Jimmy Carter[1]

We are living in a world that is becoming increasingly violent and conflict prone, and particularly on the domestic or intrastate level, where civil order is commonly expected to be found. According to the Center for International Development and Conflict Management at the University of Maryland, which for many years has been tracking the outbreak of violent conflict, the steady decline in the number of active conflicts around the globe immediately following the end of the Cold War appears now to be reversing itself with a resurgence of armed conflict and violence in many countries.[2] At the same time, there is a greatly diminished appetite in the United States, given its continuing security commitments in Afghanistan and Iraq and now its growing fiscal burdens, to intervene with Gun Power to stop the outbreak or escalation of violence in different corners of the world. Absent US leadership or willingness to intervene, others are unlikely to follow. These harsh realities underscore the vital need to identify strategies that can prevent the outbreak of violent conflict in the first place.

This is not a new challenge. In the early 1990s, in the aftermath of genocidal atrocities in Rwanda and the horrendous war in the Balkans, there was growing interest in designing strategies aimed at preventing the outbreak of violent conflict. As early as 1991, actions mandated by the UN Security Council in Resolution 687, led by the United States and Britain, imposed a highly intrusive and complex regime of monitoring to prevent Iraq from producing weapons of mass destruction. Thereafter, Council members tended to use the "international peace and security" threat that flows of refugees could pose to neighboring countries to authorize preventive action. Such arguments were advanced, notably, in the early stages of the disintegration of the former Yugoslavia, Somalia, Haiti, East Timor, the overflow of refugees into Guinea from neighboring Liberia and Sierra Leone, and the flight of refugees across the Mediterranean when the Libyan dam broke. Where action was taken, Security Council decisions aimed at preventing even worse outcomes. Yet, in general, prevention was preached more often than it was practiced.

Much of the discussion in more recent years has revolved around strengthening emerging norms associated with the "Responsibility to Protect." Although based on existing humanitarian principles, this doctrine reiterates that individuals must be protected from mass killing, in particular genocide and crimes against humanity. Protection is mandated even when these acts occur within the territory of sovereign states, redefining the concepts of sovereignty and humanitarian intervention to focus more directly on the rights of threatened individuals, rather than those of states. Unfortunately, despite some clear successes in strengthening this general prohibition and facilitating state compliance, international and intrastate violence has continued relatively unabated in many corners of the globe. There are conflicts in Darfur, Somalia, Syria, Yemen, Pakistan, Afghanistan, Colombia, Congo, and elsewhere where the international community has had little appetite for intervention. The reality is that politics all too often stands in the way of any kind of direct military intervention—the use of Gun Power—after a conflict has escalated beyond the point of no return.

Although Gun Power may be necessary to halt massive human rights violations and genocide within a nation's borders, there are other potential options that are available to prevent the outbreak of violence and conflict in the first place. One such tool is the early exercise of Talk Power, or Timely Talk, which can play a vital role in forestalling the onset of civil war and regional conflict. This is no airy theory. Think of it: Literally innumerable conflicts have been prevented by talking, as practiced in normal diplomacy. Plenty of potential conflict situations exist both between and within states that in the extreme—in fact exceptional—cases give rise to violence. In most cases, normal diplomacy and, internally, normal politics, can and indeed have handled disputes before they get out of hand. Talk works! More than half a dozen specific positive and negative examples show the breadth of the exercise of Talk Power in its Timely Talk variation.

The Uses of Timely Talk

Case #1a

In the South Atlantic in 1980, Great Britain and Argentina entered a short but bloody war, costing 1,000 lives, over a group of islands far from Britain but not very close to Argentina either. The parties engaged in some talk, but not much, and concentrated mainly in repeating their immovable positions.

Case #1b

In the western Mediterranean in July 2002, a conflict broke out over a tiny island a few hundred meters off the Moroccan mainland, where one could say, using the old rhyme,

> The King of Morocco sent a dozen men
> To march up the hill but not march down again.
> The King of Spain then sent two dozen more
> To march up the hill the Moroccans marched up before.

Since some Spanish enclaves are on Morocco's Mediterranean coast and are claimed by Morocco, the Perejil/Leila (Toura) Island conflict threatened to escalate into a nasty and costly war. Tempers rose, nasty words were exchanged, and friends of both parties lined up behind them. Many countries, notably in Europe, were friends of both sides, producing many calls for talk and reason. Spain refused EU mediation, looking for support instead. Morocco declared that "dialogue was the best way to build the future relations between the two countries." The United States was particularly active in urging the parties to meet, discuss, and settle the affair, which they did after ten tense days. Timely Talk led by the United States forestalled the onset of conflict.

Case #1c

In the eastern Mediterranean in 1995, a conflict arose over the Greek island of Imia/Kardak three miles off the Turkish mainland, composed of two even smaller pieces of rock. A Turkish cargo ship had run aground nearby. Relations between the two historic enemies were so bad that no agreement on the delimitation of maritime areas even for search and rescue operations had been established. Greek troops landed on one rock in response to the Turkish infringement, whereupon Turkish troops landed on the other rock, spiraling into a race between media and officials on both sides to see who could be more vociferously patriotic. By the end of the month, the two sides' navies trained guns on each other, on the brink of war. Both countries, members of the North Atlantic Treaty Organization (NATO), scrambled for allies. Both sides had to react once the first move was made, escalating to the point where the next step would be catastrophic. The United States stepped in and helped the parties climb down from their perilous perches, the situation returned to the status quo, and the cargo ship was refloated.

The difference between the island conflict of the South Atlantic and the two in the Mediterranean is that in the second set of cases the parties were open to talking to each other, clarifying their positions and the events which gave rise to the conflict, and winding down the tensions between them. The parties in the Mediterranean were concerned about the crisis's escalating out of control and were sensible enough to realize that the little pieces of uninhabited rock were not worth the danger, whereas in the South Atlantic the islands were seen as a major prestige stake for both parties. In the Mediterranean cases, ownership of the islands did not change but the conflict was defused. In the case of the Falklands, ownership did not change either, but at great cost in terms of lives lost in the ensuing conflict. The greatest obstacle in all three cases was saving face, commitment, and entrenched positions, which words and the effective use of Timely Talk properly used in two out of three cases, helped assuage.

Case #2

As the Federal Republic of Yugoslavia fell into pieces after the fall of the Berlin Wall, beginning in 1990, the independence of Croatia, Bosnia, and Kosovo was bought at a heavy price of some 300,000 lives, to add to the 6 million Slavs killed in the rest of the twentieth century.

Military intervention by NATO in 1999 in Kosovo, an autonomous region of the former Yugoslavia, occurred following a Yugoslav refusal to accept an internationally imposed peace settlement. NATO launched a seventy-eight-day bombing campaign that forced Yugoslav military and paramilitary forces out of Kosovo. Despite the absence of express UN authorization, many NATO states argued that the Security Council had implicitly supported their military action through its characterization of Kosovo as an impending catastrophe, bolstered by its decision, in a vote of 12-3, to reject a Russian Federation proposal to condemn the intervention. Ambiguities highlighted by NATO's Kosovo intervention led UN Secretary-General Kofi Annan to call on states to redefine and clarify the framework for responding to internal humanitarian crises using military force.

In two other cases, however, the independence of former Yugoslav republics was achieved without violence—Macedonia and Montenegro. Montenegro got its independence from Serbia following a public referendum on May 21, 2006. The process of secession was regulated by the Constitutional Charter of Serbia and Montenegro, adopted some three years earlier by both houses of the Yugoslav Federal Assembly, in accordance with the 2002 Belgrade Agreement between the governments of the two constitutive republics of the former Yugoslavia.

Macedonia's independence was somewhat more problematic. Macedonia earlier had been named South Serbia. Following the dissolution of the former Yugoslavia in 1990–91, it refused to join Serbia and Montenegro and instead opted for its independence on November 20, 1991. Neighboring Greece refused to recognize the new independence for fear that Macedonia's very name would incite irredentist designs among the Slavic Macedonians in northern Greece. At the same time, the Republic's internal stability was threatened by its Muslim Albanian minority, who demonstrated and politicked to insist on guarantees for the protection of their cultural autonomy and welfare in the new constitution and national politics. An Albanian party became part of the Socialist government coalition, policies worked to equalize opportunity, and the minority hoped for early inclusion in the European Union (EU) to assure growth and development. A mission of the OSCE High Commissioner on National Minorities urged greater attention to the Albanian minority's concerns, and a 1,000-man UN force, later named the UN Preventive Deployment Force (UNPREDEP), was authorized in December 1992 to monitor the northern border.

Throughout the decade, many of these assumptions and accomplishments fell apart, however. EU accession turned out to be more distant. Albanian hopes for improved conditions paled. Politics swung to the right and a more nationalist coalition (including Albanians) was elected in 1998. The 1998–99 war in Kosovo—fueled by an arms influx following the 1997 state collapse in Albania—piqued Macedonian Albanian nationalism, and, to add insult to injury, the Chinese in the United Nations refused to renew UNPREDEP because of Macedonian relations with Taiwan.

In early 2001, a Macedonian Albanian National Liberation Army (NLA, with the same initials in Albanian as the Kosovo Liberation Army, UCK) took to violence and called for attention to minority grievances and ultimately independence. A tripartite Western initiative of the United States, EU, and NATO intervened diplomatically, helping unite the minority groups behind a single set of demands that did not include independence, arranging for a ceasefire and disarmament and the reintegration of the Albanian parties into normal Macedonian politics by August. In 2002, when UN authorization was not renewed, NATO assumed the functions of UNPREDEP. The NATO mission, Operation Allied Harmony, was subsequently handed over to the EU in 2003. The handover was made possible following the agreements reached by the EU and NATO on access by the EU to the collective assets and capabilities of NATO for EU-led operations.

The difference between the Macedonian case and the bloody secessionist struggles of Bosnia, Croatia, and later Kosovo, did not lie in the presence or absence of talking, but more importantly in the type of talking and its response among the conflicting parties. The high level of diplomatic activity in Bosnia, Croatia, and Kosovo was disjointed, divided, and uncommitted, until finally the United States, which had stayed out of the earlier efforts and was just as disorganized and uncommitted as the rest, took over the mediation effort in Bosnia in 1995; at the end of the decade it gave up on diplomacy and resorted to the use force in the case of Kosovo. In the case of Macedonia, at the beginning of the decade and again a decade later, diplomacy was focused, coordinated, timely, and clear in what it was seeking to prevent. Among themselves and in dealing with the West, the conflicting parties were able to see that what they could gain by working together was greater than what they could win individually by pursuing their military options, and that perception was the result of some solid Timely Talk led by the international community and some of Macedonia's own leaders.

Case #3

In Colombia, the Revolutionary Armed Forces (FARC) and the National Liberation Army (ELN) started out in the mid-1960s as leftist movements speaking for social groups excluded by the National Pact that ended *La Violencia* of the 1950s and early 1960s. Both rebel groups gradually became hooked on the production and distribution of drugs and became impossibly difficult to dislodge. The ensuing conflict has led to some 80,000 deaths.

A third insurgency group, the M-19, of more urban middle class and less ideological intellectuals also arose following an electoral defeat in 1970. It committed some spectacular terrorist acts in the 1980s, including the occupation of the Supreme Court, the Dominican Embassy, and a Bogotá military base. But in the middle of the decade, its leaders came to the realization that guerrilla violence was not the path to its goal of social reform. At the same time, a new liberal government under Virgilio Barco came to power under the slogan of "rehabilitation, normalization and reconciliation." Negotiations began in 1988, followed by a ceasefire, and then participation of the M-19 in elections in 1990. The process was slow and bumpy, but continued despite the refusal of the other guerrilla movements to participate, repeated violence by the drug lords, and the rise of right-wing militias.

The difference was produced by internal debate within the government and the M-19, which led to a realization that violence does not produce reforms and that reforms are necessary to win dissidents away from violence. Once both sides had seen that their violence could damage the other but not eliminate it and that the other side was open to talking, then discussions could begin. It took dogged commitment to overcome sabotage and keep on talking, but the results were better for both sides.

Case #4a

Eritrea became independent from Ethiopia in 1993 after a million casualties from three decades of war with a border that was delimited but not demarcated. Within five years, a vicious war that was to cost 100,000 lives broke out over two small disputed and worthless segments of land. It took another two years to conclude a peace treaty. A decade later the parties were still not reconciled.

Case #4b

The "last border dispute in Latin America," a continent torn by border disputes since independence in 1825, broke out in violence between Ecuador and Peru several dozen times in the twentieth century alone, despite an agreed protocol in 1942, an arbitration award in 1945, and the subsequent demarcation of over 95 percent of the border. However, aerial photography revealed new terrain features in the dense Amazon jungle and led to new clashes in 1981 and 1995. Both sides stuck to their legal arguments, which included Peru's claim that Ecuador had not even existed at the time the border was established. In the midst of such endless arguments and inconclusive military action, the four protocol guarantor countries (Argentina, Brazil, Chile, and the United States) proposed to look beyond legal sovereignty and brought the parties to an agreement based on demarcation in exchange for access, sovereignty in exchange for ownership, and above all cooperation to develop an isolated and inhospitable region shared by both countries. The Brasilia Agreement of October 1998 overcame past disagreements by establishing the basis for future, mutually beneficial, cooperation.

The difference between the two cases began with the fact that the Andean countries learned from unnecessarily long experience, whereas the neighbors in the Horn of Africa were entrapped by their heavy investment in war and could not see beyond it. Once Peru and Ecuador could shift their attention from their past intractable differences, creative thinking on the part of the mediators opened up new political possibilities, and the parties talked their way into a pact of mutually beneficial cooperation along newly defined lines, rather than staying in a rut of dysfunctional conflict over contested border lines. Timely Talk allowed for creativity, and creativity led to satisfaction in new terms.

Case #5a

When Robert Mugabe set the stage for the 2008 elections in Zimbabwe, his regime had already killed thousands of his population running from simple peasants to opposition and civic leaders. His kleptocratic government had all but run the country into the ground, with many of its inhabitants living in destitute conditions and suffering from widespread disease. When he lost the election by all impartial counts, he called for a runoff, and when he had harassed his opponent, Morgan Tsvangirai, and driven him out of the country, he killed off some more of his countrymen. He then lured Tsvangirai into an asymmetrical coalition, while continuing to harass members of his opposition party.

Case #5b

An election that same year in Kenya challenged the incumbent regime of President Emilio Mwai Kibaki, who headed the Kenyan African National Union (KANU) party, which was supported by Kikuyu and Meru tribes. When supporters of the main opposition leader Raila Odinga saw themselves robbed of a victory at the polls, they took to the streets in many villages to wreak havoc on supporters of the president's regime. There was a major breakdown of law and order in many parts of the country, and the situation threatened to escalate into a full blown civil war with ethnic cleansing and the threat that some regions would secede from the country. Many incidents of vandalism, looting, killings, and sexual violence were reported; a UN investigation later stated that more than 1,200 Kenyans had died in the violence, thousands more had been injured, more than 300,000 people had been displaced, and thousands of farms, businesses, and homes had been destroyed. Notwithstanding the violence and destruction, the situation might have gotten a whole lot worse had not the United States, Britain, and the African Union urged calm and reconciliation while launching a Timely Talk initiative, led by former UN Secretary-General Annan and backed by the Panel of Eminent African Personalities. Annan was able to secure an agreement between the parties, later passed by the Kenyan Parliament as the National

Accord and Reconciliation Act in 2008, which provided for a power-sharing agreement between Kibaki, who would stay on as president, and Odinga, who would assume the new post of prime minister in a carefully balanced government—known as the Grand Coalition—with cabinet representatives from the country's different ethnic groups.

The difference in the Zimbabwean and Kenyan cases did not lie in the international community's response; Timely and Triple Talk were used in both cases, led by mediators. However, the pressures on the Kenyan government and opposition were much stronger and concerted than those directed against Zimbabwe, particularly from the African Union, who tried to be gentle on Mugabe. Mugabe also controlled the security situation in Zimbabwe. The Zimbabwean army was strongly opposed to giving any concessions to the opposition, so that the threat of continuing violence and anarchy weighed more heavily on the opposition and the general population than on the regime. The need to talk and to share power effectively was brought home more strongly to the parties by Kofi Annan in Kenya than by Thabo Mbeki in Zimbabwe. The fact that the conflict was at an impasse and threatened massive damage to both parties and the country in general in Kenya forced them to listen to the Tough Talk of the mediator and to step down from escalation, even if not all the way down to fraternity. The conflict was managed by talking in a way that gave the parties time to examine ways of living with the new modus vivendi without recourse to violence.

Case #6a

The most devastating genocide of the post–Cold War era was the massacre of 800,000 Tutsi and moderate Hutus in Rwanda in 1994. The return of Tutsis exiled in neighboring Uganda began the civil war by the Rwandan Patriotic Front (RPF) in 1990. Internationally mediated negotiations brought about the Arusha Agreement of 1993, setting up a new political system with a coalition regime between the Hutu government, the Hutu opposition, and the RPF. But it excluded the *akazu* Hutu extremists, who carried out the genocide the following year, and, paradoxically, brought in the RPF as a result.

Case #6b

The same year, elections were held in South Africa under a new political system negotiated between the White National Party and the African National Congress (ANC). Earlier, an Umkhonto we Sizwe ("Spear of the Nation"; also known as MK) slogan floating around stated "One White man, one bullet." But as the 1990s began, Joe Slovo, head of the South African Communist Party, said,

"Neither side won the war. The National Party couldn't rule any longer and we [the ANC] couldn't seize power by force. That means both sides have to compromise. That's the reality."[3] On the other side, President F. W. de Klerk came to the conclusion that the regime was no longer able to provide security and prosperity for the privileged minority; it was unable to control and contain the dispossessed majority; it had lost international legitimacy; and the cost of these three inabilities was rising beyond its capacity to sustain. Neither side changed its goals—political equality for the majority, security and prosperity for the minority—but both changed their perception of the means to attain them, no longer in conflict but in cooperation with the other party.

Early contacts between South African business and government and the ANC began in the mid-1980s to see if there was any change of heart on the other side. De Klerk's change of mindset at the end of the decade produced the release of Nelson Mandela and the unbanning of the ANC at the beginning of 1990. Then talks about talks began, fleshing out the original formula of "legality in exchange for nonviolence." Parties and civil society groups worked out a National Peace Accord in September 1991, laying the ground for the first session of the Convention for a Democratic South Africa (CoDeSA) at the end of 1991. In mid-1992 violence and disagreement brought a breakdown in the talks but renewed violence brought the parties back to work out a Record of Understanding in September 1992. A revived CoDeSA, renamed the Multiparty Negotiation Forum, convened in March 1993 and approved an interim constitution with some immutable principles in November, under which the new political system was voted upon in the elections of April 1994. The result was indeed a miracle—the first time in history when an ascriptive majority overthrew a ruling minority without violence.

The differences between these two cases are particularly instructive, especially considering that there was much negotiation and even an agreement in both cases. On the surface, the Rwanda talks were unconvincing and did not bring in the spoilers, the *akazu* who became the *genocidaires* the following year, but also the RPF who continued its military campaign after Arusha. In Rwanda, the two sides saw the other as an existential threat and deeply feared their takeover; in South Africa, that fear may not have entirely disappeared, but it was certainly pushed far back in people's minds. Instead, they saw their existential protection in cooperation rather than conflict with the other side, and the step-by-step behavior of each side over the four years of the process confirmed that new calculus. It is worth repeating that in South Africa the parties did not change their goals, but, after talking, they saw new ways of achieving them, while also recognizing that they could not achieve them by old methods at an acceptable cost.

Talking Before Violence

These stories, chosen out of many, underscore above all the importance of keeping open lines of communication and using them, particularly when touchy situations begin to appear. Keeping lines open is the job of "normal diplomacy." An ambassador's prime role is to maintain good relations between the home and the host country, and that means keeping one's Rolodex open and active. Then, if unusual events occur, it is easy to use those open lines to forewarn and defuse. India and Pakistan faced a mounting crisis in their extremely testy and suspicious relations in 2010 when the Indians built hydroelectric dams across Pakistan's main water supplying rivers; objectively this should not cause problems since water through power dams returns to the stream and proceeds downhill. But the appearance of "them damming our water" raised hackles. The *New York Times* commented, "The water dispute would not be nearly as acute, experts said, if India and Pakistan talked and shared data on water. Instead, the distrust and antagonism is [sic] such that bureaucrats have hoarded information, and are secretly gunning to finish projects ... in order to be the first to have an established fact on the ground."[4] Normally flowing communications can prevent crises.

But when they do not, crisis times are especially important as moments when the parties involved need to sit down and talk it out. The crisis makes talk more difficult, because now the parties find themselves entrapped in the train of events and in the demonizing and hysterical rhetoric that inevitably creates the public atmosphere of a crisis. Newspaper accounts, political campaigns, and talk shows envenom the atmosphere and undermine official attempts to return to calm. Government representatives are caught between their attempts to defuse and their need to be responsive to public pressure and not to appear to back down. Officials are tempted to respond in kind to the public provocations rather than to diplomatic efforts. Therefore, not merely is talk required but careful, skillful Timely Talk, which both reassures the other party and insures avoidance of deleterious effects. Both aspects matter: the personal subjective reassurance and the objective provision of measures to make sure that negative effects do not occur.

States working to overcome broken and suspicious relations also often resort to Confidence and Security Building Measures (CSBMs). Essentially, these are measures to restore talking in various forms. They include hotlines, prenotification of military and other activities that may be taken as threatening, and forums to discuss plans and activities.

Another type of "CSBMs extended" is engagement in joint projects. Nothing pulls parties together and forces them to talk positively like an engagement to do things together. The very fact that such activities might serve as a further platform for suspiciousness and miscomprehension forces the parties to make extra efforts to communicate carefully and talk out possible problems. One cannot work side by side in the same direction without talking out purposes and problems in order to make the common project work. Again, it is not simply working together that prevents conflict; it is through creating lasting structures that benefit both sides and tie them together in interdependence. It is often said that France and Germany were able to join in building a common European project because they had overcome their centuries-long animosity, but it is the reverse that is true: France and Germany were able to overcome their historic hostility by engaging in a joint European project that forced them to overcome animosities and collaborate.

Thus, as the stories tell us, Timely Talk is a necessary and vital tool of diplomacy. But Talk alone is not enough, it must be done constructively and creatively. Britain and Argentina, the warring parties in Yugoslavia, the rebels and the government in Colombia, Ethiopia and Eritrea, the Zimbabwean government and its opposition, and the Rwandan ethnic groups all talked to each other on the path to violence. But the talks broke down, were halfhearted, were sabotaged by spoilers, or were overridden by the parties themselves. What made the difference?

Some characteristics stand out strongly. *Parties who talked successfully were persuaded of the looming danger if they did not change the stakes of the conflict.* Sometimes talking removed any troubling doubts and uncertainties about the status quo; other times, it brought out new solutions that improved the status quo. Talk in these cases released creativity and the parties thought outside the zero-sum conflict into which they had been boxed.

Parties who talked successfully were persuaded that joint efforts and cooperation were more likely to produce reforms and other positive outcomes for each of them than continued unilateral efforts and conflict. Working together would produce positive sums and was more likely to be successful than doggedly going it alone. Their existential concerns, where such were involved, were seen to be protected better in cooperation than in unilateral defense. This meant that the parties had to communicate to each other that they were willing to work together, even before that cooperation actually began. That communication was possible only by talking together, before they started acting together. Obviously, the individual gains through cooperation were sometimes not as large as they would have been if single-shooting were to have succeeded. But the chances of success of unilateral action were deemed lower than the chances of cooperative success, and more costly. Half a loaf in hand was worth more than a full loaf in an oven that had not been turned on.

Probably the most controversial characteristic was that parties who talked successfully included everyone in their talks. This is simply an extension of the idea that one must talk with the opponent, the adversary, the enemy. "Who do you expect me to negotiate with except the enemy?" said Israeli negotiator Uri Savir.[5] The challenge comes with the recognition that there may be enemies who are beyond talking—the *akazu* in Rwanda, but also the Argentine generals and the British politicians, the Ethiopian and Eritrean presidents, and Mugabe. Extremists may have locked themselves into a spoiler position and may be out to overturn any attempts at reaching a cooperative agreement. They may either believe that no agreement is possible, that half a loaf is not sufficient even if attainable, or that they are benefiting too much from the conflict to give it up. Left out, they would upset any agreement; brought in, they would make agreement impossible. There is no general answer to the problem. But leaving such parties out will confirm them as spoilers, whereas bringing them in opens them up to persuasion, even if it makes the deal harder to achieve.

In the end, the key to all of these differences is persuasion, which is the essence of diplomacy. Talking persuasively is more important than forcing the parties into agreement, more effective in removing misunderstandings and suspicions than public assertions, more promising in achieving satisfactory results than doggedly pursuing conflict. Persuasion can come in many forms—as Sweet Talk, as Tough Talk, as Straight Talk, as Sticky Talk, and more. Together, it is the means to change the minds of parties preventively, before they escalate into disastrous conflict.

But it cannot be just talk. The parties must put their hand where their mouth is, back up their talk with demonstrations in action, provide concrete measures to show what they mean, and lock in their words with deeds.

Chapter 6
Engaging Unengageables

Msgr d'Ossat profited by everything, is firm as a rock when necessity
demands, supple as a willow at another moment, and possessed the
supreme art of making every man offer him a gift that which it was
his chief desire to secure.

—François de Callières, 1716

That's how you conduct negotiations. What you propose to the
other side is nothing. If the other side demands it, [then] it consid-
ers it an achievement.

—Shimon Peres, 1994

The world image of American foreign policy throughout most of this century's
first decade was one of use of force, a reliance on hard power, a refusal to talk,
and an instinct to go it alone. Whatever the accuracy of this picture, images
do matter. When the Obama administration came into town, its foreign policy
bumper sticker was "Engagement." Four years later it is too early to assess final
results, but it is clear that the administration's desire to create a new image and set
a new tone for US foreign policy has been only partially successful, that it takes
two to get engaged, and that US policy in some places is reverting back to old
habits. The United States still confronts the problem of dealing with countries
and foreign actors that are major "unengageables." There are countries or actors
that remain on the US foreign policy blacklist and are subject to sanctions and
other measures of isolation, including Burma, Iran, Sudan, Syria, Cuba, and
Hamas in Gaza, among others. Other unengageables, which are not subject to

sanctions but nonetheless remain on bad terms with the United States, include Venezuela, North Korea (DPRK), Ecuador, and Bolivia.

This chapter addresses the following questions: What is involved in talking with unengageables? When should the United States initiate such talk? And, finally, what are the right tools of Talk Power to deploy? The challenge is not new to US foreign policy and there are important lessons to be drawn from recent and not so recent history. It is also the case that engagement is neither a binary choice nor a linear process, and thus not one end of a spectrum where the opposite end is isolation. There are many degrees and strands of engagement as well as obvious limits to framing an effective strategy. Ultimately, however, engagement's greatest contribution may be to lower the temperature of foreign relations, exchanging an assurance to diverse regimes that the United States is not out to overthrow them, in return for some secondary elements of policy cooperation. But when engagement is refused, the atmosphere may actually be darkened by the ensuing storm clouds.

Why Talk?

When addressing the matter of engagement with today's adversaries or an unsavory regime, one must ask the prior question, "What's in it for the United States?" Assuming that engagement is reciprocated, there is much to be gained, beginning with a general reduction of tensions. Tensions and attitudes do matter. Since negotiations work best when there is an atmosphere of equality between the parties, efforts by the remaining superpower (which the United States still is) to level the playing field by changing the perception of a relationship and setting the right tone can actually help the United States attain its goals, among other things.

The prime element of this tension reduction exercise is not merely the use of Sweet Talk. It is the removal of the threat of regime overthrow under which a surprising number of countries today feel they operate. Governments in Iran, Venezuela, and Gaza (Hamas) have very good reasons to feel threatened, even if the United States is not likely to lead a military expedition against them. That is because they face major opposition internally and the United States is a useful bogeyman to bolster their own internal political support and rally their people behind them. But repressive governments in Burma, Sudan, DPRK, and Syria, which have been somewhat more secure internally because they were successful in quashing internal dissent, also feel deeply that the United States would like to see them replaced. That may be so. But policy change is not regime change, and sometimes it may be easier to achieve policy change when it is made clear to the other side that regime overthrow is not the immediate aim, regardless of broader foreign policy aims and ambitions.

In a democratic age, authoritarian leaders and despots will always be plagued by existential fears and doubts about their long-term political survival. And they are probably right to harbor such fears, especially when dealing with the United States, which, under successive administrations, has made the global advancement of democracy a key foreign policy goal. Generically, this emphasis on democracy and democratic development conveys the idea that regime change is one of America's basic goals. It is also undeniably a truism that it would be easier to work with a different government in many of these capitals. However, it is also true that US interests and relations with these countries, no matter how unsavory their leaders happen to be, need to be put on a more-or-less even keel unless the United States is really prepared to resort to Gun Power or other measures to unseat them.

The removal of this atmospheric impediment would help clear the air for more direct discourse about specific policy matters that pertain to US immediate interests. It is particularly appropriate to calibrate such overtures to external events that make the unengageables more receptive to America's entreaties. Elections that bring about a change in governments or natural disasters that invite nonpolitical cooperation are good examples of situations that can be exploited to advance US interests. Elections planned for civilian return in Burma were a disappointment, even if Aung San Suu Kyi was released. Likewise, rigged elections in Iran and Sudan at the end of the first 2000 decade could only be met by condemnation, not cooperation, and autocratic succession in the DPRK seems to be the reason for a severe policy hardening to avoid appearing soft during a time of leadership transition or takeover.

Engagement when carried through can also open up new sources of information on local conditions in the newly engaged country. That is because having diplomatic and nongovernmental foot soldiers on the ground creates multiple avenues for dialogue, discussion, and interaction with local officials and the wider populace. There is nothing like being able to see firsthand local conditions for oneself. The availability of multiple interlocutors allows the United States to assemble a multifaceted picture of churning social and political currents in a country, replacing a reliance on single sources. Engagement even when it is tentative and provisional forces the target country to open up and explain its own views and policies, which is not necessary when it has only its own, controlled population as an interlocutor. Their isolation is America's isolation. However, engagement may mean moving away from some of America's traditional partners from the democratic or moderate opposition in a country even if the government of the country in question is persecuting its democratic or moderate opposition. This does not mean the United States should abandon its principles and commitment to human rights on the altar of political expediency, or cut ties with a regime's dissidents. But unless these movements suddenly gain the upper hand, a pragmatic approach that temporarily soft-pedals these friendships may well be the price to pay.

Beyond communication and information lies the deeper, less tangible element of trust. Communication and information are necessary for building trust but they are certainly not enough. Trust comes only with sustained contacts backed by performance. While trust among nations can never be total, since bluffing and national secrets are part of the game, it can be established as a general basis for relations. In its absence, as is seen repeatedly in US relationships with adversaries, even the first attempt(s) at engagement have a major hurdle to jump, since those first messages have to show their bone fides against a background of suspicion, treachery, and insincerity.

But all of this depends on reciprocity, the return of the outstretched hand to produce a handshake. Engagement makes a couple, but it represents only a unilateral attempt if the other party does not respond. Engagement is like a trapeze act: If the artist leaving the trapeze to join hands with the other artist firmly attached to a trapeze on the other side is left hanging in midair, and then plunges into the safety net because hands have not joined, the show is ruined and egos (at least) are bruised. But the artists will live to see another day. States, however, do not always have the luxury of safety nets, and efforts to assure themselves that they have a safety net or a clear path to the exit can work against acceptance of the initial leap of faith. States can invite reciprocity by the provision of incentives and professions of sincerity, but essentially they have no means of assuring it.

How to Talk?

President Barack Obama delivered bravura addresses to the Muslim world in Turkey and Egypt within six months of his inauguration. They contained a number of noteworthy elements. First, they defined "a new beginning." Whether it was substantively new or not—his predecessor had often declared that "we are not at war with Islam," although Obama added "and never will be"—he took advantage of his election to declare a policy opening. He even proposed a new vocabulary: "extremists" instead of "terrorists," "engagement" instead of "war."[1]

Second, while reiterating familiar and constant goals such as democracy and religious and electoral freedom, Obama conveyed the impression that regime change was not an active policy goal; countries would decide upon their own regime and form of government, which the United States would then deal and live with. Such assurances, as noted, are important political capital; they not only work to remove fears but they also establish respect and equality, the basis of any sound relations.

Third, the speech contained both offers and limits, in a declaratory, business-like combination, so that the intended target would not think that this was just some ordinary campaign speech. Engagement has to be real and credible; the engagers have to demonstrate that a real change in policy is taking place. But the tiger should not try to change all of his stripes or purr like a kitten, because a total change in personality or nature would not be deemed believable and would almost certainly destroy the credibility of the initial offer. The engagers also have to avoid looking like the *demandeur* (the party which makes the opening bid in a negotiation), the traditional position of weakness in negotiation. Instead they must present themselves as making a sincere and valuable offer, without strings or catches attached.

Just starting a conversation is usually not enough to provide a solid launching pad for the engagement process. Messages need repeating and testing to overcome political inhibitions and past fears. Indeed, the initial course is usually up a very steep hill. There are many reasons why the opening demarche may face rejection, at least initially and possibly for a while. Issues of credibility, misperception, injustice, unfulfilled obligations, and reactive devaluation, among others, are likely to arise. The unengageable may find the policy change hard to believe, and may suspect it is a trick to throw them off guard. The new signals may be misperceived, coming as they will in the midst of contradictory noise and smoldering fires of past slights. The opening may be dismissed as a sign of weakness and proof that the superpower is not so powerful after all, so tighten the screws and batten down the hatches so that the bureaucratic ship of state does not leak with contradictory messages and communications. Or, it may be taken as a sign that the former hardliner is suffering, so let's make the world's Samson suffer some more. Or, it may be seen as something the superpower should be doing anyhow, so let it stand in line and not give it rewards. Finally, there is the known psychological reaction that devalues the opponent's offer and overvalues those that one makes at the outset or in return, making equilibrium and reciprocation difficult. Iran's, North Korea's, Syria's, Hamas's, Cuba's, and Venezuela's reactions to President Obama's extended hand in 2009 are cases in point.

So the effort continues. Although reciprocity is the normal mode of negotiation and diplomatic exchanges, it is unrealistic in a world of human feelings, political perceptions, and audience reactions to expect a hand extended immediately in return. The offer needs repeating, in a variety of forms and occasions. The engaging party needs to reassure the home audience that the new path is safe and to reassure the target that this is not a trick, that the hand is indeed open and outstretched. This requires Straight Talk of the clearest and firmest kind. As in any kind of demarche, a few tangible indications along the way always help—a social contact, a formal boycott lifted, and believe it or not even a holiday or anniversary greeting helps.

It bears repeating that engagement is not the same as surrender or appeasement: Reciprocity is the eventual goal. At the end of the day, one has to give in order to get, but that understanding should begin with dawn's early light. Engagement can be seen as the road to a process of mutual concessions. By moving toward the other party's position on a contentious issue, the engager invites the other to meet it halfway. The opening of contacts and dialogue is designed to allow the two parties to explore, explain, and better understand their point of view on major questions. This involves some change from both parties' initial positions, the second or substantive element in engagement; the first is the simple procedural opening of communication, or, simply put, "engagement talk."

Meeting the other party halfway is the simplest form of giving something to get something on the same issue. In the negotiations led by UN Special Representative of the Secretary-General Alvaro de Soto to end the Salvadorian civil war, the Faribundo Martí Liberation Front demanded the dismissal of a number of named officers involved in repressive measures, but in the end accepted an impartial panel's recommendations that the president was committed to carry out. In the negotiations led by former Finnish President Martti Ahtisaari to end the rebellion in Aceh, the Free Aceh Movement (Gerakan Aceh Merdeka, or GAM) initially demanded punishment for the repressive army but later accepted that the issue be noted for discussion after the self-government solution had been implemented. Further back in time, US negotiations with North Vietnam in 1972 and with Russia and China over the status of Laos in 1960–61 involved many halfway compromises, including some splitting of differences on details and on the status of South Vietnam itself.

A reciprocal exchange of concessions is not the only model of substantive engagement. There is also a second method or approach, probably the core of negotiation, of "tradable compensation." This refers to an exchange of one position for another on a different issue, and often allows each party to achieve total success on items of its choice, rather than settling for half a loaf as in the case of concessions. In fact, a key to successful negotiations requires the parties to arrange the items in dispute into two "piles"—those it values most and those its values less—and exchange the items one party values most against the items the other values most, each compensating the other with items it values least.

The United States launched a policy of constructive engagement with both South Africa and Angola over the issue of Namibia in the 1980s. South Africa had a large number of troops in southern Angola, ostensibly to protect its territory against the large numbers of Cuban troops in Angola, which Angola claimed were necessary to protect it against the South Africans. Clearly if one left, the other would not be necessary. But who would begin the process? Constructive engagement, led by Assistant Secretary of State Chester Crocker, involved building contacts with both sides so that both sets of troops would be withdrawn simultaneously, each compensating the other for the withdrawals and each achieving its full goals. In the process, Namibia achieved its independence as a buffer between the two states. Compensation left each party with a whole loaf, each baked from a different grain.

However, beyond concession and compensation negotiators have a third model of construction, or a reframing of the stakes so that the parties no longer oppose each other from incompatible positions but rather redefine the problem as one where both sides will benefit from a common solution. In engaging each other in thirteen years of talks to resolve the Panama Canal dispute, the United States under presidents Nixon and Carter, and Panama under President Omar Torrijos, constructed a formula that involved Panamanian ownership and US security, allowing the Canal to function in the interests of both parties. Engagement is at its best when it enables the parties to study the problem that they face together and devise a common understanding that leads to a common solution.

Indonesia faced a long rebellion in its westernmost province, the devoutly Muslim former kingdom of Aceh, which has enjoyed its own independent status in more distant times past. A change of government to a more democratic regime led Indonesia to explore the possibilities of engagement with the GAM after 1999. Talks continued with a variety of mediators, interspersed with violent clashes between the GAM and the Indonesian army, a force unto itself. However, in the middle of the first 2000 decade, some persistent and skillful mediators entered the talks to find a status that would satisfy both parties and that would lie somewhere between the GAM's demand for total independence and Indonesia's demand for total integration. The Center for Humanitarian Dialogue in Geneva tried its hand but stumbled over the concept of special autonomy. The 2004 tsunami interrupted further attempts at engagement. Former Finnish President Ahtisaari then took over and came up with a nearby concept of self-government that won the day. It is hard—and perhaps pointless—to decide whether this exercise of Right Talk was concession or construction; the parties indeed met each other in the middle, preserving Indonesian sovereignty and granting Aceh's self-determination within it, and it was a redefinition of the outcome that brought engagement to a successful conclusion. Yet another point is important as we look at the process of engagement: The agreement was a conclusion of conflict but also the opening of a new type of positive relations and cooperation between the two parties. Engagement begins with talk, but to be successful, needs to end up in projects that ultimately contribute to a greater understanding and interdependence between the parties. Straight Talk thus paves the way for meaningful engagement.

The Tools of Engagement

When engaging the unengageable there is also the question of deciding which Talk Power Tools to use and when. The choice of tools will vary depending on the situation and some tools—like Trash Talk—should probably not be used at all when dealing with an unpredictable or paranoid leader who will only too readily seize the bait. The history of US-Soviet relations during the Cold War is instructive about the many different kinds of tools that are sometimes required to deal with a sometimes unengageable adversary. As the examples provided below suggest, Straight Talk, sometimes preceded by Safe Talk, and followed by Sticky Talk, are the preferred tools for engagement, but persuasion must be consistent and backed by a firm hand and the occasional and properly timed use of Tough Talk, especially when an adversary is balking at proposals that are being put on the table.

Negotiations for the Austrian State Treaty, which was finally signed at the Belvedere Palace in Vienna on May 15, 1955, for example, underscore some of the dilemmas of choosing the right tools of engagement, including when to press for talks and when to suspend them. It also parenthetically points to a fourth model for constructing an agreement, namely one of "mutual denial." When both sides have diametrically opposed goals and interests, it may be best to press for a second-best solution that prevents *both* sides from getting what they want. In this instance, the Treaty not only re-established Austria's sovereign independence, but also, by guaranteeing its neutrality with the removal of troops by the four occupying powers (Britain, France, the United States, and the Soviet Union), ensured that neither the Soviets nor the West could bring Austria into their military orbit or sphere of influence.

The Grand Alliance of the United States, the United Kingdom, and the Soviet Union, which defeated Germany (and Japan), quickly began to fray after World War II ended. As large swaths of Eastern and Central Europe fell under Soviet control, the question arose about how to deal with Austria, which had joined Nazi Germany during Hitler's rule. The initial decision, which had been taken during the final months of the war, had been to divide Austria into American, British, and Soviet zones with a fourth zone being given to France after the war ended. But as Stalin's intentions became increasingly clear, Roosevelt's "Grand Design" of cooperation with the Soviets fell by the wayside and the United States sought to secure a negotiated withdrawal of Soviet troops. In a Straight Talk demarche the United States proposed to put Austria's future on the agenda in talks with the Soviets in 1946 under a proposed treaty framework that would secure the withdrawal of Soviet troops from that country. The Soviets, however, demurred on the grounds that treaties governing the future of Italy, Finland, Hungary, Romania, and Bulgaria would have to be concluded first before negotiations on Austria's future could begin. Negotiations began the following year in an atmosphere of rapidly escalating Cold War tensions following communist-led uprisings in Greece and Turkey in 1947 and communist-led coups in Hungary and Czechoslovakia.

In a somewhat surprising turn of events, the Russians began to look to the Western allies for an agreement on Austria. This time, however, notwithstanding British pressure to make concessions to Russia on Austria's future, it was the United States that was the reluctant bride. The United States did not trust Stalin and feared that the Russians would simply try to manipulate the situation to seize power in Austria the way they had in other Eastern European countries. With the Soviet blockade of Berlin in 1949, the Americans were eager to find any excuse to break off negotiations and they eventually found one when the Soviets began to tie a change in Austria's borders with Yugoslavia to negotiations about Austria's reparations owed to Yugoslavia. Stop Talk clearly had its uses.

With the fall of China to the communists and the successful Soviet detonation of an atomic bomb, the tables turned yet again. Following intensive discussions among the State Department, the Defense Department, and the White House, President Harry Truman decided that a treaty was needed at all costs to secure the withdrawal of Soviet troops from Austria, and in the words of NSC decision memorandum 38/6 to "re-establish an independent and Western-oriented Austria."[2] This time, however, it was Stalin who did not want to engage. With relations becoming increasingly strained between Moscow and Belgrade because Yugoslavian leader, Marshall Josip Tito, was intent on pursuing his own path to socialism without Soviet interference, Stalin was keen to keep Soviet troops in neighboring Austria just in case they might be needed to deal with Tito.

It would take Stalin's death and the rise of Nikita Khrushchev before negotiations would resume in earnest again. Even then the path was not easy. Conflicting US and Soviet priorities over whether the Austrian people would be allowed to have a say about the future political status of their country became entangled with issues concerning German remilitarization and its incorporation into the Western alliance. When the Austrian State Treaty was finally signed, in the words of one observer,

> it initiated a course of events that led to the Geneva Summit in 1955 and to a cooling of tensions between the two blocs. With the treaty, the postwar settlements

in Europe were completed by excepting Austria from the process of bloc formation.... In this settlement both sides gave up their original objectives in Austria
in exchange for political stability in the area.[3]

The 1955 Austrian State Treaty took ten years to negotiate and is significant
because it led to the only Soviet withdrawal from territory it had occupied in
World War II. Negotiations culminating in the treaty involved the artful use of
Straight Talk and Tough Talk along with healthy doses of Small Talk, especially
in the final round of negotiations when a deal could be clinched with a new
Soviet leader, Khrushchev, once he had consolidated his own internal political
position. But there is also an important Sticky Talk element to these negotiations.
Although the United States was prepared to suspend negotiations because it did
not trust Stalin's broader political intentions, its negotiators never completely
threw in the towel (the one time use of Stop Talk was a temporary expedient,
not a firm policy). Nor were they prepared to let the other side walk away from
the table even as relations took a tumble over Berlin, China, and the onset of
the Korean War. As US Secretary of State Shultz observed on the thirtieth anniversary ceremony of the treaty, it was "one of the greatest successes of the
postwar period," but it also taught an important lesson: "There were many who
condemned the negotiators as foot-dragging bureaucrats. Yet in the end, patience
was rewarded with success."[4]

Preconditions for Happy Talk

If the Austrian State Treaty represents one of the early Talk Power successes in the
early days of the Cold War, the 1986 Reykjavik Summit between US President
Reagan and Soviet General Secretary Gorbachev is now generally recognized
as a major, transforming event in the history of the Cold War and US-Soviet
relations; this despite the fact that the negotiation itself was a failure. The story
of the summit has been told many times before, including by some of its key
participants. What is now clear is that what made this a real turning point in
superpower relations is that the leaders of both countries engaged in Happy Talk
and shared with each other what former US Ambassador James E. Goodby has
called "an impossible dream"[5]—a world that would eventually be free of nuclear
weapons. Although that dream was not realized, the summit paved the way for
concrete agreements that saw the elimination of intermediate-range nuclear forces
and major reductions in the strategic nuclear arsenals of both sides. Reykjavik
also contributed significantly to a broader political process placing US-Soviet
relations on a new trajectory that allowed Soviet leaders to embark on an internal

political transformation eventually leading to the fall of communism and the end of the Cold War.

Why did this happen? What made Happy Talk work at Reykjavik? The outcome was certainly not foreordained. US-Soviet relations in the early 1980s with the arrival of the new administration of Ronald Reagan in Washington had taken a sharp turn for the worse. The Soviet invasion of Afghanistan in 1979 had thrown the relationship into the deep freeze as did their incursions in Southern Africa and elsewhere in the developing world. There was a widespread perception that the Soviets had exploited American weaknesses and manipulated détente and years of arms control negotiations—a variation of Sticky Talk—to secretly build up their nuclear arsenals and conventional military force capabilities. Soviet violations of key arms control agreements, like the 1969 Anti-Ballistic Missile (ABM) Treaty, reinforced the view that the Soviets were not to be trusted and that the United States should not try to do business with them.

Early in his administration, President Reagan characterized the Strategic Arms Limitation Treaty, or SALT II, which had been negotiated by the Carter administration, as "fatally flawed."[6] In his first year in office, the president embarked on what would be the biggest defense buildup and modernization of US military forces in recent history, including the deployment of new, intermediate-range nuclear forces in Europe. There was little appetite in some quarters of the administration (especially in the Defense Department, led by Secretary Caspar Weinberger) to engage the Soviets, not least because their new leader, Yuri Andropov, a former head of the KGB, was regarded as a ruthless hardliner and unrepentant Cold War warrior. On March 8, 1983, President Reagan delivered an address to a meeting of the National Association of Evangelicals in Orlando, Florida, where he called communism "the focus of evil in the modern world"[7]— Trash Talk that quickly came to be known as his "evil empire" characterization of the Soviet menace. Barely two weeks later, Reagan went on national television to deliver his famous "Star Wars" speech where he enjoined the US scientific and defense communities to begin work on developing a new strategic defense system that could shoot down incoming missiles.

Against this background of Trash Talk, Reagan also chose to embark on a Straight Talk strategy of engagement with the Soviets. Both the president and Secretary Shultz understood that pressure, including cutting the Soviets down to size, and persuasion had to go hand in hand; disengagement was not an option. Thus, the administration continued with NATO's earlier 1979 "two-track" decision to prepare for intermediate-range nuclear forces (INF) deployments while simultaneously seeking a negotiated reduction of Soviet deployments of SS-20 missiles to restore INF nuclear parity. It also went back to the negotiating table on strategic arms control with the Soviets in the Strategic Arms Control

Reduction Talks (START) in June 1982. Although the Soviets abruptly suspended talks following Reagan's 1983 announcement that the United States would proceed with research and development on a Strategic Defense Initiative (SDI), or "Star Wars," Reagan repeatedly declared that he was ready to go back to the negotiating table whenever the Soviets were ready.

That opportunity came with the installation of a new Soviet leader, General Secretary Mikhail Gorbachev, upon the sudden death of General Secretary Konstantin Chernenko in early March 1985. Within months, Secretary Shultz and Soviet Foreign Minister Andrei Gromyko met in Geneva to set an ambitious agenda for new Nuclear and Space Talks (NST), strategic nuclear arms, intermediate-range nuclear forces, and space-based defenses.

At their first meeting in Geneva in November 1985, Reagan and Gorbachev found common ground in the formula, "50 percent reductions in the nuclear arms of the United States and the Soviet Union appropriately applied." The two leaders also declared that "a nuclear war cannot be won and must never be fought."[8] In the months that followed, both leaders advanced their own proposals for nuclear disarmament. In January 1986, Gorbachev put forward his own sweeping proposal to eliminate all nuclear weapons by the year 2000, a process that would begin by cutting strategic arsenals by half, banning space-based weapons outright, and halting all nuclear testing. Gorbachev also proposed the complete dismantlement of all intermediate-range systems in Europe—in essence accepting the US's "zero option" that was such a sticking point in earlier negotiations. Reagan countered with his own proposal to cut inventories of offensive ballistic missiles, set a multiyear moratorium on the deployment of ballistic missile defenses, share the benefits of new strategic defense technology, and eliminate intermediate-range nuclear forces.

The two sides, however, were still far apart in the details of their specific nuclear reduction proposals and there was strong suspicion in many quarters of the US government and wider political establishment that Gorbachev was simply mounting a new propaganda campaign to discredit the United States and divide the NATO alliance. Nonetheless, there was still a strong desire on both sides to discuss these ideas further at an informal, exploratory meeting that would have a limited agenda and serve as a kind of "base camp" for future summit talks. That would all change with Gorbachev's surprising opener at Reykjavik to halve strategic nuclear arsenals and eliminate all INF missiles of the Soviet Union conditional on no withdrawal from the 1972 ABM Treaty for at least ten years and no testing of space-based defense systems. Later in the afternoon of the same day, Reagan countered with an offer that "[t]he USSR and the United States undertake for 10 years not to exercise their right of withdrawal from the ABM treaty.... [and] Within five years of the 10-year period ... the strategic offensive arms of the two sides shall be reduced by 50 percent. During the five following years of that period, all remaining offensive ballistic missiles of the two sides shall be reduced."[9]

As the two leaders and their aides thrashed out the details of a potential agreement over the next two days, the sense of excitement grew. "The final session," as Goodby observes,

> was a scene of high drama. Gorbachev said he wanted to eliminate all strategic forces, not just ballistic missiles. Reagan said, "It would be fine by me if we eliminated all nuclear weapons." The breakpoint began to appear when Gorbachev, following the script laid out in the initial presentation, insisted that all research and testing of space-based ballistic missiles be restricted to laboratories.... Gorbachev insisted on the word "laboratories." Over this one word, the negotiations broke off. Washington ... read Gorbachev's proposal as an attack on the missile defense program, the Strategic Defense Initiative. That one word, "laboratories," obviously rang alarm bells.... So ended "the highest stakes poker game ever played," as Shultz described it. In Reagan's words, "We proposed the most sweeping and generous arms control proposal in history. We offered the complete elimination of all ballistic missiles—Soviet and American—from the face of the earth by 1996. While we parted company with this American offer on the table, we are closer than ever before to agreement that could lead to a safer world without nuclear weapons."[10]

Some of those agreements would indeed come in the years that followed under Reagan's presidency and those of his successors.

The engagement strategy of the United States with the Soviets was based on three core principles—"regime acceptance, limited linkage, and rhetorical restraint." These principles underscored the importance of reassuring adversaries that the United States would not overthrow those with whom it is intent on doing business and engaging in talks, provided that reciprocal gestures would be matched. Straight Talk followed by Small Talk are the preferred tools of engagement. Tough Talk too has its uses, but Trash Talk has to be put aside when the conversation gets serious. As Abraham Sofaer, the State Department's legal advisor during the period, notes,

> As a matter of general tone, the notion of equality often surfaced [at Reykjavik]. President Reagan, for example, described the meeting's objectives [to rid the world of nuclear weapons] as being shared equally.... The notion of equal or reciprocal treatment is an inevitable aspect of sovereign negotiations, and regime acceptance requires a willingness to entertain and deal seriously with such claims.... When Secretary Gorbachev argues for restrictions on missile defense in order to prevent

evasion, the president said Gorbachev's remarks reflected a belief that the United States was in some way trying to attain an advantage out of hostility toward the Soviet Union. He assured Gorbachev that we harbor no hostile intentions toward the Soviets. We recognized the differences in our two systems. But ... we could live as friendly competitors.... A "'fundamental difference' existed between the two societies," [said Reagan to Gorbachev] but "the United States believes that people should have the right to determine their own form of government."[11]

Furthermore, in discussions with Gorbachev about broader issues concerning human rights, regional security, and the like, Reagan made it clear that progress on arms control would not be linked to concessions made by the Soviets in these other areas. Throughout the meeting, the tone was businesslike, cordial, professional, disciplined, and principled. It was a tone that would continue right up to the fall of the Berlin Wall and the end of the Cold War.

Although the United States is far from having a Happy Talk conversation with countries like Iran, Burma, or North Korea of the kind it had with the leader of the former Soviet Union at Reykjavik, the same preconditions and lessons apply. Advocating a policy of regime change with one's intended interlocutor via Trash Talk will almost surely thwart the possibilities for diplomatic engagement and almost certainly make a bad situation worse. It also conveys the implied threat that if negotiations fail or flag the use of force is an option. (Again, don't make threats unless you really mean it and are prepared to act on them.) The effective use of Talk Power to secure US objectives and aims begins with the recognition that negotiation is a means to an end and the right way to advance one's interests and goals even when dealing with dangerous adversaries or mortal enemies. And even if one is fortunate enough to get to the stage of Happy Talk, which itself can have a profound, transformative impact on a relationship as the legacy of the Reykjavik Summit attests, the importance of providing continued assurances that the United States is amenable to a "live and let live" world of political differences is critical to the success of these Talk Power ventures.

"Walking the Walk" as well as "Talking the Talk"

As the above illustrations have also shown, engagement cannot remain at the level of dialogue. It must lead to improved relations, policy concordance, and concrete common projects. As President Obama declared in his first news conference on January 27, 2009, six months before his Cairo speech, "Ultimately, people are going to judge me not by my words but by my actions."[12] An engagement policy cannot simply rest at the level of formal communications and a return to normal diplomatic status. The fact that relations before were exceptionally bad means that relations after engagement must be exceptionally good.

Once the United States began its policy of engagement toward Muammar Qaddafi's Libya, it did not stop at dialogue, the removal of terrorist support status, sanctions, or even at denuclearization, but moved on toward renewal of normal diplomatic, economic, and cultural relations, with insistence. What could not have been predicted with the "Arab Spring" uprisings in 2011 was that there would be rapidly mounting opposition to Qaddafi's rule and an ensuing civil war led by forces in the eastern part of the country. With the imposition of the UN's "no fly" zone over Libya when the cities of Benghazi and Tobruk seemed imperiled, Gun Power returned to the region with a vengeance as NATO bombarded Qaddafi's troops from the air. Whatever the outcome of Libya's ongoing civil war, it took large doses of Talk Power to keep the NATO countries on track in both their means and their ends with regard to Libya, and it will take large doses of Talk Power to assemble into a viable alternative to Qaddafi's regime the unruly coalition of secular liberals, Islamists, Muslim Brotherhood, tribal figures, and Qaddafi defectors who want Qaddafi out.

Other kinds of engagement led by Talk Power are also required to help stabilize countries that are experiencing difficult political transitions. The situation in Egypt is instructive. Although those courageous souls who took to the streets of Cairo, Alexandria, and elsewhere in such large numbers were ultimately responsible for toppling President Hosni Mubarak's regime, a much bigger bloodbath was averted by critical doses of Safe and Straight Talk between the United States and Egypt's military leaders who were ultimately persuaded that Mubarak had to leave sooner rather than later. These talks were accompanied by others between Egypt's military and key opposition and youth leaders on constitutional reform and setting a new timetable for parliamentary and presidential elections. The transition in Egypt is a work in progress, but it underscores the importance not just of Twitter Talk, but also Street Talk, Safe Talk, Straight Talk, and other forms of Talk Power. In sum, political stability in the region will only be achieved through the power of negotiation, engagement at all levels of society, and the constructive support of external actors, including the United States. It is a slow process, facing many rebuffs and setbacks, and demanding concrete acts as proof of the Talking. At the end of the day words must lead to real political commitments and cooperative action.

CHAPTER 7
TALKING WITH TERRORISTS

A firm stand has to be taken on the one hand against the *a priori* conviction that nothing but crude violence will succeed, and on the other against the understandable urgings ... that only abject submission will save lives. In other words, I am a believer in negotiated solutions that give neither side everything it wants.

—Dr. Frederick Hacker, psychiatrist, 1982

Throughout the 1970s and 1980s, the British (and American) governments publicly refused to talk with the members of the (Provisional) Irish Republican Army (IRA), which they outlawed as terrorists. At the same time, Israel and the United States refused contact with the Palestine Liberation Organization (PLO), labeled terrorists, and Israel even made it a crime to talk with its members. Also in the same period, the South African (and US) governments banned the African National Congress (ANC), classified it as a terrorist group, and prohibited all contact with it.

Yet contacts between individuals and political parties from both sides did develop in the mid-1980s, which led to power-sharing agreement in the 1990s. The feeling began to spread that neither side could win the struggle and that instead the stalemate was pointlessly producing victims in the population on both sides. A new British secretary of state, Peter Brooke, took office at the end of the decade and allowed that he would not rule out talks with the political wing of the IRA, Sinn Féin, if the violence were stopped; it took another half decade before the 1994 unilateral ceasefire was announced by the IRA. Four years later (through many ups and downs of talks), the conflict was ended by the signature of the Good Friday Agreement of 1998, on a formula of nonviolence in exchange for power sharing and full participation in political and social processes.

The United States recognized the PLO in 1988 and dropped it from its terrorist list after it formally acknowledged Israel's right to exist and renounced terrorism. In 1993, two Israeli scholars ran the danger of arrest by establishing contact with the PLO, with opposition support at home, and after the elections of that year, undertook regular meetings with the PLO in Oslo. They were later joined by government representatives to negotiate the Oslo Agreement, publicly signed at the end of the year at the White House, on a formula of nonviolence and mutual recognition in exchange for autonomy leading to a final solution.

In South Africa, despite the ANC ban, government ministers contacted ANC President Nelson Mandela in mid-1984, and when this was ineffective, South African business leaders made their own contacts a year later. By the end of the decade, newly elected State President F. W. de Klerk had come to see the costly hopelessness of the current apartheid situation and had swung around to the formula of nonviolence in exchange for legality, and the way to a democratic South Africa was opened.

In three salient cases, the absolute ban on negotiating with terrorists was broken under the table, by combinations of government representatives and private individuals from civil society, leading to major policy shifts and a transformation of the conflict. At some point in the conflict, the parties came to realize that they could not refuse to negotiate. Yet at an earlier point in the conflict, they proclaimed a policy of no negotiations with terrorists. There is a paradox to explain, and a role for Talk Power to clarify.

When to Talk to Terrorists

While in general, terrorists are weak, desperate groups of extremists acting for extreme causes, even small groups of extremists can serve as a warning that something is wrong, a proverbial canary in the mine. Their extremism makes them unlikely representatives of the cause that excites them, to be sure, but their appearance suggests that there is a problem in some people's mind and that some attention to it might be a good preventive measure. It doesn't always work. But in June 1990 an attack on an army post by a group of *ishumar* (from *chomeur*, or unemployed in French) alerted the Malian government to a real problem with the Tuareg minority in the north and started nearly two years of negotiation that ended in the signature of a National Pact in April 1992. But again, outbreaks of violence were necessary in mid-1992 to remind the government not only to sign, but to implement, a process that took four more years of talks. In all, extremists signaled a problem and government listened, awakened by local violent and terrorist attacks to prevent a much worse escalation of anarchy in the Sahara. It is important to listen to terrorists, and even to talk to them when possible; it can help open minds, focus goals, and sow doubts in established plans.

There are other cases of terrorists as the canary in the mine. Morocco and Tunisia were heading toward a terrorist rebellion in 1955, of the same sort that was beginning to engulf Algeria lying between them, leading the French to negotiate a gradual if rapid transfer of powers by the following year and thus head off a potential terrorist war across all North Africa. When a small terrorist protest arose after World War II in Alto Adige/Süd Tyrol, the German-speaking region of northeast Italy, Italy and Austria negotiated a more equitable autonomy status, and used it as a model for its four other autonomous regions of Sardinia, Sicily, Val d'Aosta, and Friuli-Venetzia Giulia. Terrorism arose in Mindanao after 1968 when calls for equal treatment for the Muslim Bangsamoro had failed.

These examples run from Timely Talk before much terrorist activity has begun to those that took place after some terrorism but before the conflict had run out of hand. It is easier to deal with the challenge of terrorism through negotiation before the terrorism becomes a mainstream activity than later on.

Going back to the original examples of later terrorist negotiations, there is no doubt that the National Party's coming to its senses at any number of crucial points after it came to power in South Africa in 1948 could have led to constructive talks that would have saved many lost lives and much lost time and energy—in response to the Defiance Campaign against apartheid legislation in 1952, upon the adoption of the Freedom Charter in 1956, after the Sharpeville massacre in 1960, at the time of the declaration of the Republic the following year, after the Soweto riots of 1975, during the constitutional reform debates of 1983, after the initial contacts in 1985.

It is also certain that, had the British and Irish recognized the legitimacy of their growing grievance over the centuries at the end of the 1960s, before the deployment of British troops, and subsequently the establishment of direct British rule in 1972, and begun to talk in search of a just solution, the whole time of troubles and the following quarter century of hate and death could have been forestalled.

It is arguable that dropping one side or the other's refusal to negotiate from the very beginning of the conflict in the Middle East—during the Bernadotte and Bunche missions on the founding of Israel in 1948, or after the withdrawal of the Suez campaign in 1956, or at the end of the Six-Day War and the passage of UN Security Council Resolution 242 in 1967, or after submission of King Fahd's eight-point peace plan in 1981, or in pursuit and implementation of the Oslo Agreement in 1994 and 1996, or after submission of the Arab Peace Plan in 2002—could have sent the Israeli conflict heading in a different direction, toward peace among its neighbors in the Mideast.

For a more cataclysmic example, the attack on the World Trade Center on September 11, 2001, was unequivocally not a call for negotiations with al-Qaeda nor would negotiations on Mideast questions have prevented the attack, but it was a horrible reminder that the Israeli-Palestinian problem was in need of attention and persistence in the US-led Peace Process, rather than an accompaniment to the "war on terrorism."

So why not? The refusal to negotiate is a matter of entrapment, after the initial, reflexive reaction to answer violence with violence. Even when a terrorist attack is a warning signal, it is an infringement of the law and of humane behavior, and must be met by law enforcement. Terrorism is the weapon of the weak and desperate in face of the state's power, despairing of attaining their goals by normal means. Terrorists use unconventional, repulsive means to achieve extreme, unacceptable ends. To immediately open up talks would be a declaration of feebleness by the state, a capitulation to demands that it had previously declared out of bounds, and a denial of its legitimate role as protector of security, law, and order. To talk at the first outbreak would also invite imitation by others, including perhaps weaker and more extreme movements. Similarly, by using such extreme means—murdering civilians in an effort to sway public opinion and, through it, government policy—the terrorists put themselves beyond the pale of political conversation and declare war, in their own terms. And war, once declared, goes on until victory or stalemate. Once embarked on that track, it becomes more and more difficult to reverse course.

But at this point (and at any point during the period of confrontation), it is important to take stock of the situation and ask some questions. History shows that terrorism has a limited life. Some terrorist movements can be nipped in the bud while they are still small, narrow, extremist movements, and it is perfectly natural and reasonable for the state to do so. Then where is this confrontation leading? Can the terrorists and their cause be beaten militarily? At what cost to us? Are we stuck in a stalemate, with no prospect of eliminating the terrorism, or are we gradually overcoming it? Are there splits in the terrorist side that can be capitalized on to bring the campaign to an end? Is there an alternative, moderate movement that can be encouraged and strengthened, and what can be offered to strengthen them? The key elements are outcome and stalemate, cost and moderation, and factions and alternatives.

If the outcome looks unpromising, it is wise to consider alternatives. If the confrontation process is stalemated, with neither side making headway for its cause, and that stalemate is costly, there is an incentive for both sides to consider a negotiation process. A mutually hurting stalemate needs a complementary sense that both sides feel there is an outcome that is mutually satisfactory and that both sides are willing to look for it, or what we would call "a way out," in order to be ripe. The costs of the two different policies—confrontation and negotiation—need to be weighed. Their gains must also be weighed against another measure—opportunity gains or gains to be achieved by not engaging—i.e., the chances of winning or of not losing what one had to pay to get an agreement.

Tactical moderation on the government's side needs to see tactical moderation on the terrorists' side, too. States do not stretch their hand out to negotiate unless they see signs that they will meet an extended hand. Such signs can come in many forms, from direct statements to actions amounting to policy changes either in ends or in means. One should not expect terrorists to make a confession, or to rush into an open-arm embrace, but rather to produce small, gradual steps, often hard to see and even contradicted.

A state will talk with the terrorist organization when there is no moderate alternative to deal with, and when that organization itself shows signs of moderating. Again, the same reasoning applies to the terrorist organization. Talking is designed to produce moderation, and will not be undertaken if moderation is already available elsewhere and if the extremists have not shown an ability to moderate. This means that the terrorists will be expected to show some engagement tendencies of their own before the state will take the step; the terrorist organization's steps are expected to be internal—rhetoric, hostage release, elections, ceasefire, etc.—whereas the state's first move would be interactive or external. The parallel lists illustrate the difficulty of launching a policy of engagement.

However, additional signs of terrorist moderation are usually also necessary. Terrorists may moderate themselves by coming together around a common, moderate platform with other moderate groups who rally behind the same cause. Or they may find themselves engaged in processes—electoral competition, parliamentary processes, marginal negotiations, informal conferences—whose mechanics and spirit gradually force moderation on them. Again, the hanging question is how much moderation does it take to secure a fundamental transformation in relations between the parties.

States must also feel some reassurance that their gesture will be productive and that a change in policy stance is actually possible. To gain this assurance, they need to continue active involvement in the conflict, as they add incentives to their offers of contact, without totally abandoning their previous pressure, if only as a threat to return to policies of isolation and confrontation if engagement fails. They need also feel that there are enough moderating dynamics present within the terrorist organization to signal a direction and produce a continuation of internal change. All of these elements are judgment calls, but that is what policy is made of.

Factions and alternatives are important considerations in the tactical element of the decision to negotiate. If there is a moderate group that claims to represent the terrorists' reference group, it may be better to negotiate with them instead and to strengthen their claim to representation by making concessions to them, effectively sidelining the terrorist extremists. But the moderate group has to be truly stronger and not open itself to being delegitimized by the state's embrace. And terrorist extremists have to be able to be truly marginalized and not be able to play an effective spoiler role in the conflict. Thus the strength of the moderates depends as much on how the state opponent plays it as on their intrinsic position. Similarly, the state has to keep an eye out for factions within the terrorist organization, for example a political wing distinct from the militant wing, giving the state a potential partner and an ability to split the terrorists. Again, the strength of the internal moderates depends on how the state plays it, along the same lines as in the case of the external moderates.

How to Talk to Terrorists

A growing chorus has called for a negotiated settlement between Taliban insurgents and the Karzai government, arguing that only a political solution will solve Afghanistan's problems and pave the way for a speedy exit of US and NATO forces. The latter point is almost certainly true. President Hamid Karzai, meanwhile, has also signaled that he is prepared to negotiate (and, in fact, has been doing so quietly under the table). Some senior Taliban leaders have said they are prepared to talk—but only if foreign forces leave the country and Karzai agrees to an Islamic-style democracy.

The Afghan conflict is nearly a decade—if not two centuries—old. Yet there is precious little evidence the war is perceived as a painful stalemate by both sides. If anything, the Taliban have been emboldened to increase the pace and frequency of their attacks. The insurgency also appears to be expanding from the south to the other parts of the country. Much of the available evidence points to a troubling, escalatory dynamic despite some tactical successes by NATO forces. And the direct and indirect assistance that different rebel and political groups in the country are receiving from a large number of external actors—the pro-Taliban Pashtun tribes in Pakistan among them—does not bode well for the emergence of a military stalemate that would force rival factions to seriously entertain their political options even if NATO withdrew from the country. Is this the time to talk to the Taliban?

Talk, yes, but the United States should be under no illusions that the Taliban themselves are ready for negotiations. One problem is the absence of any kind of reasonably unified coalition among Taliban forces. The Taliban are a disparate, loosely affiliated, faction-ridden entity. Although there is something of an emerging political leadership, the Taliban remain too fractured to be a reliable negotiating partner. Peeling off moderates may hold out some hope for serious negotiations, but the presence of so many factions means there are also many potential spoilers who could easily wreck any kind of nascent peace process.

Talking to terrorists is much like talking to any other adversary, although with some special twists. *The first thing to do is to talk whenever possible,* and this certainly applies to the Taliban. Safe Talk is the way to carry out these soundings because it does not precommit the parties or put political reputations on the line. Negotiation (except to arrange an opponent's surrender) is not what the terrorists want, but even for that reason talking is crucial, to find out information, crystallize goals, develop interlocutors, and set up a negotiating situation if it is to ever materialize. Talking is not negotiating, but it is the first step toward negotiation, as opposed to confrontation. Talking and negotiating are a process, not an event; the initiation of either should not be taken as a total policy demarche (in fact, one keeps the pressure of renewed confrontation as a ready alternative while negotiating). Rather it is an investigation through Safe Talk of possibilities and intentions and an attempt to sound out and attract the other side into flexibility and moderation. One element of negotiation is the changing of images, ideas, and even goals, as well as exchanging views about them. In the process of sounding out possibilities of talking and negotiating, one does not begin with a prominent authoritative figure. Talk should be carried out at lower levels; it does not involve legitimizing and recognition, and it seeks the mere exchange (or extraction) of information. Intermediaries are necessary as a first step toward communication, behind the public view of strident statements.

The next thing to remember in negotiating with terrorists (and with many others, as well) is to follow a two-handed policy and use both carrots and sticks—Tough Talk and Sweet Talk. Terrorists (like states) only move to negotiation when they are checked and cannot achieve their goals by themselves. At that point—a gradual realization—they might take refuge in millennial notions or in hunkering down behind their commitment, but they might also begin to consider alternatives. To encourage such constructive thinking and debate within the organization, the potential negotiator must have something to offer, something to make it worthwhile. The negotiator wants to obtain an end to terrorism, so something must be offered to the terrorists to buy that concession from them. At the same time, the negotiator or the state standing behind must continue to make it impossible for the terrorists to obtain their goals by continuing their tactics, and must convince them that these tactics are actually counterproductive, standing in the way of their achievement of their goals. Thus, carrots and sticks are indivisibly linked.

Admittedly, a two-handed policy is not easy. The two hands contradict each other, leaning in the direction of confrontation so the negotiator must make efforts to make the carrot side credible. Yet one element of credibility is the continuing blockage of the terrorists' efforts to achieve their goals through their terrorism, in effect to use their own sticks. This balance takes time and effort, the essence of negotiation. Negotiation is persuasion, as we have said, and terrorist leaders have to be persuaded, by credible gestures, that there is something in it for them that justifies their putting an end to terrorism.

The third thing to remember is to move forward and carry the opponent with the process. Terrorists have to be persuaded—again—that there is something at the end of the tunnel and that their own engagement in the process leaves them no room to turn back. This is a variation of Sticky Talk, but with one caveat—one has to be prepared to use a combination of Tough Talk and even Stop Talk in creative ways to sustain the momentum. To show that there is no turning back the negotiators must deliver on their promises, implement their commitments, and hold themselves and the other side to their word. The more these commitments can involve working together rather than making separate gestures, the greater the likelihood that terrorists and the negotiator's state will become locked in a joint effort from which it is hard to disengage.

But again, the contradictions of the two-handed policy appear. The best way to ensure that the terrorists implement their promises would be to defect if they defect, using the stick if they withdraw their carrots. In this way, they are "taught" that defection will be punished and cooperation will be rewarded with reciprocal cooperation, a strategy termed Tit-for-Tat. However, in fact, the truly best way to ensure cooperation is for the negotiator's state to persist in its cooperation even when the terrorists defect, at least for an initial period. Delayed defection—necessary at some point lest the negotiator's policy be one simply of unreciprocated concessions—avoids immediate downward spirals of punishment and puts the state on the moral high ground. This strategy, which game theorists (and also ethicists) show will produce the highest gains, is called Tit-for-Double-Tat. On their side, the terrorists no doubt will be erratic, slow in responding, inadequate, and inconsistent in their behavior, uncertain in the command and control of their own side, all of which makes a good solid reciprocation hard to obtain. But the negotiator's state is responsible for its own policies, not the terrorists', and it is in a training mode, trying to get across the idea that moderation is the goal, that it offers cooperation and will reward it and will continue to seek cooperation, but punish defection if it is too often repeated.

All this recalls some recent cases. Israel's and the United States's policy toward the Palestinians after 2005 has been to favor Fatah and the PLO and encourage democratic participation and accountability. In this way, progress could be made toward a solution and Fatah could wave its accomplishments at the electorate and marginalize the rival, terrorist Hamas. Only it worked out differently. Israel offered little or nothing to Fatah in the Palestinian Authority (PA), while the PA became known among the Palestinians for its corruption and ineffectiveness, and democracy produced a protest victory for Hamas. The United States and Israel then worked to break up an entente between the two Palestinian parties and Israel placed a tight blockade on Gaza as punishment for their voting for Hamas. It was a poor show in training, consistency, and persuasion. Half a decade later, the United States is pushing Israel and Fatah to try again.

A more positive example comes from Mozambique, where the preliminary talk process began in the late 1980s, using church intermediaries to contact the terrorist Renamo rebels. The Sant'Egidio lay community acted as mediators, backed by a dozen international observers, and when a drought provided the clinching element in the hurting stalemate between the Renamo rebels and the Frelimo government, talks began in 1990. It took two years to reach an agreement and another two years to hold the decisive elections; when Renamo just before the elections announced it was reneging on all the agreements, additional support money was forthcoming to support electoral activities. A steady course, patient persuasion, and ready carrots backed by the threat of returning to hostilities made the agreement happen.

To go back to the beginning, negotiations in Northern Ireland, Palestine, and South Africa all began with extensive informal talking, gradually formalized into official negotiations in which the rebels, formerly considered terrorists, came to negotiate on equal terms with the authorities. However, in all cases, it was not the militants—the IRA, the various Palestinian armed groups, the Umkhonto we Sizwe—that were the parties recognized as equal participants, but their political organizations, which then had the task of controlling them. The state made allies of the political wing to give control to militant terrorists. The negotiators on both sides then proceeded along both formal and informal tracks, talking under the threat of a return to violence if talks broke down, and they persisted in talking even when violence broke out. In the process, the pairs of sides set up mechanisms and institutions that tied them together, step by step. They could monitor each other's progress and commitment and were each obliged to carry out its part of the bargain so that the other side would carry out its part in order for the first side to gain its benefit. In fact, it was the breakdown of this latter point that caused the collapse of the Oslo Agreement. The point is that it was not a case of the state's giving in to the terrorists but one of the state's turning the terrorists into parties with whom it could cooperate.

Negotiating with Hostage Takers

A special case of talking with terrorists involves negotiations over hostages. There are many stories. In Beslan, in 2004, Chechen terrorists captured an entire school of 1,200 people. It was only on the second day that they made their demands known—independence for Chechnya—in return for which they would call off all violence against Russia. After a number of sporadic contacts, only fifty-two hours after the takeover, Russian troops stormed the building, causing 362 deaths, including 31 terrorists and 176 schoolchildren.

In 2006, Hamas terrorists finally managed to capture an Israeli soldier, Corporal Gilad Shalit. Repeated attempts were made to secure his release and some reports indicate agreements were worked out on the basis of an exchange for several hundred Palestinians held by Israel, only to be canceled by the Israeli government. The price for Shalit in numbers of detainees released continued to rise, but five years later he was still in captivity.

In 1977, an Italian biscuit maker was seized by a band of professional kidnappers, who demanded $3.4 million for his release. Frantic negotiations ensued, in which the hostage played a major role in getting the kidnappers to realize the limited amounts of money his family could actually produce. Seventeen days later he was released for nearly $1 million.

In 1999, a band of fundamentalist Kashmiri nationalists hijacked an airplane with 189 passengers. The plane, on a flight from Kathmandu, Nepal, to New Delhi, was forced to land in Amritsar in India, then Lahore in Pakistan for refueling, and then to Kandahar, Afghanistan, then ruled by the Taliban, who served as mediators and guarantors. The hijackers sought the release of some of their jailed colleagues, ransom for the hostages, and publicity for the plight of occupied Kashmir. Six days of negotiations produced the release of the hostages against the release of three prisoners held in India and safe passage for the hostage takers as well.

There are as many outcomes from hostage-taking as there are cases, with few common characteristics. But the negotiation process is clear, starting with the total demands of the hostage takers and the total refusal of the authorities to make payment in any terms for the release of the hostages. Hostages are terrorists' capital, or bargaining chips, that is, items of no intrinsic value to terrorists but created for the purpose of bargaining away. Hostage takers want to negotiate. They want to get full price for their hostages and they try to overcome their essentially weak position by appropriating a part of the opponent and trying to get the best deal out of the opponents' efforts to get that part back. The problem is that the world does not accept their deal.

But that is merely an extreme case of any negotiating situation. Terrorists tend to focus on their original terms of trade—release of hostages in exchange for fulfillment of demands—and are little inclined to look for reductions and alternatives, options that need to be developed if negotiations are to succeed. As in any negotiations, when they become convinced that a search for a solution is legitimate and acceptable to both sides, they become joint searchers for a solution to a problem rather than adversaries. In that situation, the normal approach is to begin by making efforts to turn a hostile confrontation into a common search for a joint solution, even though this may sound wildly idealistic. Treatment as equals, inculcation of the legitimacy of a solution, development of a sense of independent decision-making, attempts to understand terrorist interests, translation of those interests into politically acceptable terms, and expansion of options leading to a joint search for mutually satisfactory solutions are all ways of moving the hostage takers off positional bargaining.

There are two appropriate negotiating strategies—to lower their terms or to change their terms. To lower the terrorists' terms, negotiators must work to show that initial demands are simply impossible, that thinking smaller is more realistic, and that their concerns are understood (even if not shared). To change terms involves leading the terrorists to think of something else rather than to think of less. The key to successful negotiations is to shift the terrorists' terms of trade from their demands to their fate. When they see that there is no chance of their demands being met but that their future personal situation is open to discussion, innumerable details become available for negotiation. The two must be carried out in tandem—again carrots and sticks, indicating that while one avenue or problem is closed to discussion, the other is open and personally more compelling.

These two strategies may or may not be in contradiction with each other. On one hand, the first strategy helps the terrorists look for lesser amounts of the terms that interest them, whereas the second pushes them to investigate other terms. The second option also reinforces the asymmetric position of the authorities as holders of the upper hand rather than as equals. On the other hand, both strategies involve removing obstacles to creative negotiating by making plain the legitimacy and interest of both parties in developing a range of options and finding a solution.

There is no firm guideline for the tactics to be used. Sometimes, parties can be urged to explore alternatives and options whereas at other times firmness in the subject of negotiations is in order. On some occasions, invitations to further refinement and creative thinking are appropriate, and at others, take-it-or-leave-it offers are effective. Time is on the side of the negotiator, a point that the terrorist may seek to reverse by either killing or releasing some of his hostages. Once relations with terrorists get into the bargaining mode, however, they are open to the same shifts and requirements of tactics as any other negotiation.

All this is not to suggest either that terrorists' demands only require some tailoring around the edges or should be considered legitimate in principle. But it does emphasize that terrorists take their hostages in order to negotiate and that the only alternative to negotiation is what authorities call the tactical alternative: the use of force. Sometimes force is fine, but both its failure and its success are likely to be more extreme than those of negotiation. To go back to the beginning, force was an awful failure in Beslan where the Russians never really tried negotiation. Hamas and Israel negotiated repeatedly, using all the tricks of the trade, over poor Corporal Shalit but the price was too high for the Middle Eastern market to bear. Kidnappers, Inc. and the Lazzaroni family bargained intensely over the price, aided by Paolo Lazzaroni, the kidnap victim himself, to bring the figure within the range of reality and finally succeeding. At Kandahar, Indians, Pakistanis, Afghan Taliban, and the terrorists bargained hard, reached an agreement embarrassing for the Indians but a relief for the rest. The going price for a hostage in Beslan was infinite; in Gaza it is hundreds of prisoners, but not clinched; in Italy nearly $1 million; and in Kandahar three prisoners for 189 hostages.

CHAPTER 8

TAMING INTRACTABLE REGIONAL CONFLICTS

> When no firm and lasting ties any longer unite men, it is impossible
> to obtain the cooperation of any great number of them unless you
> can persuade every man whose help is required that he serves his pri-
> vate interests by voluntarily uniting his efforts to those of all others.
> —Alexis de Tocqueville[1]

The end of the Cold War at the turn of the 1980s saw a number of secondary conflicts turn from violence to peaceful resolution, to the point where this
important shift in world affairs is often credited with bringing peace on earth.
Recall the words of former US President George H. W. Bush about building "a
new world order, a world where the rule of law, not the law of the jungle, governs
the conduct of nations."[2] Former proxy wars, as in Angola, Mozambique, El
Salvador, Nicaragua, and Cambodia, found a peaceful solution as they no longer
served the two superpowers' purposes. Yet there are warring parties around the
world who still need to be talked into reconciliation, far beyond the reach of
the great power rivalries.

Parallel to the Soviet Union, Yugoslavia fell apart in the 1990s. While Slovenia,
Croatia, and Macedonia (and later, Montenegro) hived off from the main federation with little violence, the principal explosive device was Bosnia-Herzegovina,
parts of which were claimed by Serbia and Croatia, leaving a small landlocked
piece for the Bosniaks. Many seasoned statesmen tried their hand in devising
a formula that would respect the crazy quilt of nationalities while maintaining
the unity of the republic. Finally the United States stepped in directly in 1994,

negotiating first federal cooperation between Bosnians and Croatians, and then in 1995 an agreement, arguably tenuous, between the presidents of Serbia, Croatia, and Bosnia (sidestepping the local Serbs and Croats) to provide for a unitary state composed of the two-party federation and a Serb "republic," administered under the control of a NATO commander. The architecture of this agreement was the result of the masterful touch of Tough Talk led first by Charles Redman and then by Richard Holbrooke in consecutive meetings in New York City and then in Dayton, Ohio. The result did not establish interethnic harmony but it did end the genocidal violence and establish a recognized state.

Northern Ireland was torn by "The Troubles" from 1972 until the late 1990s when the two sides began to feel that death and violence were getting them nowhere. Gradually pieces of each side began talking to each other and finally agreed to face-to-face meetings, chaired by former US Senator George Mitchell. By Straight Talking to each other, the parties were able to put their fears and demands on the table and gradually work out an agreement to end violence and to cooperate in governing their region. Talks were conducted on the Mitchell Principles. When one party broke the agreed rules of engagement, it was suspended for a time and then returned to the talks. When violence broke out during the talks, it was regretted by the talking parties, and when a breakaway faction used violence again after the agreement, the parties rallied together to condemn the act. The two sides reached their agreement to share power in government on Good Friday 1998 in the Belfast Agreement, and the region has been inching jaggedly to cooperation and cohabitation ever since.

The War of the Zairian Succession was brewing since the early 1990s, even before the overthrow and demise of longtime dictator Mobutu Sese Seko. His regime was toppled in 1996 and the name of his country reverted to the Congo, but violence continued, burgeoning into "Africa's World War" among nine countries and two rebel groups (and their splinters). But in 1998, the conflicting parties began to talk warily to each other, overcoming not only issues of conflict between them but also issues of status between states and rebel movements. It took two years of talks during continued fighting to bring about an agreement at Lusaka in July 2000. The principles of power sharing, including the rebel movements, and of noninterference in internal affairs by the neighboring states were established and fleshed out in subsequent agreements. It would be obviously more than a bit of an exaggeration to say that they all lived happily ever after, but one phase of the Zairian Succession was settled and the rebel movements were brought into the official fold.

Further out into the Pacific, the island of Bougainville underwent a disruptive conflict since 1988 over the local population's share of mineral wealth that quickly escalated into revived demands for independence from Papua New Guinea. The conflict rose to a mutually hurting stalemate by 1997, and New Zealand seized the ripe moment to offer mediatory services, using traditional Maori practices to open the discussions. Throughout 1997 and 1998, the parties moved through a series of conflict management agreements, leading to a staged weapons disposal process, and new elections for an autonomous government. Under a UN-brokered deal signed in August 2001, the two sides agreed that Bougainville should have greater self-government and eventually a referendum on independence, within ten to fifteen years, thanks to Timely, Straight, and Sweet Talk.

These accomplishments in regional conflict management, sometimes with US assistance, sometimes without, carried into the twenty-first century. In many instances, the work of constructive talking continues. On the western-most tip of Sumatra, Indonesia's largest island, the Sultanate of Aceh has aspired to retrieve its former independence ever since the entire archipelago threw off Dutch colonial rule in 1949. Aceh's struggle turned violent in 1982, but after Indonesia over-threw its own dictator and turned to democracy in 1998, contacts were opened between the Free Aceh Movement (GAM) and the Indonesian government. Violence continued alongside of sporadic talks, drawing the attention of many mediators, generally nongovernmental organizations (NGOs). The World Affairs Council at Harvard University and the Center for Humanitarian Dialogue in Geneva both stumbled over the conflict. Then, in 2004, the region was hit by a massive tsunami that wiped out villages and populations and destroyed army camps and installations. The Crisis Management Initiative of former Finnish President Ahtisaari entered the mediation and the following year the Helsinki Accords were signed, providing Aceh with self-government. Timely Talk, Straight Talk, and Right Talk were themselves important to the achievement of an agreement, perhaps as important as the tidal wave.

If we stop and take stock of these accomplishments, we can see many causes. Certainly, all the conflicts were caught in a stalemate in one way or another and the mutual impasse was costly and inconvenient to both parties. The sides had fought to the bone, with no hope of beating each other. Objectively, one might argue (as did some of their inner councils) that there was still some fight left and a chance for victory, but the important point is that both sides felt it was time to start talking instead of fighting. Talking was not easy, as the length of time spent in talks testifies, but that is normal since Timely Talking was replacing putting one's life on the line. In all of these cases, warring parties on all sides of the conflict divide judged it better to join in a political process rather than trying to physically destroy their opponents. Each side got some of its demands, enough to be able to say that they had won, by redefining winning so as to bring out its core meaning rather than insisting on the particularities of the position, redefinition often hanging simply on the right word.

Of course, other incidental—often important—events mattered, too. In intangible ways, the Indian Ocean tsunami overwhelmed both sides in Aceh and focused them on a broader goal of survival and development. The "defection" of Congo's neighbors from the war left rebel movements without key external bases of support and caused them to revise their calculations. The same was true in Northern Ireland, where key political actors in the United States and Britain felt that an agreement was preferable and possible and twisted arms to move it forward. Backing the peace process was a public that had grown weary of ongoing violence, mayhem, and destruction. So far, so good.

The New Millennium

However, in this century something happened on the way to a successful formula for conflict management and the resolution of conflict in some of the world's most troubled regions. It is now well documented that there has been an upswing in the outbreak of armed conflict coupled with another troubling development—the long persistence of conflicts, some quite low level, in various parts of the world, for instance, Afghanistan-Pakistan, Sudan and its neighbors, Iraq, Iran, the Great Lakes region of Africa, the Horn of Africa, North Africa, Kashmir-India-Pakistan, and North Korea to name but a few.

A number of peace agreements from the 1990s have also lapsed or collapsed. The Oslo Agreement between Israel and Palestinians was not sold to home audiences by either side and negotiated commitments made toward the other party were ignored or simply broken. Attempts by the United States to save the Oslo Agreement at Wye Plantation in 1995 and then at Camp David in 2000 and to move toward a two-state solution were half-hearted and unconsummated. The Lusaka Agreements on the Congolese wars were further complemented by agreements in Sun City and Pretoria in South Africa in 2002, but the eastern part of the country continues to be mired in vicious conflict over politics and diamonds.

Many new peace agreements were signed after the end of the Cold War, only to subsequently fall apart. The Arusha Agreement of 1993 that was to bring multiparty democracy to Rwanda instead was tossed aside the following year in the carnage of a brutal genocidal civil war. The Comprehensive Peace Agreement for Southern Sudan was concluded in 2005 after half a decade of intensive talks mediated by Kenya with pressure and engagement by the United States, but the power-sharing government that it established disintegrated into bickering and ineffectiveness. Elections for a new cooperative government held in 2010 were rigged and controlled, and the referendum of the following year on Southern Sudanese secession faced enormous difficulties and renewed violence over governing arrangements and the boundary between North and South. In Darfur in western Sudan, rebel groups calling for a place of their own in the country's power-sharing agreement were subject to genocidal ravages by government militias. The killing eventually trailed off, but recurring attempts to reach a comprehensive peace agreement produced only paltry results. Northern rebels and the government in the Ivory Coast, torn by interethnic conflict since 1999, signed two peace agreements, in Marcoussis in 2003, and then again in Ouagadougou in 2007. Violence ended and the divided country was opened up again to the world, but the 2005 elections held five years late were trashed by outgoing president Laurent Gbagbo; it took five months of wrenching civil war to get him out.

A number of major peace initiatives were also launched in the first decade of this century but also fell apart before ever reaching an agreement, sometimes in brutal violence and sometimes less so. The most dramatic failure was in Sri Lanka, where conflict between Tamils in the north and the Buddhist majority had been going off and on since independence in 1948. Initially the conflict was mainly political, but in 1983 a new generation took over and it turned viciously violent. The Liberation Tigers of Tamil Eelam (LTTE) invented child soldiering and suicide bombing in the modern era. Negotiations with the Sri Lankan government proceeded for a quarter century, at one point under the mediation of India, and then, more recently, under Norway's good offices. Talks broke off in 2003, revived again and then broke as both sides used the truce to find arms. The government won the race and destroyed the LTTE in an offensive in 2009. It is not certain that the fate of the Tamils is any better as a result, or that their protest is over.

In Cyprus, where conflict between the Turks and Greeks antedated independence in 1960, Talk Power was used for conflict management after an outbreak of heavy violence in 1964. A decade later the Greeks tried to take over the entire government, the Turkish army came to the defense of the Turkish minority, and the island has been divided ever since, with a UN-run demilitarized zone running across the middle. Thereafter the situation has remained frozen. There has been no violence or resolution in a seemingly unending round of negotiations. Most recently, the process was led by UN Secretary-General Kofi Annan and his Special Representative Alvaro de Soto. In 2003, the European Union (EU) admitted the southern part as the government of the whole island; as a result, when an agreement between the two communities was reached the following year, it was voted down by the Greek Cypriots, who now had nothing to gain from it, and the situation went back to square one, managed but unresolved.

In the Western Sahara, a former Spanish colony ceded to Morocco but contested by a national liberation movement, the Polisario Front, war broke out when

Spain left in 1975 and continued until 1983. A formal ceasefire was declared by the United Nations in 1991 and the process of organizing a referendum to decide between Moroccan integration and independence began. Since the two parties could not agree on a voters' list, the United Nations called off its efforts in 2006 and the following year Morocco proposed a halfway solution—internal autonomy within Moroccan sovereignty. The Polisario, backed by its sanctuary and supporter, Algeria, refused, and the conflict remains frozen, managed somewhat but obstinately far from any movement toward resolution, as Algeria and its proxy refuse to talk about autonomy as a compromise.

What makes these conflicts different from others? Geography and regional politics, local politics, economic predation and warlordism, the compound failure of past efforts to resolve the conflict, and the length of time the conflict has endured are all contributing factors. Although the specific conditions contributing to intractability generally vary from one situation to another, these conflicts share a common characteristic: They defy settlement because political leaders believe their objectives are irreconcilable and they have a greater interest in maintaining the status quo—which may or may not be violent—than considering their political alternatives. In other words, key local decision-makers seek to resist or prevent the emergence of Talk Power politics as the arena for settling their differences. Although all intractable conflicts share this characteristic, the actual level of violence and the potential for an escalation of military hostilities varies from one setting to another. Sri Lanka experienced very high levels of violence—much of it terrorist-based—before the government annihilated the Tamil insurgents. Cyprus has not seen violence for many decades even though a political settlement has remained elusive. And the Middle East shows that levels of violence can escalate, de-escalate, and re-escalate over the lifetime of a conflict.

It is wrong to believe that intractable conflicts are confined to the borders of a single country. Many of these conflicts are interstate disputes where the parties are—or consider themselves to be—"sovereign" entities. The distinction between inter- and intrastate conflicts breaks down when contested sovereignty, or the refusal of one (or more) parties to recognize the sovereign claims of the other side, lies at the heart of a dispute. Further, the intra-/interstate distinction can be extremely artificial because many so-called "intrastate" or "civil" conflicts involve external actors, including regional neighbors, who not only try to manipulate the conflict for their own ends, but may also be actively involved in the fighting itself.

Although some intractable disputes are frozen, others are boiling off the stove. But both share a common characteristic: They are not ripe because the parties themselves have not experienced the full and direct costs of a mutually hurting stalemate. They differ, however, in some crucial ways. Frozen or abey-ant intractables are conflicts that have gone into remission, usually because a third party is willing to guarantee the terms of a negotiated ceasefire—a cease-fire that may also include the broad outlines of a political settlement, as in the case of the Cyprus. When outsiders freeze a conflict by providing the means to check violence and keep peace, they save lives and manage the problem, prevent it from spreading, and limit damage, but they may also, perversely, sustain the underlying polarity and delay political solutions. Suspended violence removes the incentive for conclusive talking. In this situation, Triple Talk becomes in-dispensable, and outsiders' eventual departure presents a security dilemma for local parties as there is real potential for escalation if those third-party security guarantees are withdrawn.

Intractable conflicts tend to take over the societies they affect. They permeate all societal institutions—politics, economics, media, religion, education—and dominate the political and social discourse. No one escapes from their impact, even in conflicts where the level of violence is low, as seen in Northern Ireland or Cyprus. The conflict shapes the way that people see their world and often determines the borders of that world. In any conflict, dealing with the "other" is always an issue. Enmity, particularly once violence has broken out, is difficult to turn to any other kind of relationship, which is the reason that arriving at rec-onciliation may take decades. But in the case of intractable conflicts, that enmity enters deep into people's daily lives. And it is often augmented by isolation, as channels for communication are cut off. The Turkish and Greek Cypriots were cut off from each other for twenty-nine years until the borders were opened in 2003 and still few Greek Cypriots go north. Israelis and Palestinians are now separated by a wall. So, too, in Northern Ireland: Catholics and Protestants live in carefully segregated neighborhoods, behind walls, and send their children to separate schools.

Why Get Involved at All?

Any discussion of Talk Power intervention strategies in intractable conflicts must start by asking why engage at all (given that prior failure is a hallmark of intractability). A related challenge is when to engage and when not. Perhaps we should just wait for the outright victory of one side, as in the recent case of Sri Lanka. Victory, it is often argued, provides greater future stability than a mediated compromise that risks breaking down over issues that never quite get resolved. Statistics show victory to be an outcome more stable than compromise, at least in the middle run. Despite short-term humanitarian and ethical problems with "letting nature take its course," there may be both ethical and prudential factors in the longer term in favor of doing so.[3]

However, this line of reasoning assumes that we have a crystal ball and can divine nature's true course. It is sometimes argued that war is akin to a forest fire. It continues to burn until all available fuel has been consumed. Fuel, in the case of conflicts, takes the form of internally and externally derived resources (human, financial, operational) to support the war effort. Letting a conflict burn itself out may be the most practical option and may eliminate future emergencies and disasters at some huge and inhuman cost. But there are also other considerations. First, in the modern era, most conflicts are not controllable and fires will not burn themselves out, in part because the forces of globalization and the disappearance of the Cold War restraints make it much easier than before for rebels to secure the requisite resources and political support to keep fighting. Losers also have many friends. Modern wars thus have a tendency to continue, to sputter on, or to reignite. Outright military victory is an elusive goal.

Second, in doing so, intractable conflicts do not get better, easier, clearer, or more amenable to ultimate resolution. On the contrary, there are ample examples—in places such as Colombia, Uganda, Cote d'Ivoire, Lebanon, Somalia, and Kashmir—of conflicts that get more and more deeply impacted by layers of local, regional, and international issues and rivalries. Conflicts may migrate from initial roots in societal grievances or neighboring rivalries into struggles based on competing creeds or identities. Over time, wars are driven by entrenched interests in the form of organizational or personal greed, factors that make them almost immune to political settlement procedures. What kind of solution can lure a Colombian, Congolese, Taliban, or Somali warlord off his drugs-and-diamonds habit?

Finally, intractability and state failure are closely interrelated. The argument against intervening in intractable cases needs to take into account the potential consequences of abstention, including the ill effects of conflict spread, conflict metamorphosis, and the broader consequences for regional and international order of conflict spawned by or within failing states, particularly when failed states become breeding grounds for terrorist groups or export their problems in the form of refugees to other countries.

Third parties should not automatically intervene whenever they perceive an intractable conflict. Rather certain criteria or conditions should serve as warnings to a potential third party not to seek mediation lightly. These conditions relate to (a) the mediator's capacity and motives, and (b) the status of the conflict and the nature of the parties' behavior. Starting with the mediator or Triple Talker, it is harmful to propose or offer mediation if the mediator is not "ready" or equipped to undertake the task. Being ready has a number of political, operational, and other components that ought to be the object of serious reflection before a proposal is made: (a) *operational and political* capacity for the extraordinary practical demands of the task and the leadership responsibilities of running a round-the-clock exercise for months and years; (b) *strategic and diplomatic* capacity to place the mediation squarely in the center of one's policy concerns and to assemble an ad hoc or structured coalition of third parties willing to act as cooperating partners; and (c) *the right mediator with the right relationships, "reach," and cultural fit for a particular conflict.*

Another circumstance in which mediation may be inappropriate is when the prospective mediator is too closely aligned with one party or too directly involved in the conflict to be capable of helping the parties produce a balanced engagement. This is not to say that a mediator must be impartial or neutral to be effective, but that the mediator needs to be politically capable of pressing and influencing both sides toward a settlement. More specifically, a "biased" mediator is expected to be able and willing to deliver the party toward which it is biased. This is what Sadat banked on in calling in the United States, friend of Israel, to mediate the end of the October War in the Middle East in 1974.

Turning to the second set of criteria, a mediator should hesitate or decline involvement when a viable Talk Power framework and negotiating mechanism already exist and a new initiative could damage or destabilize this existing peace process. To do otherwise is poor tradecraft and only plays into the hands of parties engaged in forum shopping and outbidding. The United States in Namibia in the mid-1970s, the Vatican in the Beagle Channel dispute in 1980–84, and the Carter Center in Congo-Brazzaville in 1997 made sure that they were the only game in town. Similarly, mediation may not be the right answer when the prospective mediator is eager to acquire a peacemaking role but the parties themselves do not demonstrate any serious intention to explore a political solution. Mediators can also undertake the long job of building intentions by emphasizing the costly impasse in the situation, as Kissinger and Baker did in the Middle East or the parties themselves did at Oslo. In such circumstances, the mediator needs to test parties' motives and avoid pleading for the assignment. The mediator should be cautious about involvement when it would play into the hands of a dominant conflict party, legitimizing actions that may cross the line of acceptable conduct. The best response in some conflict situations, in other words, may be police action, coercive diplomacy, or benign neglect, rather than mediation. There may also be intermediate steps or stages during the prenegotiation phase when the third party is best advised to undertake activities aimed at ripening the conflict through traditional diplomatic means or—for a nonofficial actor—through activities aimed at affecting political constituencies or influential elites.

The Importance of Street Talk

Intractable conflicts also require large, ongoing doses of Street Talk to engage different sectors of society and transform relationships that have been broken by years of civil strife and violence. Street Talk is also part of a broader process of social and political transformation that changes the relationship between armed elites and the society as a whole. It is critical to empowering the local populace so that elites are accountable to their constituents. Street Talk can help reduce the level of fragmentation and confrontation within civil society and between civil society and the government.

Street Talk played a major role in the Northern Ireland conflict as women's organizations and other groups pressed their political leaders to lead the way to peace and away from fearsome fratricide. After the Good Friday Agreement of 1998, the women's movement turned itself into a political party when the established parties did not include enough women in their leadership ranks. Organizations from civil society prepared the 1990–94 negotiation to transform South Africa, beginning with business delegations meeting with the African National Congress (ANC) and mediation councils preparing for eventual reconciliation; civil society involvement continued into the transition period when the National Peace Accord monitored the transformation of testy relations in evolution at the local level. In Israel and the Occupied Territories, Israelis and Palestinians organized widespread dialogue groups in the 1980s until the mid-1990s to prepare for eventual neighborly relations and to understand differing narratives in getting there. These initiatives withered after the first Intifada and Prime Minister Binyamin Netanyahu's election, and were difficult to revive. The pace of negotiation has suffered as a result.

Another example of Street Talk is in Jammu-Kashmir where a wide variety of civil society groups and policymakers have created a constructive space for ongoing dialogue and discussion in an effort to reduce tensions between India and Pakistan and within a shifting regional and international context. This dialogue is being led by a wide variety of national and international think tanks and policy experts such as the Kashmir Study Group, the Delhi Policy Group, the Regional Centre for Strategic Studies, and the Kashmiri American Council, all of which have broadened the discourse at the official level in ways that have generally been positive and constructive. Official diplomacy has also been reinforced by civic engagement at the local level as various women's groups have mobilized to end violence by promoting reconciliation and bridging religious, ethnic, and linguistic divides. What is significant about these developments is that they have been tacitly encouraged by the Indian and Pakistani governments in a pragmatic quest to establish a sustainable framework for dialogue and negotiation.

One of the pioneers of civic dialogue and engagement is the former US diplomat Hal Saunders who has launched a wide variety of grassroots undertakings in a wide variety of conflict settings in order to change perceptions and build public support for a nascent peace process. He has been the principal architect of the Inter-Tajik Dialogue, which was launched with Russian and US support in 1993, directed at reaching out to different political factions and groups during Tajikistan's civil war. As Saunders observes,

> When people regularly meet and deliberate freely on problems that are acute for all of them regardless of ethnic or social background, they gradually create connections and habits of cooperation that are the main preconditions for improved relationships. The subject of discussion can range from economic to social to educational issues.... In Tajikistan, discussion has focused mainly on economic and social issues because they are more acute in most communities. Whatever the subject ... a base for successful further cooperation has been created.[4]

Attitudinal change can be fostered through a variety of Street Talk instruments, including consultative meetings, problem-solving workshops, training in conflict resolution at the communal level, and/or third-party assistance in developing and designing other kinds of intercommunal dispute resolution systems that are compatible with local culture and norms and engage the local citizenry. These activities can be undertaken by both official and nongovernmental actors and are typically directed at ethnic, racial, or religious groups who are in a hostile or adversarial relationship. This dialogue process can be assisted by specialized training programs that are directed at exploring ways of establishing and building relationships, furthering proficiency in facilitation, mediation and brokering, data collection, fact-finding, and other kinds of cooperative decision-making.

What Makes the Difference?

It is hard to fault the various mediators in failed or collapsed attempts to bring about peace. Persuasion was their principal source of leverage and they were well versed in the art of Triple Talk. Former US Secretary of State James Baker in the Western Sahara, UN Special Representative of the Secretary-General Alvaro de Soto in Cyprus, and Botswana President Ketumile Masire in the Congo are accomplished diplomats with enviable negotiating records—the Madrid Talks on the Middle East, the end of the El Salvador civil war, and the management of the Botswanan multiparty political system, respectively. In all of these efforts, they had played the potential benefits of an agreement against the costs of continuing conflict and persuaded the parties that their goals could actually be achieved, at least in part, by participating in the political system and cooperating with their enemies—and that, reciprocally, these former enemies were ready to cooperate.

But in the obdurate cases these attempts to convince fell on deaf ears for one major reason—at least one of the warring parties was relatively comfortable where it was and saw no reason to compromise with the opponents. Sometimes this was a matter of objective fact, sometimes a subjective view of possibilities. The president of Sudan has assured himself of continued rule in at least the northern part of his country. The now-former president of Ivory Coast reigned ten years on a five-year mandate and had no particular reason not to continue even though he was well past his shelf-life expiry date. The government of Sri Lanka felt that the moment had come, with a split in the LTTE, for a final push to victory and events proved it correct. The Greek side of Cyprus had just been awarded legal ownership of the whole island by the EU and saw no reason to compromise with the Turkish side. The Polisario enjoys the unshakable support of Algeria and sees no reason to compromise its position, even though it actually rules only a tiny sliver of its claimed country plus squalid refugee camps. And in the Middle East, the Palestinians and Israelis alike felt that they could not trust each other not to pursue their own respective form of a single-state solution at some later time when their fortunes improved.

However, in other seemingly intractable cases, Triple Talk succeeded. To put it crudely, the parties were talked into or talked themselves into taking the chance on using politics rather than violence to achieve their goals. The costs of continuing violence were deemed to be too high, the chance of military success—especially in the short run—too low, and a political window appeared open. Note that they did not give up their goals. They may have cut back on some of them, while reconfiguring others. The Acehnese felt that self-government was what they could settle for, rather than continuing a costly war for independence that might not be recognized, a perception that the Polisario did not share in the Western Sahara. The Northern Irish came to feel that power sharing was preferable to assassination, a perspective that Sri Lankan elites on both sides (unlike the people of Sri Lanka) did not adopt. The government in Kinshasa agreed to talk with the rebel opposition movements controlling the eastern Congo. They were able to separate the rebels from their external sponsors and gain real sovereignty over their territory at the price of bringing the ethnic opposition into the government, a political calculation that the government of southern Cyprus was unwilling to make.

In all of the successful cases, the elements of Talk Power and persuasion were accompanied by concrete assurances that violence was at an end and that cooperation would work. These included formal DDRRR (disarmament, demobilization, resettlement, reintegration, and where applicable, repatriation) programs, a matter that held up full pursuit of the Belfast Agreement for a while. Many an agreement has been "guaranteed" by the deployment of foreign peacekeeping forces, such as the UN Mission to the Congo (MONUC), Somalia (UNOSOM), and Rwanda (UNAMID), however imperfect they may have been in all cases. Institutions of accountability, such as the various forms of truth and reconciliation commissions, increasingly play an important role in conflict resolution processes as the varied experiences in Argentina, South Africa, El Salvador, and Rwanda show.

Some agreements in conflicts that had previously seemed intractable have lasted because they were not implemented. They lasted because they lasted. The lesson for effective talk is crucial: Words must lead to action, effective implementation, continued attention and monitoring, and further talking to handle old problems in new forms (and forums) and new problems that may turn ugly. Talk without works is a dead end. Because an agreement is obtained principally by persuasion, it needs immediate action to confirm the persuasive reasoning that brought the parties to drop violence and begin cooperation. They await a sign of works, not just faith, from each other, and down payments on the agreement are due right away.

It was the absence of follow-through that buried the Oslo Agreements. The Agreement's key to success was its key to its failure: secrecy. Closed proceedings were necessary to bring the parties to overcome their distrust of each other, but open explication and enactment of its provisions were required to convince the home audiences as well as the opponent that the deal was real. It was the absence of effective monitoring and enforcement that allowed the Rwandan genocide to occur and the Arusha Agreement to collapse. It was the absence of focus on the real problems to the east and appropriate, timely action on the part of MONUC (which needed extensive expansion both in size and in mission) that have allowed nearly a decade of murderous anarchy to terrorize the people of Eastern Congo.

As in many phases of real life, constructive talk is the key to changing bad situations. But after the door is unlocked, action is required to keep open to a better future.

PART III

TEAMING

CHAPTER 9
BUILDING "TEAMS OF RIVALS"

Diplomatic success won by methods which confer reciprocal benefits must be regarded not only as firmly founded but as the sure promise of other successes to come.... The secret of negotiation is to harmonize the interests of the parties concerned.

—François de Callières, 1716

Conflicts are no longer bilateral in this world. India versus Pakistan draws on Afghanistan, China, Uzbekistan, Turkmenistan, Tajikistan, Russia, and Saudi Arabia; Ethiopia versus Eritrea involves Somalia, Sudan, Egypt, Libya, and by extension, Kenya, Uganda, and Chad; Colombia versus its rebels overflows to Venezuela and Ecuador, not to speak of the United States; and so on. Furthermore, the bystanders who seek to do some good, pull the warring parties apart, and bring peace to the region are just as numerous and frequently just as diverse in their interests as the warring parties themselves. They do have a common interest, however, in bringing the conflict under control, and they often have to do it while handling an undermining opposition at home. This situation constitutes arguably the toughest challenge for negotiation—to build "teams of rivals" to manage regional crises.

There are important examples of Team Talk. In the early 1990s, the five permanent members of the UN Security Council (P5) plus the neighboring countries of the Association of Southeast Asian Nations (ASEAN) had rather divergent and even contradictory interests over the future of Cambodia. The United States skillfully brought these many countries together into an agreed solution. Or again, in much of the first decade of the 2000s, the Democratic

People's Republic of (North) Korea (DPRK) singlehandedly held off a group of world leaders as it pursued its nuclear security objectives. But the five most concerned nations with often diametrically opposed interests were brought together into the Six-Party Talks by China and the United States, playing very different roles, to produce some basic documents necessary to any further progress. Or, going back to the 1960s, the leading countries of the old (colonial) and new (Cold War) world order overcame their differences to negotiate a momentary solution to the beleaguered position of Laos. But also, in an even more previous era, in 1830–33, the leading powers of the Concert of Europe eventually overcame a stalemate among their opposing positions to produce a stable status to the new state of Belgium that has lasted to this day (even if with some breaches and maybe not much longer). Yet still, in things to come, it is only when the most important of Afghanistan's immediate and distant neighbors—Pakistan, India, China, Iran, Russia, and the United States—take a hard look together, despite their differences, and negotiate a regional entente that stability in the Asian heartland can be achieved. These cases are worth a closer look, to draw some conclusions about a particular challenge to Talk Power.

The problem of engaging hostile, partisan, or indifferent neighbors in a diplomatic process of regional settlement that is intended to end conflict and stabilize a situation is not a new problem facing American diplomacy. It is an old challenge of getting others to work as a team, a pact that is formed out of a "team of rivals" who are global or regional competitors but have the wisdom to realize that they share a common problem or project that can only be resolved together. If successful, such a pact or entente can advance a peace process because it brings the affected interests to the negotiating table, creates potent sources of leverage, and forces warring parties and factions to work together. It takes real leadership to build these kinds of pacts. Like President Abraham Lincoln who understood that if he was to succeed in his presidency he would have to bring his bitterest political rivals—Salmon P. Chase, Edward Bates, and William H. Seward—on board into his cabinet and use their particular talents to keep the Union together and win the war, American diplomacy achieves broader effectiveness when it marshals the resources, political will, and leverage of both friend and foe alike, both globally and locally, in compacts that are committed to the pursuit of peace.[1]

Building a team of rivals to deal with the hottest zones of conflict is a challenging task and a high-wire balancing act. It requires a special kind of leadership that is prepared to take risks. It requires calm patience and dogged persistence. It also means building and sustaining political support for new diplomatic initiatives not just internationally but also on the home front—with Congress and various domestic interests who may oppose new diplomatic initiatives for sound or partisan or self-interested reasons and are in a position to undercut the work of the negotiators. Bipartisan executive-legislative support for new diplomatic initiatives no matter how noble or honorable the cause, especially when they involve rivals or real enemies of the United States, should never be taken for granted.

Team building involves a variety of roles to play. Parties can Drive, Conduct, Defend, Brake, Derail, Ride, or Leave. Drivers try to organize participation to produce an agreement that fits their interests and positions. Conductors also seek to produce an agreement but from a more neutral position, with no interest axe of their own to grind or at least one that is less sharp. Defenders are single-issue players, concerned with incorporating a particular measure or position in the agreement if there is to be one rather than with the overall success of the negotiations. Brakers are the opposing or modifying resistance, brought into action by the progress being made on either the broad regime or on specific issue items. Derailers are spoilers, out to destroy the agreement, not merely soften or slow it down. Riders are filler, with no strong interests of their own and so are available to act as followers. Leavers pursue an exit policy, either partially through individual exceptions and derogations, or wholly through withdrawal from the negotiations and the regime.

Building a Team of Rivals in Cambodia

There is no better illustration of this global and local team-building approach than the role played by the United States and its assistant secretary of state for East Asian and Pacific affairs at the time, Richard H. Solomon, in the run-up to the Paris Peace Agreements of October 23, 1991, for a comprehensive settlement of the civil war in Cambodia.

For almost thirty years prior to the Paris Agreements, Cambodia had been wracked by a vicious civil war. In 1963 Pol Pot, the ruthless communist leader of the Khmer Rouge, led an insurrection against Prince Norodom Sihanouk, the phlegmatic and somewhat mercurial leader who had governed the country since its independence ten years earlier. The US intervention in Vietnam in 1964 created further difficulties for Sihanouk, as the war led North Vietnam to develop infiltration routes and safe areas in Cambodia, and the United States began to bomb these targets. To prevent the North Vietnamese army from supporting the communist insurrection against his regime, Sihanouk allowed Hanoi to run supply lines to the Viet Cong through eastern Cambodia. When he severed Cambodia's diplomatic relations with the United States over its Vietnam deployment in March 1970, he was overthrown by Lon Nol, who restored relations and allowed American and South Vietnamese troops to launch military incursions into Cambodia to remove North Vietnamese and Khmer Rouge bases. The communists simply moved deeper into Cambodian territory, prompting deeper US bombing.

The 1973 Paris Peace Agreements between the United States and North Vietnam brought little relief to war-torn South Vietnam or Cambodia. The United States continued bombing North Vietnamese supply routes and peasant support intensified for the Khmer Rouge, who ousted Lon Nol in April 1975. Once in power, Pol Pot began to forcibly implement his ideology of "de-urbanization," leading to some of the most brutal mass killings since World War II. Perceived traitors, religious opponents, foreigners, intellectuals, professionals, and members of the governing classes were eliminated in mass executions. Fearing that Vietnam had designs on Cambodia, the Khmer Rouge began purging Vietnamese settlers who had moved across the border during the Vietnam War. Pro-Vietnamese elements in the Khmer Rouge ranks (or those perceived to be so by the increasingly paranoid Pol Pot) were also purged and in January 1977 Khmer Rouge forces crossed into Vietnam and massacred hundreds of Vietnamese, beginning two years of war back and forth across the border. Finally, on December 25, 1978, Vietnamese forces surged into Cambodia, overthrew the Khmer Rouge, and installed a pro-Vietnamese communist government under the presidency of Heng Samrin. The new government, renamed the People's Republic of Kampuchea (PRK), was not recognized in the West and was supported only by the Soviet Union and Eastern bloc countries. The Khmer Rouge escaped to the Cambodian jungle and refugee camps on the Thai border, to carry out insurrections against the Vietnamese puppet regime, with Chinese assistance channeled through Thailand. With no clear winner and no clear strategy for either side's victory, the conflict made for dangerous enemies and unstable partners on the world scene and continued civilian casualties in the region.

Mikhail Gorbachev's accession to power in the Soviet Union in the mid-1980s brought changes in the interests and positions of major outside parties. As part of an overall effort to normalize relations with China, the Soviet Union began to step up its own efforts to resolve the conflict, by encouraging Vietnam to withdraw its army units from Cambodia and threatening termination of its military and economic aid to Vietnam. Prince Sihanouk, who had decamped to Beijing, announced that he was willing to meet with Cambodia's new leader, Hun Sen, to discuss terms for a peace settlement. Feeling pressured by these developments, China decided to support the idea of national reconciliation under the leadership of Sihanouk. However, it remained interested in preventing Vietnam, emboldened by its defeat of US forces, from dominating the region and so maintained its support for the Khmer Rouge against the Phnom Penh regime of Hun Sen. Cambodia's neighbor to the west, Thailand, also feared a

Vietnamese expansion across Indochina. Thailand hosted several refugee camps used by Cambodia's resistance factions for incursions against the Phnom Penh regime, and rogue Thai military officers were conducting profitable illicit trade in gems and timber with the Khmer Rouge. US policy was to support a coalition government led by Prince Sihanouk, which included Pol Pot's Khmer Rouge. Both Washington and Beijing were keen to restrain Vietnam's regional aspirations but the Chinese government's brutal crackdown on student protestors in Tiananmen Square in June 1989 dampened any US inclination for cooperation. Efforts to secure a secret Safe Talk channel of communications with the Chinese imploded in the political firestorm when news of the overture hit the press. Although the hard-line positions of China, Thailand, the Soviet Union, and Vietnam began to soften in the late 1980s, agreement on a settlement of the Cambodian conflict was still beyond grasp.

In March 1989 the USSR delivered a secret warning to the Vietnamese that it would no longer subsidize Vietnam's occupation of Cambodia and its tug-of-war with China, and on March 24, Vietnam announced that it would withdraw its troops from Cambodia. Sensing that there was an opportunity for the United States to take the lead on Indochina issues, newly appointed Assistant Secretary Richard Solomon began to reach out to other key diplomatic players. In a special French embassy breakfast meeting for Claude Martin, director of the Quai d'Orsay's Asia-Oceania Division, Solomon gave his support for a conference on Cambodia's future, which was scheduled by France and Indonesia for August. The immediate friendship that Solomon developed with Martin was to prove invaluable as France and the United States began to work closely together on Cambodia's future.

Solomon understood that the Chinese were deeply sensitive to the damage that the Tiananmen crackdown had caused to their international reputation and that China might be more willing to work with the United States on a political settlement for Cambodia, even to the point of distancing themselves from the Khmer Rouge, if it would help restore China's tarnished image. But Solomon also knew that he would have to fend off attacks in the Congress and the media if the White House and State Department were seen to be getting too cozy with Beijing.

The first session of the Paris Peace Conference, held throughout August, was attended by the various Cambodian factions, as well as Vietnam, Laos, Japan, Canada, Australia, India, Zimbabwe, the five UN Security Council permanent members, and the six members of ASEAN. The Vietnamese delegation made clear its opposition to any inclusion of Pol Pot and his Khmer Rouge faction in the peace process because of its fear that this genocidal murderer might return to power; other conference participants felt that it was better to have the Khmer Rouge inside the negotiating tent than outside of it where they could do much greater mischief. The Khmer Rouge delegates, on the other hand, resisted the characterization of "genocide" and stressed the need for a coalition government under Sihanouk as the only way to restore Cambodia's sovereignty after a decade of "colonial" rule by Vietnam's surrogate regime under Hun Sen. Unable the break the deadlock, negotiations in Paris broke apart without reaching an agreement, and Vietnam's troop withdrawal was followed by an escalation of the civil war between the resistance and government forces.

Faced with a deadlock, Solomon turned to the five permanent members of the Security Council, an idea originally floated by US congressman Stephen J. Solarz, chairman of the House Subcommittee on Asian and Pacific Affairs, and the Subcommittee on Africa. US strategy in putting Cambodia firmly into UN hands was driven by two considerations: to prevent Cambodia from becoming a US problem, and to get others to share the financial burdens of the massive reconstruction effort that would be required to put the country back on its feet if the peace process were to get some traction. The only way to wean the various Cambodian factions from their regional and great power backers was through a concerted, P5 team–based effort that would, in effect, force Cambodia's factions to compromise and make concessions at the negotiating table. Just as important, it would help control the Khmer Rouge who were largely political outcasts and potential spoilers in the peace process by giving them a seat at the negotiating table. Solomon also realized that if the Khmer Rouge were engaged in the political process they would have to participate in elections where they were bound to lose because of their massive unpopularity with the Cambodian people, scarred by Pol Pot's brutal regime.

After the first meeting of the P5 on January 16–17, 1990, the US and British delegations retired to the American embassy to draft a set of basic principles that would govern the work of the group. The second day, the delegates reviewed the principles and agreed that the United Nations would play an "enhanced" role in managing Cambodia's political transition and ensuring a "free and fair" electoral process to an elected government where Cambodian "sovereignty" would be preserved under a body called the Supreme National Council. UN observers would also verify that Vietnam had completely withdrawn from Cambodia and that Khmer Rouge refugees would be afforded proper security in their return from Thailand. The details of the emerging architecture for a UN-supervised political transition were thrashed out in subsequent meetings of the P5 that were held in February, March, May, June, and July in New York, Paris, and Tokyo. During these Small Talk negotiations over key details there was a real tug-of-war between the Soviets and the Chinese about the ultimate degree of UN control and involvement in implementing a peace plan. The Soviets wanted a minimal UN role so as to allow the Hun Sen government to position itself favorably for the elections, but also called for controls on Pol Pot, with explicit references to the Khmer Rouge's genocidal policies in the formal text of the agreement. The Chinese objected with a call for the complete disarmament of the Hun Sen government in order to weaken it in the run-up to elections.

While these negotiations were underway, Solomon found himself coming under increasingly tough criticism from Congressional critics and in the media. A bipartisan group of sixty-six senators wrote to Secretary James Baker to urge the administration to immediately withdraw its support for Prince Sihanouk and his Khmer Rouge allies and shift its support to the Vietnamese-backed Hun Sen government, or face the threat of Congress's termination of all financial assistance to the noncommunist resistance in Cambodia. To make matters worse for the administration, *ABC News* anchorman Peter Jennings hosted a special program "From the Killing Fields" in April 1990, which alleged that the United States was providing secret financial and material assistance to Prince Sihanouk that was finding its way into the hands of Khmer Rouge. And the night before one of Solomon's appearances before Congress, *ABC News* broadcast a story stating that Sihanouk's own forces were fighting alongside the Khmer Rouge in the jungles of Cambodia—an allegation, which if true, would have spelled doom for the negotiations and Solomon's own diplomatic career. Administration allies counterattacked with hearings before Congressman Solarz's subcommittee, where the critics were invited to appear and then their testimony demolished, point by point.

However, following a meeting with Soviet Foreign Minister Eduard Shevardnadze, Secretary Baker announced that the United States would no longer recognize the UN representative of Cambodia's coalition, which included Sihanouk and the Khmer Rouge. Although China feared the shift would embolden Hun Sen and harden his position, the effect was just the opposite: Vietnam saw the shift in US policy as an opportunity to improve its relations with its former enemy, while China, fearing it would be blamed if the Khmer Rouge walked away from the table and the talks collapsed, told the Khmer Rouge that it had to stay the course and reach a political settlement.

The shift in the constellation of political forces as a result of Baker's announcement broke the final logjam and opened the way to progress in the negotiations. On August 28, 1990, after eight months of talks, the five permanent members of the Security Council agreed to a framework for a comprehensive settlement. Cambodia would be represented in the pre-election period by a Supreme National Council (SNC) comprised of all the major political factions and chaired by Prince Sihanouk. Administrative authority and responsibility to organize free elections would be transferred to a UN Transitional Authority in Cambodia (UNTAC), with its own civilian and military components to supervise, monitor, and verify the ceasefire agreements and to monitor the withdrawal of all foreign forces in the country. Free and fair elections would be held by the United Nations to choose a parliament that would draw up a new constitution and appoint a new government. The protection of human rights in light of "Cambodia's tragic past" would be the basis of the new settlement. Finally, Cambodia would be declared an internationally guaranteed neutral state.

The framework agreement resolved the power-sharing dispute that had dogged negotiations between Cambodia's different factions from the outset. It formally recognized that there could not be a settlement without the participation of all factions and that the Khmer Rouge had to be included to avoid the continuation of the civil war. The next step was to turn to Small Talk to reach a detailed agreement that would incorporate these basic principles and outline the concrete steps for the political process. It took another 14 months to craft a comprehensive settlement plan for Cambodia, finalized on October 23, 1991, in Paris. The Khmer Rouge were marginalized in the ensuing elections and did not return to power, none of the Cambodian factions won a decisive electoral advantage, Vietnam withdrew its troops, and foreign interference in Cambodia's affairs all but ceased. The final outcome of the Paris Accords was generally what the team of great powers had intended, with the United States in both a Driver's and a Conductor's role.

Building a Team of Rivals in North Korea

A second instance of building teams of rivals emerges from the Six-Party Talks on North Korean denuclearization, which took place between 2003 and 2008. Unlike the first example, the problem was not brought to closure, although two important sets of principles were established as a basis for continuing negotiations. Principal players, in addition to the DPRK, the target, were China and the United States, represented by Assistant Secretary of State for Asian Affairs Christopher Hill. The talks are perhaps best summarized by the Chinese expression *qiutong cunyi* ("seeking common ground while preserving differences").

North Korea has been in an erratic state of war with the United States since the Korean armistice of 1953. After a decade of internal reorganization, Pyongyang began a gradually intensifying campaign of violence, conventional and unconventional, ostensibly designed to force the United States into a bilateral peace agreement and to assure DPRK security, two goals that often tripped over each other. In the midst of sporadic confrontations, attempts were made at negotiations as well, primarily multiparty since the Korean War was a UN operation despite the predominant US role. Secretary of State Henry Kissinger called for four-party talks with the United States, China, and North and South Korea in September 1975, dismissed a year later by DPRK. The United States and South Korea revived the proposal two decades later, which held six sessions between December 1997 and August 1998, but ran up against the same North Korean insistence on only bilateral talks. Earlier, through troubled times that included the death of Kim Il-Sung and succession of Kim Jong-Il, sanctions, the threat of war, and a deus ex machina appearance by former President Jimmy Carter, the two parties signed an important set of agreed principles on October 21, 1994. But the agreements broke down, and the arrival of a new administration in Washington in 2001, shocked by the attacks of September 11, brought an end to diplomacy and brought about the dominance of hardliners in US policy. Once again, the conflict teetered on the edge of dangerous confrontation with no resolution in sight and accidental (or even irresponsibly purposeful) escalation in view. Concerned leaders again began to feel "it can't go on like this."

In this situation, the Japanese Prime Minister Junichiro Koizumi suggested a larger circle of talks while visiting Kim Jong-Il in September 2002, supported by phone by Russian President Vladimir Putin. It was China that then picked up the initiative as a Conductor. Following phone calls between President George W. Bush and the outgoing and incoming presidents of China, Jiang Zemin and Hu Jintao, respectively, in early 2003, Chinese officials met with North Korean officials and passed messages between Pyongyang and Washington. As a result, Triple Talks began in Beijing in April in a Chinese effort to keep the standoff on Korean nuclear weapon development from escalating away. When the trilateral talk bogged down, China pressed for a broader group and in August assembled the first round of the Six-Party Talks in Beijing, with the two Koreas, the United States, Russia, and Japan. Worse than the classical troika, the Six were heading in a diversity of directions, often with individual interests only to be divined. However, they were not merely six free-floating parties, but six parties arrayed in two sets of alliances with varying strengths at any one time: China with DPRK, the United States with South Korea and Japan, all playing different roles and all enmeshed in a six-sided box of bilateral and multilateral relations that they sought to keep in balance.

China's aims were broad: peace and stability in northeast Asia, a nuclear-free Korean peninsula, and security for the extant DPRK regime. As a Conductor, it therefore sought damage control, to head off worse possibilities such as DPRK collapse or nuclearization, or war. Beijing also enjoyed hosting the talks, as a boost for its prestige. If there were hawks and doves behind the scenes in Beijing, the cockfight in Washington was out in the open. The camp of Vice President Dick Cheney, Defense Secretary Donald Rumsfeld, and Undersecretaries of State John Bolton and Robert Joseph looked simply to regime change and the collapse of the DPRK; this camp, from the president on down, threw inappropriate verbal rocks of Trash Talk at the process on numerous occasions, giving North Korea the opportunity to utilize Stop Talk tactics and delay proceedings. The opposing camp, led doggedly by National Security Advisor and then Secretary of State Condoleezza Rice and Assistant Secretary Christopher Hill, worked for the complete, verifiable, irreversible dismantlement (CVID) of North Korean nuclear facilities and Pyongyang's integration into the world security system. At the same time, the United States was also concerned about keeping its ties to Japan and South Korea solid. But neither of them facilitated the task. Japan was a Defender, interested principally in the fate of Japanese held in North Korea and rather adamant on that issue. South Korea wavered election by election, but during the period of the Six-Party Talks followed a conciliatory policy toward the North to above all prevent its collapse and to achieve denuclearization. DPRK was the target of the talks, and it continued on the nuclear path throughout the period (and after), continually raising the stakes and making dismantlement more and more difficult. It skillfully played its coercive deficiency, as Thomas Schelling has termed it, convincing the world by its behavior that it just might do the crazy things it threatens.[2] Its strategy seems to have been twofold and reinforcing. On one hand, it pursued a sibylline bargaining tactic to show what would continue to happen if the opponents did not agree, and on the other it pursued a security goal of getting its own nuclear assurance, using the talks to give it time to develop its weapons capability, the latter goal removing any flexibility from the first. North Korea wanted bilateral talks and a peace treaty with the United States, economic assistance, and absolute security. These very divergent goals posed a complex challenge to the Chinese Conductor and the internally beleaguered US Driver to maintain coherence with the other four parties at a meaningful level.

The Six-Party Talks went through five disjointed rounds and produced two statements of principles. The first session in August 2003 included plenary and bilateral meetings; Assistant Secretary James Kelly declared that the United States had no intention of invading the DPRK, but Pyongyang proposed full diplomatic relations before its nuclear facilities would be dismantled. China issued a summary of the parties' consensus on rather broad principles about continuing the talks, but Pyongyang announced its decision to focus its nuclear efforts away from electricity and on to creation of a nuclear deterrent force. The second session in February 2004 was preceded by unusual bilateral pre-talks and proceeded in a more relaxed atmosphere. China continued to pursue consensus, the United States continued to insist on CVID, and DPRK in response attempted to insert a last-minute item that scuttled what was to be the first joint communiqué.

China continued its shuttling efforts for working talks in preparation for the third round that eventually began in June 2004. In a series of Right Talk exercises, the United States agreed to trade the CVID phrase in for "comprehensive dismantlement," and China introduced the principle of "word for word, actions for actions," in part to establish effective reciprocity and in part to limit the effects of Trash Talk so generously practiced by both sides. The United States again held bilateral talks with the DPRK, which renewed its threat to hold nuclear tests; the closing ceremony was then canceled. The talks took a year-long recess, in part to await the results of the US election and in part because of DPRK's "indefinite" suspension of its participation.

The period was filled by vigorous shuttle diplomacy by China, working over the DPRK, developing a closer understanding with South Korea, who then joined in shuttle diplomacy of its own, holding off the US demands for greater pressures. The election over and new officials (Rice and Hill) in place, the United States held a prolonged policy review, adopting an approach of serious bilateral contacts and diplomacy, paced by parallel "defensive measures" or pressures. Beijing and Seoul worked to open a bilateral channel between Hill's office and DPRK at the United Nations in New York to end Trash Talk and return North Korea to the Six-Party Talks. The fourth round, in August 2005, involved thirteen days of intense activity, including bilateral meetings, but produced no breakthrough; the parties agreed on a three- (and more) week break. Renewed talks on September 12 deadlocked over North Korea's right to peaceful nuclear energy, which the US distrusted; chief Chinese negotiator Wu Dawei exerted enormous energy through four drafts to avoid the inconclusiveness of the previous rounds and finally arrive at a joint Statement of Principles on September 19, after twenty days of fourth-round talks, five drafts, and a take-it-or-leave-it offer to the United States. North Korea would drop its nuclear weapons program (US demand); it had the right to a peaceful nuclear energy program (China, Russia, South Korea, DPRK demand); and the external parties would later discuss the provision of Light Water Reactors (LWR) to North Korea (DPRK demand), but only after verifiable denuclearization (US demand posted after the statement was announced); the United States had no intention to attack North Korea (DPRK demand); DPRK would move to normalize bilateral relations with the United States and Japan, and the parties would negotiate a permanent peace regime for the peninsula. The trick was in the timing in the "word" and "actions" exchange; the next day, DPRK declared that it would not dismantle until the LWR was received, and the agreement staggered.

The parties scrambled for bargaining chips, which the United States found in sanctions against North Korean money laundering activities and North Korea found in a consequent refusal to attend more Six-Party Talks. The first session of the fifth round in November 2005 lasted only a few days in the face of the North Korean boycott. On October 9, 2006, North Korea conducted its first nuclear test (which it said "does not contradict the September 19 joint statement" under which it committed itself to dismantle nuclear weapons and abandon the existing nuclear program. "On the contrary, it constitutes a positive measure for its implementation."). Instead, the United States shifted focus of the five powers to the United Nations where UN Security Council Resolution 1718 invoking Chapter VII passed unanimously. The United States picked its Driver role in strength, and Rice traveled to the powers' capitals to rally support for a two-handed policy. Hill suggested bilateral talks and indicated a willingness to resolve the money-laundering issue separately from the Six-Party Talks. Thus, again after a year's intermission, the fifth session of the talks was held in mid-December 2006 for another brief meeting. The next month Hill and his North Korean counterparts met again, in Berlin, to pursue an agreement on "words for words" and "actions for actions," as in Washington many of the hardliners—Rumsfeld, Bolton, Joseph—left the administration, finally leaving Rice and Hill freer to pursue team-making among the six rivals. The third phase then opened on February 8, 2007, and after four days of Small Talk arrived at the details of an action plan for implementing the Joint Statement of September 2005. The North Korean nuclear facilities at Yongbyon would be shut down in sixty days while the other parties would supply heavy fuel oil for emergency energy. Then DPRK would declare and dismantle all nuclear programs, US-DPRK relations would be normalized, and North Korea would be removed from the US list of states supporting terrorism; money-laundering sanctions would also be lifted. Gradually these engagements were accomplished. More details were added in the sixth round in late July and early October 2007 with an agreement on Second Phase Actions for the Implementation of the Joint Statement. Work on implementation, imperfect and sporadic, continued; Hill was last in Pyongyang pursuing the details of the agreement on October 2008, just before the US elections. In response, the DPRK tested a long-range missile in April and set off a nuclear test in May, to mark the new administration's offer of renewed engagement. Over a year later after Hill's last visit, his successor, Stephen Bosworth, was back to press for a return to the Talks. Herding the team of rivals to a series of agreements and their implementation required great skill and tenacity from the Chinese and also persistence and dedication from the US diplomatic team as it struggled loose from hawk attacks at home.

Building Teams of Rivals at Other Times

These examples are not rare. Negotiation as bilateral problem solving or as high politics between cohesive power blocs does indeed occur, but negotiating to pull together a team of diverse, competing, if not opposing, parties into an agreement that serves them all satisfactorily, if not equally, is a common challenge for Team Talk and its associated ways of talking. Other cases of rival Team Talk bear analysis; two stand out. One was the effort of coercive diplomacy to devise a status for Laos that met the interests of the invading communists—Russia, China, North Vietnam, and their local allies, the Pathet Lao—and also those of the West—the United States and France and their local allies, the Royal Lao government—in 1960–61. The salient solution was a neutralized Laos, on which the positions converged; in reality, the outcome was a divided Laos on which positions separated, with the communists keeping the mountainous north with its supply trails for the Viet Minh and the Royal government keeping the fertile south that blocked communist access to Thailand.

An older case of Team Talk was the 1830–33 London Conference to decide the status of Belgium, which had just proclaimed its independence. It was a Franco-British coalition of rivals that imposed recognition on the London Conference in January 1831. The initiative and formal motion was introduced by Lord Palmerston and seconded by Prince Talleyrand on December 18, 1830. But the conditions and details were not spelled out until the next year, and then not accepted by the king of the Netherlands and his supporters until after a seven-year standoff. The conference failed because of the obduracy of the kings of Holland and Belgium (its breakaway province) and the failure of the Concert of Europe, composed of Britain, Russia, Prussia, Austria, and France, to coordinate their positions into an effective mediation team of rivals.

The world is now (and will be for a while) facing another significant challenge to team-building of rivals, in Southwest Asia, the land of the nineteenth-century Great Game between Russia and Britain. Whatever happens inside Afghanistan, it will not be stable without a "Great Jirga," a meeting of the surrounding and distant powers to forge an agreement to consecrate the internal settlement and establish their own relations with it. The diversity and even incompatibility of interests surpasses anything that was earlier present in Cambodia, Korea, Laos, or Belgium.

After its 2001 invasion of Afghanistan to drive out al-Qaeda and its friendly host, the Taliban, the United States and other NATO countries spent three years cleaning out the country, but without any effective follow-through. A new state was created at the Loya Jirga held in Bonn under the mediating leadership of Lakhdar Brahimi. The new government was dominated by the Northern Alliance of non-Pashtun warlords, leaving the south governed rather than governing. President Hamid Karzai, a minor Pashtun figure, was twice elected more or less fraudulently. By the end of the decade, the Taliban had returned in the Pashtun south and toward the turn of the decade had begun to make inroads into the north. The base of the Taliban was located in Quetta in northwest Pakistan where the Haqqani family held sway, and al-Qaeda in Afghanistan felt comfortable there, too. President Barack Obama's surge of an additional 30,000 US troops made inroads into the Taliban area, without a decisive outcome—despite some dramatic change of military leadership—by the end of 2010. Some in the administration, notably Vice President Joseph Biden, talked of a retreat to the cities, leaving the countryside to the Taliban, without addressing questions such as supply logistics, intercity connections, and economic viability. Negotiations between whoever among the Taliban would negotiate and the government were undertaken in 2010 with US support. But the effort was inconclusive, tentative, and more of a search for a security blanket and impunity for Karzai in the event of Taliban takeover than a real search for a national unity government.

By the end of the decade the fortunes of both sides—the Taliban and the International Security Assistance Force (ISAF) with the Karzai government somewhere in the middle—remained uncertain, as did the mechanics of convening a "Great Jirga" involving principal neighbors—Pakistan, Iran, Tajikistan, Uzbekistan, China, and India (close and involved enough to be considered a neighbor)—plus Russia and the United States. Pakistan's interest has been to obtain a friendly and even dominated government in Afghanistan, both to contain its own Pashtun question and to keep out India; it is not on friendly terms with the Karzai government. India's interest has been the reverse, to eliminate Pakistan's influence, principally by cooperating with the Northern Alliance. Iran's interest has lain less in the form of government than in the elimination of US-NATO presence, although it has never had a close relationship with the Sunni al-Qaeda; it has developed a strong link within the Karzai government. China's interest has been in the prevention of a militant religious movement in control in Afghanistan because of the danger of religious movements in its western provinces, but also in avoiding Indian dominance in the area. Tajikistan's and Uzbekistan's interests favored the Tajik and Uzbek elements in the Northern Alliance. The United States has had an interest above all in destroying al-Qaeda but also in securing the withdrawal of its troops (possibly mutually exclusive goals); democracy lay somewhere in its ideological vision but stability was more important, if undefined.

In this situation, where concerned parties seemed bent on obtaining a favorable outcome that other concerned parties seemed bent on preventing or undermining—everyone was someone else's spoiler—and every bilateral relation between interested parties was soured by the conflict, the feeling rose that "it can't go on like this." This conclusion was reflected internally in the tentative and inconclusive negotiations between the Taliban and Karzai's government; externally, it was producing discussions of the need for the formation of a team of rivals to bring stability (if not democracy) to the region. The United Nations was the most prominently mentioned candidate for the Conductor's role, as in the case of the Bonn Jirga. What lessons can experience bring to the prospects of a Great Jirga over Afghanistan or any other attempt to building a team of rivals?

Team Talk Lessons

The first lesson is that a broad range of concerned neighbors and other interested parties should be invited to the negotiation table and made part of the negotiating "team," because there are more than two parties to the conflict. Even civil wars tend to have many parties and many outside sponsors who have special relationships with the warring parties and a vested interest in keeping the conflict going. Even if they cannot win, continuing the conflict is for them better than losing. It is also relatively easy for spoilers, from the Khmer Rouge to the Kim government to al-Qaeda, to acquire tangible resources and external sources of political support. Today's wars have a tendency to continue, to sputter on, or to recur rather than lead to lopsided victories because local factions have external allies who have a vested interest in seeing the conflict continue. These conflicts do not get better, easier, clearer, or more amenable to ultimate resolution with the passage of time. In fact, they get more deeply impacted by mounting layers of local, regional, and international issues and rivalries. In the process they become more and more susceptible to an accidental or deliberate precipitant of escalation that requires an appropriate response and so can rapidly bring about an extremely volatile stage of conflict far wider than the immediate parties.

The second lesson is the need to break the bonds between those factions who are fighting on the ground and their external sponsors. Umbilical cords that feed a conflict can be eventually cut if neighbors who are considered to be part of the problem are brought into the negotiating process and are engaged in finding a solution, as the Cambodian case all too well demonstrates. China and Thailand's bonds with the Khmer Rouge were weakened by making them members of the pact that was committed to a political resolution of the conflict in Cambodia, and Vietnam was weaned from Russia by Russia's own involvement in the P5-led negotiation process. China's ties with North Korea were strained, even if not always broken, by its larger need to act as Conductor of the Six-Party Talks. President John F. Kennedy's proposal of a neutralized Laos split the solidarity of the communist supporters of the Pathet Lao. England's support for the Netherlands was loosened by a chance to meet France in recognition of Belgian independence. The challenge is daunting in Afghanistan, where the Pashtun Taliban have a cross-border "state" of their own, even stronger than the ethnic ties on the northern border.

The third lesson, which follows from the first, is that these conflicts have to be worked on at different levels—the local, the regional, and the global—through negotiating teams that are not necessarily comprised of likeminded, ideological soul mates but are "teams of rivals" who develop mutual respect and a common understanding that they share wider strategic interests and goals that go beyond the conflict in question. Building such a team depends on reaching beyond current positions into wider and longer interests of the parties faced with a costly situation. In the case of Cambodia, Solomon forged an "entente of sorts" as he called it between the region's long-standing strategic rivals—China, Russia, and Vietnam—that was focused on disengaging from military commitments that were becoming very costly in financial and reputational terms. The diplomatic and institutional framework for managing this partnership was the United Nations and the P5, which spearheaded negotiations when they became deadlocked between the different local Cambodian factions. In Northeast Asia, North Korean actions confronted the UN P5 with situations calling for sanctions that DPRK saw as a "declaration of war" and threatened a "sea of fire" in return. Concerned neighbors near and far reached for a concert of powers that China, the convener, and the United States, despite the Trash Talk back home, worked to keep involved. In the case of Laos, the institution was already available in the International Commission for Supervision and Control (ICC), which the United States worked to revive. In Afghanistan, as in Cambodia, the UN P5 provides at least the venue and at least the beginning of the team.

A fourth lesson is that the potential members of a team have to be shaken loose from their rigid positions in order for the team to form. Often this involves a key party's change of position, other times it requires a new or newly revived idea. Solomon adroitly used American diplomacy and carefully timed announcements that were delivered for maximum impact through his boss, James Baker, to shift US support from one group to another during these negotiations. While China was busy holding the meeting of the Six Parties together, the United States on a number of occasions offered a package incorporating other positions compatible with its own, just as—it must be admitted—North Korea on occasion came forth with its unchanged priorities rearranged into a new package. The US "tacit ultimatum" for a ceasefire in Laos would free it from the need to intervene militarily, its previously declared threat position. Britain's shift to recognition of Belgium before the negotiation skills of Talleyrand broke the European deadlock. These interventions were intended to keep the parties off balance and force them out of their entrenched negotiating positions so as to move the process forward.

The fifth important lesson is that team building is about leadership not just on the international front but also on the domestic. There are two sides to this observation: the link between domestic settlement and external team building in the conflict area, and the link between diplomatic talk efforts and domestic support from the team builder. The first concerns the need to provide or accompany the local parties in the conflict with a settlement of their own; the external team cannot simply lock the locals into a hermetic tank and let them fight it out, for they will inevitably break out and break up the fragile entente of the team of rivals. Internal peace making may be imposed, it may be the natural consequence of cutting loose external ties (lesson one), or it may be the result of internal fatigue and stalemate. But it needs to accompany the external entente.

Within the team builder, leadership is not just about taking the helm during rough seas but also about being prepared to take one's licks domestically as one builds political support for new initiatives. Solomon and his congressional critics, Rice and Hill and their opponents within the executive, Kennedy and his opposition in upcoming elections, Palmerston and his anti-French parliamentary opposition created a situation that made life tenuous and perilous for the external team builder. The lesson that practitioners repeatedly emphasize is that the diplomatic mandate must be clear and the administration support solid, but politics often makes this a counsel of perfection.

A sixth lesson is that patching together rivals involves making tough trade-offs. It is negotiation par excellence, giving something to get something. The dramatic moves of the third lesson often involved giving in on a significant point in order to buy the agreement of the parties to make the team, and in any case the final outcome brought parties off their initial positions. To do this, team makers looked beyond positions to seek out compatibilities among rivals' interests. In Cambodia, the United States traded off its support for the incumbent coalition against support for an open electoral competition. In Korea, the United States traded support for a peaceful nuclear program against its demand for CVID (and threw in a softening of name for the demand in addition). In Laos, the United States gave up a call for Pathet Lao and Viet Cong withdrawal for an agreement on neutralization. In Belgium, Palmerston gave up support for the Netherlands in exchange for Belgian assumption of much of the Dutch debt. There are plenty of potential trade-offs in Afghanistan, all of them at some price and none of them adopted as yet by the parties.

Seventh, team-making efforts must overcome the problem, defining cooperation and successful outcomes in terms of the lowest common denominator. Substantive weakness is often the easiest way to gain procedural coherence: It is easier to get rivals to agree on little or nothing than on something meaningful. China faced this problem, particularly in the first three rounds of the Six-Party Talks as it sought a joint communiqué and only could come up with a pretty anodyne chairman's summary. Even a more meaningful agreement needs to have a Small Talk follow-up that nails down the details of implementation, as done in the

Cambodian process, as undone on occasion in the Six-Party Talks, and as delayed for seven years in the Belgian case.

Finally, team building among rivals demands that they play different and complementary roles while relinquishing those that are not complementary. Conducting and Driving are the strategies that best fit team formation. They depend on a leader who agglomerates parties into procedural and then substantive agreement. While pursuing its own interests, each party is brought to play its own score in the right way to bring a harmonious result. The team builder could be a Driver with its own interest-related agenda but willing to cut its corners in order to get a generally satisfactory agreement: Solomon and Baker in Cambodia, Kennedy in Laos, Talleyrand in Belgium, even Rice and Hill in Korea. States more often choose a Driver's over a Conductor's strategy, for many reasons: Usually no state is powerful enough to be hegemonic, interests are usually defensive and partial rather than global, and driving allows parties to pull back to make the tradeoffs necessary to team building. In this situation, the procedural Conductor is actually welcome, since it allows parties to pursue their interests more effectively, facilitating agreement. Yet if none of the parties can play the Conductor, an impartial, procedurally oriented, external agency such as the United Nations—either a Special Representative of the Secretary-General (SRSG) or the collective Security Council—has the role cut out for it.

CHAPTER 10
TALKING WITH FRIENDS AND ALLIES

> It is a constant truth that allies are kept only with care, with attention, and with reciprocal advantages.... One must inspire confidence to obtain true and useful allies.
>
> —Charles-Maurice de Talleyrand-Périgord, 1798

At her Senate confirmation hearings, US Secretary of State nominee Hillary Clinton signaled that the Obama administration would chart a bold new course in US foreign policy. It would be driven by the use of "smart power" she said. Smart Power is based on the notion that military power is not sufficient to address the world's most pressing global threats such as terrorism, the spread of weapons of mass destruction, climate change, the current financial and economic crisis, or global poverty. It deploys the full range of diplomatic, economic, cultural, political, and intelligence assets in the foreign policy toolbox.[1] It is also premised, as Clinton stressed, on the notion that "America cannot solve the world's most pressing problems on [its] own."[2] It needs the help of its friends and allies.

America clearly needs its friends. But the use of Smart Power should not be equated with the promise of being nice or the proposition that America's friends or allies will necessarily behave differently from adversaries in a bargaining or crisis situation. One would like to think that a cooperative relationship is one that is based on trust, reciprocity, and feelings of mutual respect such that when a dispute arises parties will sit down at the negotiating table to settle their differences amicably and peacefully. Alas, there is too much evidence of a historical, circumstantial, and even biblical nature, which suggests that friends, allies, or even family members will not always do so and that a conflict between friends can escalate out of control. The Bible, for example, is filled with accounts of close relationships that turned sour as a result of a breakdown in interpersonal trust (Judas Iscariot's betrayal of Christ), and where close family members failed the test of loyalty and friendship in a crisis (Jacob and Esau, Job and his three sons, Joseph and his brothers, Cain versus Abel). The history of international relations likewise is filled with stories of similar kinds of conflicts (though usually not with such high moral drama), including those involving betrayal between allies or close friends. In some instances these conflicts have escalated and led to a major disruption in relations; in others disputes have been handled more or less successfully by talking it out.

This chapter examines the role of Talk Power tools in dealing with those disputes that can arise between the United States and its key allies and trading partners. A cooperative dispute is a dispute that occurs in a peacetime relationship. Such relations are marked neither by indifference nor by enmity but by what the late Richard Neustadt called "variegated" and "tight" ties between governments as well as a network of relations at the nongovernmental level between polities.[3] The mere existence of a cooperative relationship does not mean that conflicts will not arise. But when there is conflict, the parties can talk out their differences and coordinate their behavior and interests so that the relationship is preserved, even as they test the institutional foundations and personal ties that go to its very heart.

This chapter addresses the following questions: First, what are the roots or origins of these kinds of cooperative disputes? Second, what kinds of bargaining and negotiating strategies and/or tactics are available to manage such disputes? Third, when is it desirable to enter into formal negotiations to manage such disputes and when is it not?

Origins of "Cooperative Disputes"

There are many potential sources of friction that can arise between countries in situations of complex interdependence where a basis for cooperation already exists because the parties are already involved in some form of joint decision-making. These frictions, in turn, may put a strain on existing mechanisms and trigger demands to negotiate new institutional arrangements and develop new ways of managing relations and coordinating expectations, but they may also generate conflict in the process of trying to do so. A number of different kinds of disputes can arise between the United States and its key friends and allies, and such disputes are likely to grow as US power and influence are challenged by the rise of other centers of economic and military power and influence in Asia and elsewhere.

Thomas Friedman opined in the *New York Times* that "during most of the post–World War II era, being a leader meant, on balance, giving things away to people. Today, and for the next decade at least, being a leader in America will mean, on balance, taking things away from people."[4] This is somewhat of an exaggeration. The United States is still a $14 trillion economy and a nuclear superpower that poses formidable conventional military assets. Its closest rival, China, has an economy that is still less than half the US GDP. Large sectors of the Chinese population live in abject rural poverty. It is, however, closer to the truth to say that the terms on which the United States has traditionally provided various global public goods to the world will be renegotiated in the years to come as the United States faces mounting internal economic challenges. Moreover, the forces of globalization as discussed below are transforming US relations with its economic trading partners so as to create new pressures on US diplomacy and the way the United States has traditionally talked to its friends and trading partners.

Conflict over the Provision of Public Goods

The provision, distribution, and consumption of global public goods can generate a number of different kinds of disputes in a cooperative situation. Public goods are defined by economists as goods (1) that can be consumed by all or from which no one can be denied (i.e., they are nonexcludable), and (2) whose cost is not increased by the addition of more consumers (i.e., they are nonrival or possess jointness of supply). Another characteristic that is implicit in the first two is that everyone benefits from such goods (i.e., they are universal). The benefits of "pure public goods" (goods with all three characteristics) are consumed by all members of a community almost as soon as they are produced for, or by, any one member. Public goods are often equated with particular values prized by humans—e.g., life, physical safety, economic well-being, health, and freedom of expression. Central to this understanding of such "end goods" is that everyone gains from other people's enjoyment of these valued conditions.

Such goods have the potential to generate conflicts between their producer and their consumers, who have different interests beyond the enjoyment of the goods. "Free riders" consume the public good without making any contribution to its production. In international security relations, for example, the provision of security (a public good) by the key leader in an alliance, such as the United States, can lead to friction if that country's smaller allies are seen as taking a free ride and not living up to their alliance responsibilities by contributing their fair share to a collective security undertaking, as in the NATO mission in Afghanistan. The classic free rider problem may, in fact, take a somewhat different turn in the second decade of the twenty-first century as the United States increasingly finds itself cash strapped as a result of its mounting fiscal and debt crisis and is less able to assume the lion's share of responsibility for maintaining global peace and security with its military—i.e., Gun Power—assets. This problem may become especially acute as US allies facing similar fiscal pressures cut their own defense spending. As a troubled US Defense Secretary Robert Gates observed just prior to a meeting of NATO leaders in November 2010, "My worry is that the more our allies cut their capabilities, the more people will look to the United States to cover whatever gaps are created."[5]

The United States will have to work more closely with its friends and allies to secure their assistance in the provision of these (and other) global public goods while also looking to new ways to consolidate defense expenditures and eliminate major duplications of effort not just on both sides of the Atlantic but also within Europe. The United States will have to resort to a different kind of diplomacy (as discussed in greater detail in the next chapter) that places a higher premium on Team Talk, coordination, and the formation of new kinds partnerships that will allow NATO's European members to "punch above their weight" in the maintenance of global peace and security.[6]

In an increasingly economically competitive world where knowledge and innovation are the drivers of the global economy, the United States also finds itself in disputes with its economic partners because modern communications and information systems have made it relatively easy for companies abroad to take technological innovations developed elsewhere and incorporate them into their own product lines. In the absence of patents or licensing laws, companies making use of these innovations have acted as free riders because they have been able to make use of those innovations at no extra cost to themselves and without having to compensate the original knowledge producers.

The intellectual piracy "free rider" problem is a major (and growing) irritant in relations between the United States and its key trading partners (e.g., Canada–United States; United States–Japan; United States–China) in a wide range of areas such as cultural properties (movies), computer software, telecommunications, etc. Ongoing negotiations to address this problem have been directed at developing an international property rights regime based on the extension of domestic patent legislation to cover foreign firms, bilateral treaties, and also strengthening the World International Patent Organization (WIPO), set up to register patents and copyrights internationally. But the international regime is still weak and the

United States has had to resort to Tough Talk and other measures to deal with this problem, most notably in its relations with China, which continues to be the world's greatest infringer of intellectual copyright.

In the case of international joint goods characterized by jointness but excludable, disputes can arise between members over club membership and size (i.e., who should be in the club and who should be excluded). The GATT/WTO system (General Agreement on Tariffs and Trade/World Trade Organization), for example, has extended trade liberalization, but its rules apply only to members. Those who are not members are denied key benefits such as most-favored-nation trading status. The question of expanding current club membership to other countries like China (which has now become a member) and Russia (which still has not) has been a matter of active discussion among WTO members and been an issue marked by strong differences of opinion between the United States and other GATT/WTO members.

Adding members may have other consequences, too, which may be deemed undesirable by current members, such as inducing changes in distributional and allocative relations. Some of these tensions are evident in current concerns about the implications of adding new members, like Turkey, to the European Union (EU) or helping the EU's most indebted members deal with their growing levels of public debt and ongoing financial difficulties as in the case of Greece, Ireland, Spain, and Portugal. This issue is also playing out in new global economic forums, like the G20, where the United States and other G8 members are coming under increasing pressure to abandon the smaller G8 club in favor of the larger and more representative grouping. And there are other countries like Norway and Chile who are unhappy that they are marginalized and excluded from the larger G20 grouping.

Serious disputes may also arise over the terms on which the public good is provided, particularly when a key supplier like the United States decides to unilaterally change the terms of the bargain or to withdraw the good being offered. For example, one of the most serious disputes in international monetary relations occurred in the early 1970s when the United States decided unilaterally to take the United States off the gold standard and to suspend convertibility of the dollar. In this case, the United States as the world's most powerful economy suspended the provision of a public good in order to establish a new international monetary order. There may be a dangerous precedent here as we look to the future of global security and the difficulties the United States may experience playing its global military superpower role in the future. It is the United States that will be facing Tough Talk from its friends and allies and must find ways of effectively talking back.

Externality Disputes

"International externalities" or unwanted side effects may also be a source of conflict between countries since they are by definition unintended and uncompensated byproducts of the transactions among public or private agents. If actions create nonexcludable and uncompensated costs for third parties, we have a negative externality or an external diseconomy. Most international environmental pollution problems are negative, aggregate externalities, or what might be termed "collective social bads." Problems like acid rain resulting from industrial emissions carried across interstate borders, pollution or depletion of shared water resources among neighboring riparian states, etc., are all manifestations of this kind of problem.

So, too, is the problem of climate change, which is both an externality problem in the classic sense because greenhouse gas emissions from any one country affect everyone, but also an equity issue or distributional conflict. At the December 2009 climate change Conference of Parties in Copenhagen, key developing countries, led by China, India, and Brazil, said they would cut their own carbon emissions, if rich developed nations, especially the United States, cut their own emissions and also provide major funding for technology transfer and adaptation to developing countries. Since negotiation is giving something to get something, much more talk is necessary.

Coordination Disputes

Coordination disputes involve situations where the parties have divergent or conflicting interests and there is no obvious single preferred outcome between a "go-it-alone" approach to dealing with a problem and a range of joint, cooperative solutions. In these kinds of situations, there are usually strong incentives to "beggar thy neighbor" as each country pursues its own national interests.

The problem is illustrated in the difficulties the world's industrialized countries have experienced coordinating their macroeconomic policies in the aftermath of the financial crisis of 2007–09. One of the key features of a globalized, economically interdependent world is that domestic macroeconomic policies neither fully insulate economies from external shocks, nor protect neighboring countries from financial disruptions and macroeconomic spillovers. This is not a new phenomenon. For example, the fully autonomous policies practiced in the 1930s by the world's major economies, including competitive devaluations, bank panics, and insufficient money creation were a prime cause of the Great Depression.

Starting in 2007, the collapse of the housing market in the United States and the ensuing financial crisis had contagion effects that quickly spread to other countries and jurisdictions. The crisis shook the global economy to its very foundations and we are still living with its aftershocks. To address the initial crisis, the American president at the time, George W. Bush, convened a meeting of the leaders of the world's most powerful economies in Washington, D.C., in November 2008. This was followed by further summits in London (April 2009), Pittsburgh (September 2009), Toronto (June 2010), and Seoul (November 2010).

The resulting G20, which began as a club of financial ministers, has evolved into an important forum for world leaders to meet, address, and talk over a wide range of pressing new economic challenges. These include promoting economic recovery and growth at a time when there are serious current account imbalances between surplus and deficit countries and budgetary deficits in many countries are growing worse, compounded by political instability and uncertainty; banking and other financial regulatory reforms with a focus on enhancing stability and preventing future destabilizing "excesses"; and restoring confidence in the international trade regime by recharging "standstill agreements" to avoid further protectionism and spurring the completion of the stalled Doha Round on trade. Securing international cooperation through Team Talk to deal with these issues is not easy, as countries struggle with the continuing political and economic fallout of a global financial and economic crisis that refuses to go away. And as the United States and other countries face their own international domestic pressures to take independent measures to promote economic and financial recovery, the incentives to defect from cooperative solutions may grow absent coordinated actions that boost recovery and yield positive benefits to all. As seen in other challenges of Talk Power, talk has to mesh with up-down, domestic back-and-forth talk among friendly nations.

Summits are a key forum and venue for the application of Straight Talk—a place to have sober and honest discussions among world leaders about the world's economic future and to discuss what must be done to rectify continuing economic and financial problems. One of the myths about summits whether they are of the G8 or G20 variety is that these are gatherings where world leaders make new rules. This myth has been perpetuated by many critics of globalization who see something akin to a global conspiracy when leaders get together. In reality, summits are largely talkfests or forums for the exchange of views and information between world leaders. But when properly organized they can accomplish a lot more. Through discussion and personal interaction leaders can develop the bases for mutual understanding and strengthen the incentives for cooperation. Summits also provide a critical opportunity for leaders to use their political position and influence to break deadlocks and logjams at the bureaucratic and international institutional levels. The purpose of summits, in the words of the distinguished British diplomat, Nicholas Bayne, is to "concentrate the mind," "resolve differences," and have a "catalytic effect" on international cooperation.[7]

Distributional Conflicts

Distributional conflicts are conflicts over equity, income, and even property rights. In these kinds of situations, before they can negotiate countries have to agree on the formula or rules of justice to be used for allotting fair shares of a given good: Do you allocate according to the basis of simple equality, social equity, population size, basic needs, degree of development, future generations, or some other formula or criterion? Although this problem is less serious in a domestic setting because most societies have rules for settling certain kinds of disputes that are enshrined in law (e.g., disputes about property and inheritance), in the international setting, such rules are less well developed, despite a large and developing body of international case law. One only has to look at some of the difficulties negotiators have experienced in dealing with the income distribution aspects of a problem like global warming to see that there is precious little consensus in the international community about the principles that should be used to assign responsibility and share costs for adaptive or preventive response strategies to address this problem.

To complicate things further in the cross-cultural context of international negotiation, cultural, religious, and even historical factors often inform the notion of justice and the underlying principles behind allotment and allocation. Within the state, there is a rough domestic consensus on cultural values such as notions of justice, but internationally no such cultural consensus exists. In the absence of shared standards or norms about fairness and justice—and some degree of accommodation when those values clash—there is no agreed way to negotiate to divide the pie and talks get stuck on the basic principles before any discussion of actual distribution can begin.

Distributional disputes lie at the heart of many interstate conflicts and frequently arise between close trading partners or countries whose relations are marked by close dependence. Distributional disputes between the global North and South have been at the heart of virtually every major international negotiation since the early 1970s, particularly in UN forums like the UN Conference on Trade and Development (UNCTAD) and the WTO. In spite of the high levels of rhetoric in the North-South debate, in particular, these conflicts have not demonstrated any great propensity to escalate because of deep asymmetries in economic power between the world's most powerful economies, including

China and India, and the poorer countries of the South with their ineffective use of linkage and other bargaining tactics and strategies. International income redistribution continues to be of deep concern, especially when it comes to addressing problems like trade, energy, climate change, and global warming, and the United States and its European partners are coming under growing pressure to negotiate new international arrangements that provide economic and financial support to developing countries. The lessons from Teams of Rivals can apply to such problems, and not just military-political conflicts.

The deliberate framing of a conflict in distributional terms may also make it more difficult to reduce tensions in a conflict even when close allies are involved and the basic issue itself is not distributional. Consider, for example, the Helms-Burton legislation in the United States, which has turned a foreign policy difference between the United States and its Canadian and European allies over how they should deal with Cuba into a major dispute over property rights. The extraterritorial application of US law and the imposition of tough penalties on foreign investors who do business in Cuba are based on the premise that these business transactions are illegal because they make use of expropriated assets and properties of exiled Cuban Americans. What was hitherto a rather general disagreement between allies about whether to engage Cuba or isolate it has been turned into a zero-sum dispute, not about property rights and restitution for Cuban Americans dispossessed when Fidel Castro seized power, but about economic relations between allies.

Finding the Right Tools to Negotiate with Friends and Allies

A key dilemma for the United States when dealing with allies and economic partners is to choose the right negotiating tools. When is it appropriate to use Tough Talk to deal with a recalcitrant ally? When should the United States use Straight Talk, Small Talk, or some other bargaining tool to secure cooperation? As we argue here, context matters a lot in selecting the right set of negotiating tools and US negotiators need to pay close attention to the situation they are dealing with in developing an effective negotiating strategy.

Disputes about the provision of public goods and externalities, for example, are more likely to invite Tough Talk rather than Sweet Talk, particularly because the United States, as the dominant partner, has a habit of talking tough. Ingrained attitudes and habits of hegemony die hard. The problem is sharpened when it is one of getting other countries to internalize costs and accept a greater (or fair) share of the burden—e.g., the problem of burden-sharing in an alliance or tackling cross-border pollution. In these instances, there are powerful incentives for the United States to use threats, sanctions, and other Tough Talk tactics in order to wrest concessions from its negotiating partners. The ultimate threat is Stop Talk—to withdraw the public good in question or unilaterally change the terms on which it is offered, cutting off one's flows to spite one's friends, a clear case of a coordination problem. For example, during the Cold War the United States on a number of occasions threatened to reduce its troop commitments unless the Europeans carried more of the defense burden. Such was the case when Senator Sam Nunn introduced an amendment in the US Senate in 1984 that called for a phased reduction of American troops in Europe unless Western European members of the Alliance assumed a greater share of the costs of collective defense. But these threats were not entirely credible because US allies knew that the United States would not withdraw its troops from Europe if doing so would leave the door open to a Warsaw Pact invasion at a time of mounting tensions and buildup of communist forces.

Tough Talk between the United States and its allies works only if both sides know their limits and understand each other's bargaining capabilities and interests. Where such information is lacking, Tough Talk may be more difficult to sustain as a bargaining tool because there is a risk that the conflict will escalate and the other side will simply walk away from the negotiating table or hold out perhaps indefinitely for a better deal. To continue with the above example, even in a close alliance like NATO, cooperation among the allies should not be taken for granted, especially in a post–Cold War world where there are widely divergent perceptions of security threats. This calls for judicious consultation and consensus building, especially when the parties are dealing with a troubling security situation like the one in Afghanistan where many of the United States' allies increasingly feel that NATO is powerless to rid Afghanistan of the Taliban and deal effectively with the mounting cross-border Pashtun-led insurgency from Pakistan. In such a situation, it is Straight Talk that is necessary to coordinate information, evaluate alternatives, and develop consensus before responsive measures can be agreed upon.

Large recurrent doses of Straight Talk are also needed in US relations with its key Asian allies like Japan. As the Pacific Forum of the Washington-based Center for Strategic and International Studies notes,

> The U.S. financial system has been harder hit by the crisis than has Japan, but the real economy in both countries is hurting. The crisis has done particular damage to the U.S. It accentuated and accelerated the decline of the United States in the regional balance of power, decreased U.S. assets while increasing its debt, shaken the foundation of its banking system, damaged the capitalist and regulatory model the U.S. had backed, and forced the U.S. to refocus on domestic issues. While

the crisis offers opportunities for U.S.-Japan cooperation, they have not been exploited.[8]

The Japanese are also concerned that closer relations between the United States and China will come at their expense. They worry about the long-term credibility of the US deterrent in their region. Straight Talk with nervous regional allies like Japan and South Korea must also be accompanied with generous doses of Sweet Talk to provide reassurance and demonstrate the US commitment to maintaining its long-standing partnerships.

The timing of toughness among friends is also a consideration. It is inadvisable to start tough in the early stages of negotiation in such coordination and distributional disputes. The threat, for example, to undertake beggar-thy-neighbor policies (e.g., "Buy American") will not bring others to the bargaining table if they consider their best option is simply to reciprocate and do the same. Coordination disputes are characterized by the existence of many possible solutions or outcomes, not just one. If parties have serious disagreements about which outcome is preferred, Tough Talk, with its use of threats and sanctions to raise one's security point in the negotiation, will likely not only prove ineffective, but also escalate the dispute.

The failure of negotiations in the early 1990s within the Organization for Economic Cooperation and Development (OECD) to reach a Multilateral Agreement on Investment (MAI) that would enhance the mobility of capital can be understood, in part, as a coordination dispute characterized by serious differences among the parties. Issues included the scope and applicability of the agreement (e.g., whether and how to include "cultural" industries), the chief mechanisms appropriate for liberalization, and even the appropriate negotiating forum (the United States preferred to adopt standards within the OECD, whereas Canada and the EU preferred to negotiate binding rules within the WTO). Talks collapsed when it became apparent that Tough Talk by the United States and some of its European negotiating partners could not secure a deal because both sides had other alternatives, including sticking with the status quo.

Similarly, in a distributional dispute, in the absence of agreement on how the pie is to be divided, as well as agreement on general principles and the conception of justice upon which distribution will be decided, a Tough Talk approach to bargaining is likely to be ineffectual at best and counterproductive at worst. The use of threats and bullying tactics in order to force the issue or get one's way will only escalate the dispute or encourage the other side to walk away from the table in exasperation. This problem is all too evident in the dispute between Canada and the United States over Pacific salmon in the 1990s. Although elements of the dispute lie in their 1985 Pacific Salmon Treaty, which was badly drafted and had a weak mechanism for allocation setting, it also lies in the concept of equitable sharing, which has never been properly established or agreed upon. As salmon stocks declined in the late 1990s, the dispute intensified with Canada's claim that US fishers were catching more salmon than Canadians in both Alaska and Canada, and then upping their catch when the talks broke down. The British Columbian government added oil to the fire by announcing that it would cancel a US lease of a weapons testing ground and British Columbian fishers took matters into their own hands by blockading a US ferry in Prince Rupert Harbor.

Standards of fairness and justice cannot be imposed or simply mandated by fiat via Tough Talk and the use of threats or sanctions. Rather, they have to be created through a search process of mutual accommodation and consensus, i.e., the artful use of Straight Talk—a sober assessment of the problem in order to arrive at a new negotiating formula that reconciles the competing visions of the parties about a "just" future—followed by Small Talk focused on the application of the formula to the details. Even so, these negotiating tools are unlikely to work if parties are wedded to fundamentally different views about the basis of equity and the terms of reference about what constitutes a "fair" solution. In a highly asymmetrical bargaining situation, the stronger side may try to force the other side to concede to its view about who should get what and on what conditions, thus obviating the true sense of negotiation or, indeed, of a fair solution.

In coordination and distributional disputes, the more productive bargaining strategy is one where the parties resort to Straight Talk and a healthy measure of Small Talk. The use of these tools will help the parties identify shared norms and settle on a common focal point in negotiations. In a distributional dispute the main challenge of negotiation is ultimately to identify key principles and standards of fairness and justice upon which the parties agree and on which a new allocative formula can be based and subsequent negotiations can center. This can only come about through the exchange of views and the development of shared understandings setting the problem on the other side of the table as the parties sit together to face it, as Jean Monnet advised, rather than have the parties face off against each other over the problem. If the parties are far apart on just what those principles are, or should be, any attempt to force the issue through threats, sanctions, or bribery will be counterproductive, particularly if the agreement is to be the product of joint, noncoerced behavior.

In sum, the choice of negotiating tools in cooperative disputes may well depend upon the fundamental characteristics of the dispute itself. Some disputes over public goods and externalities may indeed call for a Tough Talk approach. On the other hand, coordination and distributional disputes generally tend to require a Straight Talk/Small Talk approach to negotiations at their outset if there is to be any prospect of reducing tensions and reaching an agreement.

The selection of bargaining tools will also be affected by each party's perceptions about the long-term nature of their relationship with the other side and the value they place on friendship and trust. If friendship is deeply valued, parties may be careful to avoid threats and brinksmanship even if a distributive approach to bargaining is warranted by the dispute at hand, as on public goods. They may also be less concerned about balancing concessions over the short term because they believe reciprocity will be rewarded over the long run. Even where relations are less historical or emotional, maintaining the relationship for its practical benefits can be a powerful incentive to compromise. In its broadest sense, reciprocity in relations among states is the basis of a stable international community.

Likewise, if negotiations take place within the context of an existing regime where negotiating forums are clearly identified and a culture or climate of accommodation already exists and/or formal dispute and negotiating mechanisms are clearly identified, parties may be more predisposed to a less threat-based approach to bargaining and/or to defer contentious issues to a later date or a more propitious moment.

Talking Out Cooperation

This chapter has argued that cooperative disputes between the United States and its allies represent a special kind of problem and require careful use of Talk Power because of the nature of the relationship that exists between negotiating partners. Such disputes arise in joint decision-making situations where parties have strong incentives to cooperate but fail to reach an agreement. Recognizing that the exact nature of these disputes will vary considerably from one setting to another, this chapter has argued that not only are there different kinds of cooperative disputes—public goods disputes, externality disputes, coordination disputes, and distributional disputes—but that different kinds of negotiating strategies and tactics may be required for each. Although disputes over public goods and externalities create strong incentives for distributive bargaining, these strategies should not be employed indiscriminately, not only because of the risks of miscalculation, but also because distributional and other kinds of conflicts often also lie at the heart of these disputes. In talking with friends or allies the United States should choose its negotiating strategies and tactics carefully, especially as it looks to a world where it is going to need them more than ever.

CHAPTER 11
TALKING LATERALLY ON
NEW GOVERNANCE CHALLENGES

For men to live together in a state of society implies a kind of continuous negotiation.... Everything in life is, so to speak, intercourse
and negotiation, even between those whom we might think not to
have anything to hope or fear from one another.

—Antoine Pecquet, *Discours sur l'art de négocier*,
Nyon Fils, 1737

All the inventions of recent years have tended the same way: to narrow the world, to bring us closer together, and sharpen the reactions
before the shock absorbers are ready.

—Sir Anthony Eden, 1945

We live in a time of bewildering financial connectivity and advancing political
complexity. Our unipolar world is passing into history, yielding to a multicentric system in which the United States seems likely to remain preeminent, albeit
less predominant, as a global power, particularly with the rise of China, India,
Brazil, and other centers of political and economic power and influence. Our
international governance systems and institutions, constructed out of the Great
Depression and the ruins of World War II, have been steadily lagging the steepen-
ing curve of globalization. The financial cataclysm of 2007–09, which is forcing
us to put out the fire and rewrite new fire codes at the same time, has made the
search for governance alternatives and innovations urgent.

In the last 100 years, the world has gone from a multipolar to a bipolar to a unipolar system in which the United States has been the predominant power. The economic and financial meltdown of 2008–09 whose consequences we are still living with seems likely to accelerate the return of a multipolar world around a diluted hegemon, as the great powers of Asia, China, and India, in particular, are drawn by ambition or necessity (or both) into playing larger roles on the world stage. This emerging set of pluralistic relationships does not inherently pose a threat to world order. However, a new kind of leadership and diplomacy to manage real or imagined rivalries is required as was the case during the Concert of Europe that began after the Napoleonic wars and lasted until the beginning of the twentieth century.

Many are now championing the virtues of multilateralism to tackle a wide range of global problems such as climate change, new security threats, and the proliferation of nuclear weapons. Strobe Talbott, who served as deputy secretary of state under Bill Clinton, has argued that the United States can only truly exercise effective leadership in the world by pooling its sovereignty in cooperative institutional arrangements with others: Global governance accordingly is both a necessity and an ultimate political good.[1] Talbott reports that President Clinton in a quiet, unguarded moment opined that American preeminence in the world after the Cold War was an aberration in world politics and that US leadership could only be secured through the creation of new global institutions and multilateral cooperation. Currently the Obama administration appears to be putting greater store in partnership than dominance with other states in the international system.

What role does Talk Power have to play in building new partnerships in an increasingly multicentric world? And how should the United States use its formidable Talk Power assets to advance its core national interests through new and evolving multilateral cooperative arrangements? There is no easy answer to this question because the shape and trajectory of emerging international governance arrangements is still very much of a work in progress. As former Assistant Secretary of State Chester Crocker has written,

> Moments of geopolitical change often produce new institutions as a response to that change. The end of World War I brought the League of Nations, which attempted but failed to create a global order through international cooperation on security matters. The end of World War II produced a host of institutions, most of which still function today—the United Nations, the North Atlantic Treaty Organization, the International Monetary Fund, the World Bank, and the European Coal and Steel Community which has transformed over time into the European Union. However, the end of the Cold War did not result in much new global

institution-building. Instead, the past two decades have seen existing institutions adapt their missions and doctrines, expand their membership, and engage in a series of agonizing reappraisals of their identity and purpose.[2]

Moreover, as the Princeton scholar John Ikenberry argues, there is not a single logic, fixed set of principles, or enshrined practice to the current liberal international order and the way it operates. The postwar internationalism of the second half of the last century, which was based on the regulatory principles of President Franklin Roosevelt's New Deal, is yielding to a new "post-hegemonic liberal internationalism" that is based on an expanding membership of non-Western states, post-Westphalian principles of sovereignty, and an expanded set of rules and cooperative networks.[3]

As the United States and other countries struggle with a wide range of new economic, financial, environmental, and security challenges that do not respect national boundaries, like terrorism, transnational crime and drug trafficking, climate change, or the lingering aftershocks of the global financial and economic crisis, new forms and varieties of Team Talk are going to be required to muster viable international coalitions and develop new governance arrangements to address these challenges. However, in order to be effective these new "horizontally" directed conversations will typically take place outside the boundaries of formal international institutions.

There are a number of reasons for this. First, many of the world's formal international institutions have demonstrated that they are not up to the task of dealing with the most burning global issues. International treaties, conventions, and international organizations generally work too slowly and major intergovernmental conferences often lack proper follow-up mechanisms.

Second, there is growing disenchantment in many parts of the world with the legitimacy and accountability of formal multilateral institutions. This debate plays out at two levels. At one level, many would like to see a better representation from the South in the major decision-making organs of the UN and the Bretton Woods institutions. At another level, many would like to see international institutions become more accountable to the public by engaging citizens to a much greater degree in their decision-making processes.

Therefore, as a matter of necessity, new forms of multilateral diplomacy and Team Talk will have to be largely informal, ad hoc, opportunistic, inventive, and improvised at least for the time being until new institutional regimes come to be established. As an active participant in these new cooperative ventures, the United States will sometimes want to be the instigator and sometimes stand aside and let others take the lead, especially if there are partners who can carry the freight. These new varieties of Team Talk in the twenty-first century will have to be accompanied by new forms of Street Talk that engage and mobilize key sectors of civil society, including business, labor, and nongovernmental organizations, sometimes in "unholy" alliances or partnerships, to work alongside governments. Fortunately, some compelling examples of the new kinds of Team Talk/Street Talk diplomatic ventures are emerging from which we can learn more about how to deal with the world's new governance challenges.

Team Talk and the Evolution of Global Summitry

Surprising to some perhaps, the history and evolution of global economic summitry is instructive of the kinds of Team Talk innovations that are often required in the midst of crisis to tackle new global challenges. It is useful to recall that the first economic summit of world leaders, which took place at Rambouillet, France, in November 1975, was born out of a major global monetary and economic crisis. The Rambouillet summit was a small, informal gathering, convened at the initiative of French President Giscard d'Estaing to break the deadlock between the United States and Europe and Japan over reform of the international monetary system after the United States abandoned the gold standard by suspending the convertibility of the dollar. The summit also discussed international trade issues and generated a political commitment to resist protectionism and complete the Tokyo Round of trade talks. It was initially a summit of six—France, Britain, the United States, Japan, and Germany, with Italy added at the last minute; Canada was invited to be a summit member in 1976 and the president of the EEC (now the European Union [EU]) was added in 1977. It was the very informality and improvised nature of this gathering that proved to be the key to its success. Furthermore, this first meeting of world leaders took place at the initiation not of the United States but of France, although the United States was a willing, enthusiastic, and active partner who would go on to play a key leadership role in the annual summit gatherings that followed.

The G7, founded in the mid-1970s as group of the wealthiest, most developed countries with an initial focus on financial and economic issues also gradually transitioned into more political and security terrain. Over twenty years later, in 1997, Russia would join the group (a possible consolation prize for having stood aside and watched NATO and EU expansion), thus making it the G8. By 2005, leading European members pressed for the inclusion of emerging and developing nations, and the so-called Outreach Five (Brazil, China, India, Mexico, and South Africa) joined some of the proceedings.

Today's G8 summits are ambitious, elaborate, and highly scripted affairs. They are preceded by extensive meetings not just of summit "Sherpas"—the senior bureaucrats who organize these meetings—but also of key ministerial groupings to whom much of the responsibility for developing agendas and fostering policy innovation on specific issues has devolved. With so many actors, institutions, and interests involved in the preparation of these high-profile gatherings of world leaders, agendas have expanded. Recent summits have addressed everything from finance to terrorism, African development, climate change, and maternal health. Arguably, in preparing the agenda for global summits there is a tendency to overdecorate the proverbial summit Christmas tree. As result, the effectiveness of these gatherings has diminished.

The history of G8 summitry thus points to a broader lesson. A successful Team Talk venture is one that focuses leaders' attention and discussion on just a couple of critical issues rather than diluting it with a long list of "declarations" and "initiatives" scripted by well-intentioned bureaucrats who want to dress up official communiqués for their own purposes. Informality is also vitally important as the earlier exercises in summitry attest insofar as it helps leaders to get to know each other, develop trust, and foster the requisite political will to take collective action.

Since 1999 the G20 meetings of finance ministers and central bank governors have developed into the premier body for consultation on governance of the international financial system, as discussed in the previous chapter. After several years of increasingly insistent argument that the G8 was inadequate to the times, which until the 2008–09 financial and economic crisis had fallen on deaf ears in several G8 capitols, the G20 political leaders' summit was born as an important forum for world leaders to meet, discuss, and address the new economic challenges—the brainchild of President George W. Bush to address the economic crisis. At that first meeting in November 2008 and those that followed, the G20 promised and subsequently provided the IMF and the regional banks new resources to help countries deal with the crisis, issued new Special Drawing Rights (SDRs), undertook a series of measures to stimulate the global economy, and adapted the governance structure of the financial institutions to changing political and economic realities. Governments also committed themselves to resist the pressures of protectionism while asking the WTO to monitor lapses. Importantly, profound differences of opinion between Europe and the United States about the need for greater regulation of financial regulation and the need to stimulate economic growth did not disrupt the ongoing summitry process. As the *Los Angeles Times* concluded after the London summit in April 2009, "[t]he measures announced at the Group of 20 summit ... may not constitute the 'new global deal'.... But the outcome still surprised many observers with its unusually substantive achievements...."[4] The G20 result underscores the value of improvised and then institutionalized cooperative leadership and dialogue.

The early experience of the G7/8 and more recently the G20 also under-scores another lesson of Team Talk, namely, that minilateralism (sometimes also termed plurilateralism), especially of the more informal variety, may be a more useful venue for tackling pressing global issues—especially if there is an actual or looming crisis—than collective undertakings in larger, more formal maxilateral or multilateral forums. (In the recent economic crisis, the Bretton Woods institutions proved themselves woefully inadequate.) Mini-Team Talk, even within the enlarged summit forum of the G20, is sometimes necessary to make bigger institutions work and mobilize foot-dragging bureaucrats in large unwieldy organizations. The G20 has thus been a spur to the reform of the operations and membership of the Bretton Woods institutions.

These Team Talk ventures in global summitry are proving enormously valu-able in dealing with the still floundering global economy. However, there is a real tension between the G7/8 and the evolving G20 summit processes. The original G7 represents those countries who used to dominate the world economy but whose position has been eroded in the recent economic and financial crisis and by high unemployment rates, indebtedness, and sluggish economic performance. Although this group of countries has ceded much of its responsibility for steering the global economy to the G20, which includes the emerging economic power-houses of the developing world like China and India who pumped billions—if not trillions—of dollars into the global economy to help reverse the financial downturn of 2008–09, G7 financial ministers and central bankers continue to meet (as do their leaders) because they see themselves as a like-minded group whose cooperation, especially on regulatory matters, is key to wider coopera-tion in the G20. It is also the case that together the original G7 members still account for roughly two-thirds of global economic output and remain the major banking and financial centers of the globe and the world's major bilateral and multilateral institutional donors. However, many non-G7/8 members of the G20 are unhappy about the continued existence of this smaller minilateral group and are strongly opposed to the notion that the G7/8 might serve as the *directoire* of the enlarged forum of the G20. At some point, the relationship between these two levels of Team Talk will have to be reconciled with the United States play-ing a key if not central role as first among equals in determining the future of these global leadership forums and where the real center of gravity will reside.

Team Talk to Promote Collective Security

Generally speaking, institutional innovation in the field of international security has been modest when compared to the fields of economics and finance. The end of the Cold War initially seemed to augur positive change for the United Nations as a new spirit of cooperation among its permanent members emerged. In the late 1980s and early 1990s, the United Nations was successful in ending violent conflict in places like Namibia, Mozambique, Cambodia, El Salvador, and more recently in East Timor as discussed in earlier chapters. However, the United Nations was ineffective in Israel-Palestine, Bosnia, Kosovo, Somalia, Rwanda, and Haiti, and found itself increasingly marginalized in the face of the September 11, 2001, terrorist attacks on the United States, which were followed by US-led invasions of Afghanistan and Iraq. At the same time, scandals, such as the siphoning off of funds from the United Nations' oil for food program in Iraq by senior UN officials, the rape of Congolese women by UN peacekeeping forces, and administrative inefficiencies continue to plague the institution. Critics have called for the UN's dissolution notwithstanding ongoing efforts to reform the institution and make it more relevant to the security challenges of the twenty-first century.

Different problems confront the North Atlantic Treaty Organization (NATO), which has been remarkably active in tackling a wide range of out-of-area security challenges since the end of the Cold War, notably in the Balkans and Afghanistan. However, as some of these operations have floundered, especially in the case of Afghanistan, NATO has increasingly been wracked by internal divisions and self-doubt and its role in a post–Cold War environment.

As both the United Nations and NATO struggle to define their respective missions and mandates in the twenty-first century, the level of disquiet, confusion, and discord within these two bodies has grown. It is probably time to change the channel and recognize that there are other ways to secure international security cooperation, notably through the formation of ad hoc coalitions that have been formed through Team Talk. Consider some of the newer varieties of security cooperation to address some of the emerging threats to global security.

Tackling Piracy

Piracy is one of the world's oldest professions, certainly as old as merchant shipping itself. Since ancient times, traders who have plied the seas have risked attacks from marauders and buccaneers. Piracy played a key role in bringing the Spanish Empire to its knees. One of the most famous buccaneers of the seventeenth century was Sir Henry Morgan who was rewarded for his efforts by gaining a knighthood and the governorship of Jamaica.

Today's buccaneers are a less glamorous but no less lethal lot. From the Malaccan Straits of Southeast Asia to the Chittagong anchorages of Bangladesh, and the waters off Lagos, and the Bony River in the Bight of Benin off of Nigeria, mariners face the constant threat of attack. The most dangerous waters in the world lie off the coast of Somalia in the Gulf of Aden and the Indian Ocean where Somali pirates have boarded and hijacked everything from oil tankers returning from the Persian Gulf to cruise ships to fishing trawlers to even small pleasure craft piloted by unsuspecting yachters. Many of these attacks take place far out at sea at distances that exceed 1,000 nautical miles from Somalia's coastal capital Mogadishu.

In 2009, of the 406 piracy incidents reported worldwide more than half (217) originated from Somalia. In some instances, captured crew and vessels have been held for many months until ransom has been paid for their release. Ransom payments have soared into the millions of dollars. In early 2010 a Greek-owned oil tanker was released only after its owners agreed to pay more than $5 million. By some estimates, these attacks are costing the commercial shipping industry almost $100 million a year. Beyond ransom, some have paid with their lives.

With the escalating number of attacks, international naval antipiracy patrols in the region increased last year. But the task has proved daunting. Not only is the Somali coastline vast—almost 3,000 kilometers long—but if one includes the entire Horn of Africa and Yemen (which is also a growing source of attacks), the patrol area extends to almost 9,000 kilometers of coastline. It is also clear that Somali piracy is a booming, growth industry run by close to 2,000 pirates who are members of some seven "syndicates" controlled, financed, and brokered by "bosses" operating out of Kenya, Dubai, Lebanon, Somalia, and even Russia. Most of the pirates are young men who come from one of Somalia's two major clans and/or were militia members who fought in Somalia's brutal civil war.

There are two pieces of good news in this otherwise troubling picture. The first is that Somalia's pirates do not have ties—at least not yet—to al-Shabab, the powerful Islamic fundamentalist movement in the southern part of the country, which has links with al-Qaeda. The second is that although the number of pirate attacks is on the upswing, the proportion of successful attacks—where ships are captured and crews taken hostage—is falling.

This is because in 2009 as a direct consequence of Team Talk led by the United States with the support of its European and NATO allies, a combination of intergovernmental, regional, state, and private actors mounted a collaborative effort to address this threat. Team Talk has led to a combined effort to deal with piracy involving joint, ad hoc naval coordination among key NATO, EU, and Coalition Maritime Forces; a major parallel role of the private sector, especially among those companies whose ships transit these waters; the critical cooperation of Kenya in handling captured pirates; and more effective efforts by distinct Somali nonstate entities. Although there is no unified command structure among the three naval contingents, there has been extensive coordination at the tactical level.

Another positive development of Team Talk is seen in improved joint efforts by merchant shipping lines to protect their own vessels. Up to 70 percent of pirate attacks are now being defeated by merchant ships' crews themselves. As a consequence, pirates face significant risks and less likelihood of reward if they attack merchant ships. Furthermore, Kenya has agreed to prosecute pirates who are apprehended, although other regional states lacked the necessary legislation or political will to cooperate with international efforts to provide legal support for direct naval action against pirates. One account summarized the picture this way:

> [I]n 2009, the combined maritime operations of NATO and allied forces disrupted 411 pirate operations of 706 encountered; delivered 269 pirates for prosecution under prevailing legal interpretations to Kenya and other jurisdictions (of whom 46 were jailed); and killed 11 pirates. The combined operations also destroyed 42 pirate vessels; confiscated 14 boats, hundreds of small arms, nearly fifty rocket-propelled grenade launchers, and numerous ladders, grappling hooks, GPS receivers, mobile phones, etc.[5]

At the end of day, naval operations are no substitute for greater efforts to tackle the sociopolitical and economic challenges within Somalia itself. Even here there has been some modest progress as a result of encouraging political developments in the autonomous regions of Somaliland and Puntland, where local officials and communities have taken to Street Talk to ostracize those who engage in piracy and launch community awareness campaigns to show that piracy hurts local interests. Does this mean that the threat has diminished? It does not. However, there is something of an evolving cooperative network of global, regional, and state and nonstate actors, at least in this part of the world, to address the piracy problem.

The long-term challenge will be to sustain these efforts, especially to break the stranglehold of Somali warlords and "bosses" who bankroll and profit from piracy and to create incentives that strengthen the local Somali economy with employment opportunities for Somali youths. As Indonesia's successful efforts to combat piracy in the Straits of Malacca have shown, local authorities have a key role to play in curbing piracy and armed robbery in their littoral waters alongside those of the international community, but this too depends on the effective use of Team Talk, locally, regionally, and globally.

Countering Nuclear Proliferation

Another interesting example of Team Talk is the Proliferation Security Initiative (PSI) launched by President George W. Bush in Krakow, Poland on May 31,

2003, in cooperation with ten countries—Australia, France, Germany, Italy, Japan, the Netherlands, Poland, Portugal, Spain, and the United Kingdom. Many other countries have since committed themselves to supporting the initiative. PSI participants have downplayed the concept of membership in the joint initiative, explaining that PSI is "an activity not an organization." Nevertheless, the PSI is now endorsed by some ninety-five countries whose act of adherence consists of officially subscribing to a set of principles. The PSI aims to detect and intercept WMD materials and related finance, and its operation is described in official US statements as "a flexible, voluntary initiative geared toward enhancing individual and collective partner nations' capabilities to take appropriate and timely actions to meet the fast-moving situations involving proliferation threats."[6] Emphasis is placed on "voluntary actions by states that are consistent with their national legal authorities and relevant international law and frameworks." The PSI has principles in lieu of a formal charter, and it conducts operational and training activities rather than regularized meetings or summits. It has no headquarters or dedicated facilities and no intergovernmental budget. Interestingly, President Barack Obama has described the PSI as "a durable international institution."[7]

Securing Troubled Borders

In some cases, the United States has decided to let other countries take the lead in Team Talk ventures. Until his untimely death, Richard Holbrooke, the president's special envoy for Afghanistan and Pakistan, held the ring in trying to promote the two countries' working together on shared security problems while also talking to some of Afghanistan's other neighbors to advance greater levels of regional engagement for stability. The United States has strongly supported the efforts of one of its closest NATO allies, Canada, to secure greater levels of cooperation between Afghan and Pakistani government officials on cross-border management issues.

Major, long-standing disagreements between Afghanistan and Pakistan over the issue of the Durand Line, the de facto border between the two countries, have for many years thwarted any kind of dialogue or security cooperation between the two countries on a wide range of border problems. These include the cross-border movement of insurgents; the absence of proper infrastructure and customs management at key, legal border crossing points (Waish-Chamam, Ghulam Khan, and Torkham); smuggling to avoid customs; the illicit cross-border flow of narcotics; and illegal migration.

A cross-border joint dialogue between the two countries was initiated and facilitated by Canada when Pakistan's former president, Pervez Musharraf, threatened to mine the border in response to pressure from the international community for stricter control of his country's borders. Canada, a long-standing champion of the antipersonnel landmines treaty, stepped in to suggest an alternative approach to dealing with the myriad problems in the disputed border region. Following the 2007 Potsdam Statement by G8 foreign ministers and the foreign ministers of Afghanistan and Pakistan (and the Pakistan-Afghanistan Joint Peace Jirga), the two countries have met on a regular basis under Canadian auspices in a series of technical, working-level workshops to discuss border management cooperation. The five working areas of what is now referred to as the Dubai Process (after the Persian Gulf Emirate where the first meeting took place) include customs, counter-narcotics, managing the movement of people, law enforcement in border areas, and connecting government to people through social and economic development. The meetings are part of an internationally recognized process that promotes dialogue between Afghan and Pakistani officials to advance cooperation in each of these areas. Importantly, the process has engaged and mobilized a wide range of partners and stakeholders not only in the two countries, but also at the international level, including the US Border Management Task Force in Kabul and Islamabad, the UN Office on Drugs and Crime, International Security Assistance Force (ISAF) Regional Command (South), the World Bank, the UN Assistance Mission in Afghanistan, the UN High Commissioner for Refugees, the International Organization for Migration, other organizations working on border management, and key donors such as Germany and Denmark.

In addition to serving as a key strategic focal point for dialogue, discussion, and cooperation between Afghanistan and Pakistan on a wide range of "soft" security issues, the Dubai Process has also helped identify and develop key projects to promote government-to-government cooperation such as the development of compatible biometrics systems at the border, coordination in counternarcotics, joint efforts to inhibit the illegal shipment of precursor chemicals, improved information sharing, and the provision of much-needed equipment and training to border agencies. Team Talk is being backed by some concrete results.

The three examples discussed above are important illustrations of a new kind of Team Talk to promote collective security in a post-9/11 world. These cooperative undertakings build on the traditions of collective defense and collective security. However, unlike collective defense and collective security, which involve formal obligations to undertake joint action in response to the actions of an aggressive state, these Team Talk–based initiatives are voluntary and improvised. They represent a new form of collective action in response to diverse security challenges ranging from traditional security threats to nontraditional threats such as organized crime, piracy, kidnapping, arms trading, narco-trafficking, illegal migration, and conflict-related commodity trade.[8]

These cooperative security undertakings through Team Talk offer a different vision of multilateral cooperation: one that is *not* based on striking a formal consensus where each state has the right of veto (as in the European model), but rather on cooperation that emerges out of an informal process of consultation and where final, decision-making authority continues to reside with national authorities (which is historically how the United States has approached many of its international undertakings). Using Team Talk, the United States has also looked for partners where they are available—from international agencies, regional organizations, and bilateral official or nonofficial partners—to address these new security challenges.

Building "Unholy" Transnational Alliances with Street Talk

The globalization phenomenon has taken many forms. On the one hand, the communications revolution is allowing many different messages to be carried on a global scale. This revolution is also transforming individual and communal self-identities and images while empowering local communities in ways that were unthinkable in earlier times, building alliances between High and Low politics. On the other hand, powerful social, economic, and technological pressures are opening up the boundaries of national life. A spreading web of global issues networks (GINs), involving vigorous and innovative new partnerships among public, private, and civil society actors, is pressuring national governments—and simultaneously enhancing their capacity—to enact conforming legislation and take practical action on global problems like the management of the biosphere, population growth, and global warming.

Successful negotiations to conclude the Ozone Accords, which led to a worldwide ban on the production and use of chlorofluorocarbons (CFCs), halons, and other ozone-depleting substances through the Vienna Convention (1985) and subsequent Montreal Protocol (1987), were a widely recognized landmark in international diplomacy and environmental cooperation. The depletion of ozone in the upper atmosphere because of manmade emissions of ozone-harming gases posed a threat to global survival, and scientists who studied the problem recognized early in the 1980s that it would take unprecedented levels of international cooperation to address it.

Although some have argued that these treaties were concluded because of the growing influence and impact of the scientific community, this is only half the story. First, public opinion fueled by fears about the link between ozone depletion, growing levels of ultraviolet radiation, and skin cancer played a crucial role in bridging the gap between science and policy by forcing the issue onto the political agenda. Second, a growing sense of crisis moved the issue from the US national to the international stage, especially as the Green Movement took hold of the issue in European and other countries. Third, once the issue became a subject of international discussion and negotiation, the exercise of skillful leadership and mediation by a variety of different actors, including the United States, the then executive director of the UN Environment Program (UNEP), and several small states, helped to sustain talks, bridge key bargaining impasses, and bring the parties to agreement. Fourth, and no less important, key US industrial stakeholders, in particular the US du Pont de Nemours and Company, the largest producer of CFCs at the time controlling some 26 percent of worldwide production, threw its support behind the treaty. Dupont was joined by other major global producers of CFCs, including ICI, Farbwerke Hoechst, and ATOCHEM. Street Talk thus led to an unholy alliance between major industrial (interest) groups and environmental (ideological) nongovernmental organizations who were also strong supporters of a ban. This included the Green Movement in Germany and the United Kingdom, in particular, and groups like the Natural Resources Defense Council in the United States.

The formation of this somewhat unique alliance of private corporate interests and environmental NGOs via Street Talk in the development of the Ozone Accords is instructive for today's efforts to secure a climate change agreement that would reduce carbon emissions into the atmosphere to arrest global warming. The two-week UN Summit on Climate Change in Copenhagen and Cancun in November 2009 and 2010, respectively, failed to produce anything resembling a legally binding agreement to reduce greenhouse gas emissions. This after many years of international negotiations and significant levels of heightened public awareness about the problem.

Although key developing countries, led by China, India, and Brazil, indicated they would cut their own carbon emissions in the run-up to Copenhagen, it readily became quite apparent that they were all marching to a different drummer in terms of baselines, specific reduction measures, and legal obligations. They also sought major concessions from rich developed nations to cut their own emissions while providing major funding for technology transfer and adaptation to developing countries. Although the United States said that it would cut its own emissions to 17 percent below 2005 levels by 2020, it remains to be seen whether the US Congress will agree to such a deal. In contrast, the EU, which played a key role at Copenhagen and Cancun, plans to cut its own emissions by 20 percent from 1990 levels by 2020 if other countries follow suit. Following allegations that a key climate change research unit at the University of East Anglia had fudged key data on global warming, Saudi Arabia, the world's biggest oil producer, declared that it opposed any new climate change agreement.

As past efforts at multilateral diplomacy attest, there are creative ways to break negotiating deadlocks and impasses. The United States and/or other countries could, for example, form a new coalition of the like-minded states to take the lead. When the antipersonnel landmines treaty process headed into a cul-de-sac, for example, Canada invited those who wanted to sign a treaty to participate in a separate forum, the Ottawa Process, which quickly concluded an agreement under a tight deadline by those countries who wanted it. This was a bold move but it shamed many of the treaty holdouts to join the club or at the very least support its goals. For those countries prepared to take decisive action to reduce their emissions this is an option. However, it would likely wreak havoc on world trade if those inside the coalition penalized polluters and trading partners who don't play by their rules. We would all pay a heavy price.

A second option is to take an incremental approach by scaling down ambitious targets to reduce emissions via a lot of Small Talk. Baby steps are sometimes a way to generate momentum and build political support before you do something big. The problem is that many scientists say we need drastic reductions now to forestall disaster—a more modest, phased approach to reducing emissions simply will not work. That may be true, but right now there are precious few stepping stones to move forward. Going slow may be the better political and economic option.

A third option is for countries to work harder to develop effective compliance and verification mechanisms. There is still an enormous lack of trust among those sitting at the table at Copenhagen and Cancun. Many countries fear that others will not honor their negotiated treaty commitments because of the difficulties of monitoring carbon emissions under a voluntary reporting system. We can take a lesson here from the history of arms control negotiations between the United States and the Soviet Union. As President Ronald Reagan used to say, "trust but verify." The World Trade Organization offers a good model for dealing with these problems via its disputes-settlement procedures and monitoring mechanisms for the review of trade policies. Like the WTO, a climate change agreement will also need clear rules, effective monitoring, and penalties for noncompliance.

One of the other main challenges for the Obama administration and others who want to conclude a climate change agreement is to join Team Talk with Street Talk in order to energize a new coalition of business and environmental interests who will work together for imaginative solutions. It is undeniably the case that some businesses could benefit from carbon reductions, e.g., the insurance industry and those manufacturers and industries that are in the business of producing alternative carbon substitutes for energy development, heating, transportation, etc.

Major change occurs when advocacy and key business interest groups come together in support of a common endeavor. That is what produced the Montreal

Protocol to protect the ozone layer. It is not too late to galvanize such a co-alition now, and it would take real leadership to do it. Former Vice President Al Gore did not succeed because he made less of a pitch to business interests than to environmentalists. Yet ultimately such a coalition will be necessary if any agreement is to be reached. The negotiating impasse at Copenhagen and Cancun is not insurmountable. But it is going to take creativity, new varieties of Team Talk, and a lot of hard thinking outside the box of traditional multilateral diplomacy to break it.

Chapter 12
Negotiating America's Interests

In a society of states each state has interests ... which connect it
with the others. The great axioms of political science derive from the
recognition of the true interests of *all* states; it is in general interests
that the guarantee of existence is to be found, while particular interests—whose cultivation is considered political wisdom by restless and
myopic men—have only a secondary importance.

—Prince Klemens Wenzel von Metternich, 1807

It was a negotiation among unequals, but one that ended badly for both sides.
It was a bungled negotiation whose very failure would sow the seeds of ruin for
one of the world's greatest empires. It is a story that bears retelling in some detail
because it captures some of the central messages of this book.

In 416 BC Athens sent a landing force to the independent island state of
Melos to try to bring it to the negotiating table.[1] The island had great strategic
significance for Athens, lying as it did midway in the Aegean Sea on the sailing
route to Sparta. Sparta had been at war with Athens since 431 BC, heading its
own coalition of states that feared Athens' growing economic and political clout
in the region. Athens' superior naval capabilities had fought Sparta's armies to a
draw and for several years there was an uneasy truce between the two sides. But
when hostilities resumed Athens sought to bring Melos into the Delian League,
which would allow it to exact tribute from its new colony and also make use of
the island's important port facilities for its navy.

The Melians were a proud people, however. For hundreds of years they had
zealously maintained their independence, staying neutral in the recurring battles

and wars that engulfed the region around them. They were also deeply suspicious of Athens' intentions. Like many other states, they saw Athens as arrogant and power hungry and were not interested in joining its rapidly growing empire, the Delian League.

Generals Cleomedes and Tisias, who commanded the heavily armed landing force, led negotiations on the Athenian side. Melos was represented by twelve members of the Melian Council, the island's governing body comprised of its wealthiest and most powerful families.

The ensuing "negotiation" is a textbook case of how not to negotiate, one that was driven not by interests but positions and by the perception that power alone talks. Both sides chose to lecture each other, stating and restating their positions, appealing to principle, and taking the moral high ground. As the dialogue continued, they stuck to their guns instead of trying to find some common ground. Instead of helping the other side find a door that led it out of the bargaining impasse, each side did its best to back the other side into a corner. This was positional bargaining at its worst.

The Athenians wrongly thought that threats were the way to secure concessions from Melos and that capitulation was Melos' only option. Athens also believed that its unrivaled power meant that the gods were on its side and that Melos would simply succumb to Athens' superior military might. Rather than trying to reassure the Melians and showing respect to their leaders, Athens through both its actions and words seeded a climate of suspicion and hostility that was not auspicious for any kind of Straight Talk, which could have helped to defuse the crisis. Neither was Athens' brutal Tough Talk complemented by any Sweet Talk inducements or any kind of desire to give in order to get something in return. Athens was also impervious to the notion that Melos prized its independence and would do anything to keep its reputation and honor intact even if it meant annihilation. "For ourselves," its generals remarked at outset of talks, "we shall not trouble you with specious pretenses—either of how we have a right to our empire because we overthrew the Mede, or are now attacking you because of wrong you have done us—and make a long speech which would not be believed … for you know as we do that right, as the world goes, is in question only between equals in power; while the strong do what they can and the weak suffer what they must." Melos was backed into a corner with no way out.

If diplomacy was to bear any kind of fruit and avoid war, a way would have had to be found to recognize Melos' dignity, sovereignty demands, and independence, if only symbolically, in order to secure concessions on those things that mattered most to Athens—securing tribute payments and basing rights for its navy. This was not an insuperable challenge. But it is one that required much greater flexibility and imagination at the negotiating table than Athens demonstrated.

The elders of Melos did no better. Instead of recognizing their own vulnerability to attack they tried to raise their security point in the negotiations by arguing that the Spartan (or Lacedaemonian) alliance would come to their assistance if negotiations with Athens failed. "You may be sure that we are as well aware of the difficulty of contending against your power and fortune, unless the terms are equal. But we trust that the gods may grant us fortune as good as yours, since we are just men fighting the unjust, and that what we want in power will be made up in the alliance of the Lacedaemonians, who are bound, if only for very shame, to come to the aid of their kindred. Our confidence, therefore, after all is not so utterly irrational." This was folly, pure and simple. There was no way that Sparta could have mobilized its troops and sailed to Melos in time to defend it from Athens' invasion.

Like Athens, Melos also thought that the right side of the argument was on their side and that justice would prevail. Its elders posed the following rhetorical question to Athens: "But do you consider that there is no security in the policy which we indicate? For here again if you debar us from talking about justice and invite us to obey your interest, we also must explain ours, and try to persuade you, if the two happen to coincide. How can you avoid making enemies of all existing neutrals who shall look at our case and conclude from it that one day or another you will attack them? And what is this but to make greater the enemies that you have already, and to force others to become so who would otherwise have never thought of it?"

The subsequent course of history would prove Melos right as other states, fearful of Athens' imperial intentions and lust for power, joined forces with Sparta. But the argument couched as it was in terms of principles or speaking truth to power was unpersuasive. Confronted with an unyielding lesser power, the patience of Athens' generals ran out. The Athenian army razed Melos to the ground, murdered its male citizens, and forced the women and children of Melos into slavery, losing in the process the very thing it prized to secure: Melos intact.

Both sides lost this war of words. Both failed to use Talk Power the right way at this propitious moment in history to achieve their goals. Had they used Straight Talk to shed some light on their respective core interests (Melos in dignity and survival, and Athens in the long-term viability of its reputation as a benign imperial power that was not looking to create new enemies), the outcome might have been different. Sweet Talk was also needed to reassure the other side and induce concessions. Other options such as finding a mediator who could secure a peaceful resolution to their dispute via Triple Talk should have also been considered.

The story of the Melian dialogue underscores a key point of this book and a bigger set of lessons. Diplomacy is not simply a matter of going through the motions of negotiation. Parties have to be committed to the negotiation process.

They also have to select the right tools in the Talk Power toolkit in order to secure their interests and achieve their goals. Talk Power when used wisely can avert conflict and escalation. The story of Athens and Melos also shows how a bungled negotiation can alter the course of history. There are clearly some parallels with the failure of US diplomacy prior to the onset of the first Gulf War, which, too, shaped the course of history and US foreign policy in the Middle East, as we saw in chapter two.

Weight, Wallets, Words, and Wits

The United States enters the second decade of the twenty-first century a challenged—some believe diminished—economic and military power. US public debt, which now hovers around $14 trillion, is close to the total output of the US economy (94 percent of the GDP). Some 15 million Americans are out of work, and unemployment levels in 2010 were stuck at 9 percent. The US government recorded a budget shortfall of $1.3 trillion in the 2010 fiscal year, the second worst since 1945. With a deficit running at nearly 9 percent of total economic output, many economists believe that such high levels of deficit spending are not sustainable and are well above a desired 3 percent target.

Total US defense spending, which accounts for roughly a quarter of the total federal expenditures and almost 5 percent of GDP, dwarfs that of other countries. Since the beginning of this century, US defense spending has grown at roughly 9 percent per annum. But this level of expenditure is not sustainable. US Secretary of Defense Robert Gates admitted so publicly in the summer of 2010 as he looked to find ways to "save" $100 billion in expenditures over the next five years.

In earlier times, the fortunes of great imperial powers were tied to the health of their economies and the success of their untutored rulers in mastering the mysteries of economics.[2] In the latter half of the sixteenth century under King Philip II, the Spanish Empire reached the height of its power and influence. However, poor economic management by his successors, inflation (caused by the accumulation of massive gold reserves and spendthrift policies), and war itself weakened Spain's power. In the seventeenth century, Spain fought a series of disastrous wars against the Netherlands, France, England, and Portugal eventually losing most of its colonial possessions.

Although historians continue to debate the reasons for the decline of the British Empire, they are in general agreement that Britain's lagging industrial growth in the first half of the last century and its inability to finance the costs of imperial control and management—what some refer to as the dangers of imperial overstretch—contributed to Britain's decline.[3]

Today, the United States is the world's "weary titan."[4] Its public has grown tired of foreign wars and misadventures. Its power is severely challenged by a tidal wave of fiscal red ink that threatens to engulf the economy. But we should not trumpet America's demise just yet. Like Samson who was seduced by Delilah to give up the secret of his great strength, America's own greed and lust have left its economy seriously weakened. Like Samson, however, America is down but not out, and unlike Samson, it is not blind. The United States continues to enjoy a monopoly on the use of military force and the fundamentals of its economy are still strong. It is the world leader in the value of high-end manufactured goods like aircraft, heavy equipment, and pharmaceuticals. It remains a knowledge leader because of the high quality of its universities and applied research. It also possesses one of the most diversified economies in the world so its ability to bounce back from the current crisis is greater than that of many other countries.

However, the United States cannot dig itself out of its problems all by itself. It needs the engagement and cooperation of others. The forces of globalization and the bonds of economic interdependence have put much of the world on the same moving escalator. When the escalator jerks to a sudden halt, as it did during the economic and financial crisis of 2008–09, everyone takes a tumble.

That is China's problem. China's trade dependence on the United States has been the foundation of its economic growth. As the US economy sank into deep recession, millions of Chinese were laid off as factories shut down because export markets dried up. Although China has accumulated massive foreign exchange reserves, its ability to use this surplus to stimulate its own domestic consumption is limited. Much of China's wealth is held in US Treasury Bills and other US-based assets, and it still depends on foreign trade, especially with the United States, for its own economic growth.

The United States still possesses formidable hard and soft power assets notwithstanding the rise of China, Brazil, and India, as well as the resurgence of Russia in its own "near abroad." The United States with its $14 trillion economy is still by far the world's biggest and perhaps the most innovative. US conventional and nuclear military power capabilities dwarf those of other countries, including China, which is in the process of rapidly building up its military. Importantly, notwithstanding the dent to US prestige as a result of foreign policy misadventures, most of the world's democratic nations still look to the United States to provide global leadership and secure global security and economic stability. To paraphrase Mark Twain, reports of America's demise are to say the least, "premature."

Talk Power is the motor that drives America's hard and soft power train. America cannot win others over to its side just by using Gun Power and Tough Talk. At the same time, its soft power assets—what some refer to as America's enormous powers of attraction through its economy, society, culture, and democratic traditions and political institutions—are, like gravity, a weak rather than a strong force in the political universe. They cannot by themselves secure America's interests in a world where there are increasingly other poles of attraction and where others have soft power instruments at their disposal. Weight and wallets matter, but they are useless unless a country also uses its words and wits at the negotiating table as well.

On one front, economic and cultural globalization, coming from the West and led by the United States, has spread into every nook and cranny of the world, arousing in some areas a reaction of self-assertion and self-defense. A new multinational corporation, with its diverse centers, international staff, and multiple sources of financial support—al-Qaeda—has arisen to try to reclaim the cultural and political purity, hiding behind a deformed interpretation of its religion, using the weapons of the weak and desperate—terrorism. Meeting the threat requires many counter-weapons, but underneath the immediate clashes is a war for the hearts and minds of the huge Muslim world, which can only be won over to ideas of tolerance and pluralism and away from forces of hate and backwardness by effective use of Talk and commitment.

On a different kind of front, the world is still—and perhaps increasingly—riddled by conflicts arising from inflated and competing senses of identity, where groups fight over holy land, or find their self-realization only in putting down others, or claim discrimination for who they are. Though these may be far from the United States, they create spreading cancers in important regions of the world, destroy lives, and damage economies, eventually calling in the United States because interests are involved and, more basically, because Americans care for humanity. Finding solutions demands careful Triple Talkers, with all of their wits about them, because taming the implications of identity is a delicate business. Palestinians and Israelis, Serbs and Kosovars, Indians and Pakistanis, Buddhist Sri Lankans and Tamils, and many others still have not learned to be themselves without putting down the other party and live side by side or together; they will not do so without the help of third-party mediators, even if the final reconciliation must be their own doing.

Or, on another front, the problems of securing global economic recovery and the challenges of developing a credible medium-term plan for global economic growth must be talked out. Because the United States cannot lead a global recovery on its own, China, Germany, Japan, and other surplus countries will have to provide the impetus for global recovery by increasing domestic consumption, reducing current account surpluses, and shifting government spending to increase domestic demand and to support those who bear the burden of adjustment, including aging members of their own populations. Surplus countries, notably China, will also have to move toward flexible exchange rates. Otherwise, they will eventually be forced to adopt policies that penalize their own consumers and producers. None of this will happen overnight.

This presents a major challenge for ongoing negotiations within the G20 framework where the United States clearly has a key leadership role to play. The costs of inaction are huge, especially on the one issue that unites all world leaders—the problem of a jobless recovery. The International Monetary Fund (IMF) and Organization for Economic Cooperation and Development have shown that if the G20 adopts effective collective measures to rebalance the global economy, world output will increase by a further $1.2 trillion and more than 13 million new jobs will be created. However, if there is a failure of collective will to rebalance, an additional 23 million jobs will be lost, 60 million will fall into poverty, and world output would be 3 percent lower.

But the G20 is a disparate group. Many are inward-looking, with self-interest too often trumping global coordination. But as we have seen, Talk Power works when it is focused and infused by large doses of Straight Talk, Team Talk, and Small Talk. There has been progress in the area of financial regulation because of the successful application of these Talk Power tools. The Basel III financial commitments, negotiated by key regulators and finance and treasury officials in G20 countries in 2010, are important in developing an integrated approach to financial reform to help avert future financial crises. The same is true of IMF reform, particularly with respect to quotas and governance, where emerging economies are being given a bigger seat at the table. However, Talk Power still has yet to work its charms in the area of international trade. There is growing consensus but not yet a formula for agreement in the stalled Doha Round of trade negotiations in the World Trade Organization.

The credibility of global governance and national security is at stake. America acts on the world stage through the leadership of its words and works. And words still matter. The postwar order was constructed by Talk Power in a succession of summits at Yalta, Dumbarton Oaks, San Francisco, and Bretton Woods, plus the large arena for a Team of rivals in San Francisco. It is an order that has survived and adapted to changing circumstances largely through a continuous process of negotiation and renegotiation. As we have argued here, there is a wide range of new and recurring global and regional security and economic challenges that must also be dealt with through negotiation and the skillful application of different Talk Power tools. This requires a higher level of competence, negotiation, stamina, staying power, and leadership in the Talk Power game by America's leaders and a supportive awareness of these challenges and needs by the American people.

NOTES

Chapter 2

1. See, for example, David M. Malone, *The International Struggle Over Iraq: Politics in the UN Security Council 1980–2005* (New York: Oxford University Press, 2007).

2. See, for example, Bob Woodward, *Plan of Attack: The Definitive Account of the Decision to Invade Iraq* (New York: Simon and Schuster, 2004); Christopher Cerf and Micah L. Sifry, *The Iraq War Reader: History, Documents, Opinions* (New York: Touchstone, 2003); James DeFronzon, *The Iraq War: Origins and Consequences* (Boulder, CO: Westview Press, 2009); and Richard N. Haass, *War of Necessity, War of Choice* (New York: Simon and Schuster, 2010).

3. Bruce W. Jentleson, *With Friends Like These: Reagan, Bush, and Saddam 1982–1990* (New York: W.W. Norton, 1994): 150.

4. Ibid., 156.

5. Ibid., 161.

6. As the *Washington Post* reported on April 3, 2008, "During the run-up to the war, the Iraqi government released a transcript of Glaspie's meeting with Hussein on July 25, 1990, which suggested that she gave tacit approval for an invasion. Glaspie managed to convince lawmakers that the transcript was inaccurate and that she had forcefully warned Hussein not to invade. But her credibility eroded after the leak of her classified cable to the State Department about the meeting, which suggested a more conciliatory conversation with Hussein. In the interview, Glaspie insisted that the Iraq transcript "was invented by Tariq Aziz," the deputy prime minister. "Tariq was a master of words as a previous Minister of Information and editor of a newspaper," she said. Glaspie asserted that she told Hussein to "keep your hands off this country." Glaspie's cable was declassified after a Freedom of Information Act appeal by the National Security Archive at George Washington University. The cable, along with others obtained by the archive, suggests that she was largely carrying out a policy, pushed by State at the time, of seeking to improve relations with Iraq. Glaspie's cable says that President George H. W. Bush "had instructed her to broaden and

deepen our relations with Iraq," adding that Hussein in turn offered "warm greetings" to Bush and was "surely sincere" about not wanting war. In the interview, Glaspie recalls that her meeting with Hussein was interrupted when the Iraqi president received a phone call from Egyptian President Hosni Mubarak. Glaspie said Hussein told her he had assured Mubarak that he would try to settle the dispute. Her cable backs up this version of events, though the Iraqi transcript has Hussein saying that Mubarak called before he met with Glaspie. Glaspie said the Mubarak call was crucial in convincing her that any sense of crisis had passed. She said that she was "foolish" to believe that Hussein would not lie to both her and Mubarak, and that she left Baghdad to go on a short vacation. Before she left, she sent another cable titled "Iraq Blinks—Provisionally," also obtained by the archive. Hussein, "a megalomaniac," thought "that my government did not have any guts, that we would not fight and certainly not for that little [piece] of desert that was Kuwait for him," Glaspie told al-Hayat. Ever a diplomat, Glaspie sidestepped a question about Baker cutting her loose, answering simply that then-President Bush "was superb." Asked what she thought of the 2003 invasion of Iraq, Glaspie noted that the British Empire nearly 100 years ago had failed to control the country.

7. William B. Quandt, *Peace Process: American Diplomacy and the Arab-Israeli Conflict Since 1967* (Washington, DC: Brookings Institution, 2005): 339.

8. Jake Tapper, Sunlen Miller, and Karen Travers, "Obama in Turkey Says U.S. Not at War with Islam," *ABC News*, April 6, 2009. Available at: http://abcnews.go.com/Politics/story?id=7268063&page=1.

Chapter 3

1. Fortune Barthélemy de Felice, *Dictionnaire de justice naturelle et civile* (Yverdun 1778), trans. in *The 50% Solution*, 47f.

2. James A. Baker III, "The Road to Madrid," in Chester A. Crocker, Fen Osler Hampson, and Pamela Aall, eds., *Herding Cats: Multiparty Mediation in a Complex World* (Washington, DC: United States Institute of Peace Press, 1999): 187.

3. The quotation is attributed to Abba Eban, the Israeli diplomat and politician, who was quoted as saying "the Arabs never miss an opportunity to miss an opportunity." Available at: http://en.wikiquote.org/wiki/Abba_Eban.

4. Harland Cleveland, *Nobody in Charge: Essay on the Future of Leadership* (San Francisco: Jossey Bass, 2002): 224.

5. François de Callières, *The Art of Diplomacy* (Lanham, MD: University Press of America, 1994): 81–2.

6. Jan Egeland, "The Oslo Accord: Multiparty Facilitation Through the Norwegian Channel," in Crocker et al., *Herding Cats,* 533.

7. De Callières, *The Art of Diplomacy,* 22.

8. "United Nations: Until Hell Freezes Over." *Time*, November 2, 1962. Available at: http://www.time.com/time/magazine/article/0,9171,874589,00.html. Also quoted in Robert F. Kennedy, *Thirteen Days* (New York: W.W. Norton, 1968): 54.

9. Recollection of I. William Zartman who was a member of President Carter's negotiating team.

10. Baker, "The Road to Madrid," 203.

11. Department of State Telegram Conveying President Kennedy's Reply to Chairman Khrushchev, October 28, 1962. Available at: http://www.jfklibrary.org/jfkl/cmc/cmc_correspondence.html.

12. Robert F. Kennedy, *Thirteen Days: A Memoir of the Cuban Missile Crisis* (New York: W.W. Norton, 1971): 105–6.

13. See, for example, Thomas Blanton, "Annals of Blinksmanship," *The Wilson Quarterly* (Summer 1997). Available at: http://www.gwu.edu/~nsarchiv/nsa/cuba_mis_cri/annals.htm.

14. Quoted in *Current Issues Briefing* (Washington, DC: United States Institute of Peace, September 28, 2005).

15. Nicholas Berry, "Why Saddam Hussein Approved UN Inspections," *Foreign Policy Forum*, September 17, 2002. Available at: http://www.foreignpolicyforum.com/view_article.php?aid=19.

16. John Petrie's "Collection of Winston Churchill Quotes." Available at: http://jpetrie.myweb.uga.edu/bulldog.html.

17. Both quotations appear in Jane Macartney, "President Bush Condemns China Human Rights Record on Eve of Olympics," *Sunday Times,* August 8, 2008. Available at: http://www.timesonline.co.uk/tol/news/world/asia/article4476593.ece.

18. Paula Wolfson, "Bush Warns Gulf States of Iran Threat," Voice of America, January 13, 2008. Available at: http://www.globalsecurity.org/wmd/library/news/iran/2008/iran-080113-voa01.htm.

19. Harry de Quetteville, "Iranian Leader Mahmoud Ahmadinejad Taunts 'Wicked' President George W. Bush," *The Telegraph,* June 11, 2008. Available at: http://www.telegraph.co.uk/news/worldnews/middleeast/iran/2111093/Iranian-leader-Mahmoud-Ahmadinejad-taunts-wicked-President-George-W-Bush.html.

20. President Wilson's Fourteen Points, Delivered in Joint Session, January 8, 1918. Available at http://wwi.lib.byu.edu/index.php/President_Wilson%27s_Fourteen_Points.

21. Jan Egeland, "The Oslo Accord," 530.

22. Saunders, "Prenegotiation and Circum-negotiation: Arenas of the Peace Process," in Chester Crocker, Fen Hampson, and Pamela Aall, eds., *Managing Global Chaos: Sources of and Responses to International Conflict* (Washington, DC: United States Institute of Peace Press, 1996): 419–32.

23. Ambassador Stephen Low, "The Zimbabwe Settlement, 1976–1979," in Saadia Touval and I. William Zartman, eds., *International Mediation in Theory and Practice* (Washington, DC: Johns Hopkins University, SAIS, Foreign Policy Institute, 1985): 93.

24. Jean Monnet, *Memoirs* (New York: Doubleday, 1978): 216.

25. Baker, "The Road to Madrid," 188 and 196.

Chapter 4

1. Anwar Sadat quoted in "Sadat: Hour of Decision," *Time,* December 5, 1977. Available at: http://ca.mg4.mail.yahoo.com/dc/launch?.gx=1&.rand=0gh3mh3dv5slg.

2. Richard M. Nixon, *RN: The Memoirs of Richard Nixon* (New York: Grosset and Dunlap, 1978): 921.

3. Henry Kissinger, *Years of Upheaval* (Boston: Little, Brown and Company): 467–68.

4. Ibid., 1253–54.

5. Baker, *Herding Cats,* 186.

6. Ibid., 205.

Chapter 5

1. Jimmy Carter, *Negotiation: An Alternative to Hostility* (Macon, GA: Mercer University Press, 1984): 13–4.

2. Joseph J. Hewitt, Jonathan Wilkenfeld, and Ted Robert Gurr, *Peace and Conflict, 2010* (College Park, MD: Center for International Development and Conflict Management, University of Maryland, 2010).

3. Quoted in I. William Zartman and Alvaro de Soto, *Timing Mediation Initiatives: Peacemakers' Toolkit* (Washington, DC: United States Institute of Peace Press, 2010): 18.

4. Lydia Polgreen and Sabrina Tavernise, "Water Dispute Increases India-Pakistan Tension," *New York Times,* July 20, 2010. Available at: http://www.nytimes.com/2010/07/21/world/asia/21kashmir.html?pagewanted=2.

5. See Uri Savir, *Peace First: A New Model to End War* (San Francisco: Berrett-Koehler Publishers, 2008): 68.

Chapter 6

1. Jake Tapper, Sunlen Miller, and Karen Travers, "Obama in Turkey Says U.S. Not at War with Islam," *ABC News,* April 6, 2009. Available at: http://abcnews.go.com/Politics/story?id=7268063&page=1.

2. Kurt Steiner, "Negotiations for an Austrian State Treaty," in Alexander L. George, Philip J. Farley, and Alexander Dallin, eds., *US-Soviet Security Cooperation: Achievements, Failures, Lessons* (New York: Oxford University Press, 1988): 53.

3. Ibid., 68.

4. Quoted in ibid., 76.

5. James E. Goodby, "Looking Back at the Reykjavik Summit," *Arms Control Today,* September 2006. Available at: http://www.armscontrol.org/act/2006_09/Lookingback.

6. Quoted in Fen Osler Hampson, *Unguided Missiles: How America Buys Its Weapons* (New York: W.W. Norton, 1989): 245.

7. President Ronald R. Reagan, "Address to a Meeting of the National Association of Evangelicals," Orlando, Florida. March 8, 1983. Available at: http://www.nationalcenter.org/ReaganEvilEmpire1983.html.

8. Goodby, "Looking Back."

9. Quoted in Hampson, *Unguided Missiles,* 263.

10. Goodby, "Looking Back."

11. Abraham D. Sofaer, "A Legacy of Reykjavik: Negotiating with Enemies," in Sidney Drell and George Shultz, eds., *Implications of the Reykjavik Summit on Its*

Twentieth Anniversary: Conference Report (Stanford, CA: Hoover Institution Press, 2007): 135–36.

12. Barack Obama, Interview on Al-Arabiya Television, Washington, DC, January 26, 2009. Available at: http://www.presidentialrhetoric.com/speeches/01.26.09 .html.

Chapter 8

1. Alexis de Tocqueville, *Democracy in America* (New York: Doubleday, 1969): 517.

2. George H. W. Bush, "Address to the Nation on the Invasion of Iraq," delivered January 16, 1991. Available at: http://www.americanrhetoric.com/speeches/ ghwbushiraqinvasion.htm.

3. The discussion in this section draws on the arguments about effective mediation strategies, the reasons for engagement, and mediation "readiness" in Chester A. Crocker, Fen Osler Hampson, and Pamela Aall, *Taming Intractable Conflicts: Mediation in the Hardest Cases* (Washington, DC: United States Institute of Peace Press, 2002).

4. Harold H. Saunders, *Politics Is About Relationship: A Blueprint for the Citizens' Century* (New York: Palgrave Macmillan, 2005): 144.

Chapter 9

1. Doris Kearns Goodwin, *Team of Rivals: The Political Genius of Abraham Lincoln* (New York: Simon and Schuster, 2005).

2. Thomas C. Schelling, *Strategy of Conflict* (Cambridge: Harvard University Press, 1981): 31.

Chapter 10

1. See Center for Strategic and International Studies, *Smart Power Initiative* (Washington, DC: CSIS, 2009).

2. Statement of Senator Hillary Rodham Clinton, Nominee for Secretary of State, Senate Foreign Relations Committee, January 13, 2009. Available at: http://www .america.gov/st/texttrans-english/2009/January/20090113174107eaifas0.6630213 .html.

3. Richard Neustadt, *Alliance Politics*. (New York: Columbia University Press, 1970): 2.

4. Thomas L. Friedman, "Superbroke, Superfrugal, Superpower?" *New York Times,* September 4, 2010. Available at: http://www.nytimes.com/2010/09/05/ opinion/05friedman.html.

5. Quoted in James Blitz and Daniel Dombey, "Uncertain Destination," *Financial Times,* November 17, 2010: 9.

6. Ibid. As Blitz and Dombey also argue this includes a greater role for Europe in policing its own "back yard."

7. Sir Nicholas Bayne, "The G8's Past Performance, Present Prospects, Future Potential," *The Kyushu-Okinawa Summit: A G8-Developing Country Dialogue,* July 17, 2000, United Nations University, Tokyo. Available at: http://www.g8.utoronto.ca/scholar/bayne20000713.

8. Brad Glosserman, rapporteur, "Japan-U.S. Security Relations: A Testing Time for the Alliance," Pacific Forum, Center for Strategic and International Studies, Vol. 9, No. 14 (March 2009). Available at: http://www.docstoc.com/docs/49872577/Japan-US-Security-Relations-A-Testing-Time-for-the-Alliance.

Chapter 11

1. Strobe Talbott, *The Great Experiment: The Story of Ancient Empires, Modern States, and the Quest for a Global Nation* (New York: Simon and Schuster, 2008).

2. Chester A. Crocker, Fen Osler Hampson, and Pamela Aall, "Collective Conflict Management: A New Formula for Global Peace and Security Cooperation?" *International Affairs* 97 (1) (2011): 6.

3. G. John Ikenberry, "Liberal Internationalism 3.0: America and the Dilemmas of Liberal World Order," *Perspectives on Politics* 7 (1) (2009): 71–87.

4. Henry Chu, Jim Puzzanghera, and Paul Richter, "G-20 Summit Surprises with a Show of Unity," *Los Angeles Times,* April 3, 2009. Available at: http://articles.latimes.com/2009/apr/03/world/fg-g20-summit3.

5. Robert I. Rotberg, "Combating Maritime Piracy," Policy Brief 11 (Boston: World Peace Foundation, January 26, 2010). Available at: http://www.worldpeacefoundation.org/WPF_Piracy_PolicyBrief_11.pdf.

6. Proliferation Security Initiative, US Department of State. Available at: http://www.state.gov/t/isn/c10390.htm.

7. "Obama Supports Initiative Combating Nuclear Terrorism: Effort Now Has the Support of 75 Nations," America.gov Archive, June 30, 2009. Available at: http://www.america.gov/st/texttrans-english/2009/June/20090630111842xjsnommis0.7028009.html.

8. For a further discussion of this phenomenon, see Crocker, Hampson, and Aall, "Collective Conflict Management."

Chapter 12

1. The following excerpts of Thucydides's account of the "Melian Dialogue" appears in Heinz Waelchli and Dhavan Shah, "Crisis Negotiations Between Unequals: Lessons from a Classic Dialogue," *Negotiation Journal* 10 (2) (1992): 129–46. For other analyses, also see James V. Morrison, "Historical Lessons in the Melian Episode," *Transactions of the American Philological Association* 130 (2000): 119–48; and Michael G. Seaman, "The Athenian Expedition to Melos in 416 B.C.," *Historia: Zeitschrift für Alte Geschichte* 46 (4) (1997): 385–418.

2. See Paul Kennedy, *The Rise and Fall of the Great Powers* (New York: Vintage, 1989).

3. See, for example, Aaron Friedberg, *The Weary Titan: Britain and the Experience of Relative Decline, 1895–1905* (Princeton, NJ: Princeton University Press, 1989).

4. Ibid. The term is used by Aaron Friedberg to describe Britain's decline prior to World War I.

⮵

Suggestions for Further Reading

Further Readings for Chapter 1

Allison, Graham T., and Philip Zelikow. *Essence of Decision: Explaining the Cuban Missile Crisis*. 2nd edition. New York: Longman, 1999.

Allison, Roy. "Russia Resurgent? Moscow's Campaign to 'Coerce Georgia to Peace.'" *International Affairs* 84 (6) (2008): 1145–71.

Antonenko, Oksana. "A War with No Winners." *Survival* 50 (5) (2008): 23–36.

Asmus, Ronald. *A Little War That Shook the World: Georgia, Russia, and the Future of the West*. New York: Palgrave Macmillan, 2010.

Blight, James G., and David A. Welch. *On the Brink: Americans and Soviets Reexamine the Cuban Missile Crisis*. 2nd edition. New York: Noonday, 1990.

Bundy, McGeorge. *Danger and Survival: Decisions About the Bomb in the First Fifty Years*. New York: Random House, 1988.

Garthoff, Raymond L. *Reflections on the Cuban Missile Crisis*. Washington, DC: The Brookings Institution, 1989.

Hampson, Fen Osler. "The Divided Decision-Maker: American Domestic Politics and the Cuban Crises." *International Security* 9 (3) (Winter 1984–85): 130–65.

Kennedy, Robert. *Thirteen Days: A Memoir of the Cuban Missile Crisis*. New York: W. W. Norton, 2000.

Lebow, Richard Ned, and Janice Stein. *We All Lost the Cold War*. Princeton, NJ: Princeton University Press, 1994.

Nash, Philip. "Nuisance of Decision: Jupiter Missiles and the Cuban Missile Crisis." *The Journal of Strategic Studies* 14 (1) (1991): 1–26.

Pious, Richard M. "The Cuban Missile Crisis and the Limits of Crisis Management." *Political Science Quarterly* 116 (1) (2001): 81–105.

Rumer, Eugene, and Angela Stent. "Russia and the West." *Survival* 51 (2) (2009): 91–104.

Ury, William L., and Richard Smoke. "Anatomy of a Crisis." *Negotiation Journal* 1 (1) (1985): 93–100.

Further Readings for Chapters 2 and 4

Albright, Madeleine. *Madam Secretary.* New York: Hyperion, 2003.

Baker, James. *The Politics of Diplomacy: Revolution, War and Peace, 1989–1992.* New York: G. P. Putnam's Sons, 1995.

Carter, Jimmy. *Keeping Faith: Memoirs of a President.* Toronto: Bantam Books, 1982.

Christopher, Warren. *Chances of a Lifetime.* New York: Scribner, 2001.

———. *In the Stream of History: Shaping Foreign Policy for a New Era.* Stanford: Stanford University Press, 1998.

Clinton, Bill. *My Life.* New York: Alfred A. Knopf, 2004.

Cooley, John K. *Alliance Against Babylon: The US, Israel and Iraq.* London: Pluto Press, 2005.

———. "Pre-War Gulf Diplomacy." *Survival* 33 (2) (1991): 125–139.

Corbin, Jane. *The Norway Channel: The Secret Talks That Led to the Middle East Peace Accord.* New York: Atlantic Monthly Press, 1994.

Freedman, Lawrence D., and Efraim Karsh. *The Gulf Conflict, 1990–1991: Diplomacy and War in the New World Order.* Princeton, NJ: Princeton University Press, 1993.

Hiltermann, Joost. *A Poisonous Affair: America, Iraq, and the Gassing of Halabja.* New York: Cambridge University Press, 2007.

Hinnebusch, Raymond A. "Does Syria Want Peace? Syrian Policy in the Syrian-Israeli Peace Negotiations." *Journal of Palestine Studies* 26 (1) (1996): 42–57.

Jentleson, Bruce W. *With Friends Like These: Reagan, Bush, and Saddam 1982–1990.* New York: W. W. Norton, 1994.

Kurtzer, Daniel C., and Scott B. Lasensky. *Negotiating Arab-Israeli Peace: American Leadership in the Middle East.* Washington, DC: United States Institute of Peace, 2008.

Parker, Richard B. *The Politics of Miscalculation in the Middle East.* Bloomington: Indiana University Press, 1993.

Pressman, Jeremy. "Visions in Collision: What Happened at Camp David and Taba?" *International Security* 28 (2) (2003): 5–43.

Quandt, William. *Peace Process: American Diplomacy and the Arab-Israeli Conflict Since 1967.* 3rd edition. Washington, DC: Brookings Institution Press, 2005.

Rezun, Miron. *Saddam Hussein's Gulf Wars: Ambivalent Stakes in the Middle East.* Westport, CT: Praeger Publishers, 1992.

Ross, Dennis. *The Missing Peace: The Inside Story of the Fight for Middle East Peace.* New York: Farrar, Straus, and Giroux, 2005.

———. *Statecraft and How to Restore America's Standing in the World.* New York: Farrar, Straus, and Giroux, 2007.

Slater, Jerome. "Lost Opportunities for Peace in the Arab-Israeli Conflict: Israel and Syria, 1948–2001." *International Security* 27 (1) (2002): 79–106.

Stein, Janice Gross. "Deterrence and Compellence in the Gulf, 1990–91: A Failed or Impossible Task?" *International Security* 17 (2) (1992): 147–79.

———. "Structures, Strategies, and Tactics of Mediation: Kissinger and Carter in the Middle East." *Negotiation Journal* 1 (4) (1985): 331–47.

Wanis-St. John, Anthony. "Back Channel Negotiation: International Bargaining in the Shadows." *Negotiation Journal* 22 (2) (2006): 119–44.

Wheeler, Michael. "Fighting the Wimp Image: Why Calls for Negotiation Often Fall on Deaf Ears." *Negotiation Journal* 8 (1) (1992): 25–30.

Further Readings for Chapter 3

Azar, Edward E., and John W. Burton, eds. *International Conflict Resolution: Theory and Practice.* Sussex, UK: Wheatsheaf Books, 1986.

Bazerman, Max H., Jared R. Curhan, Don A. Moore, and Kathleen L. Valley. "Negotiation." *Annual Review of Psychology* 51 (2000): 279–314.

Bercovitch, Jacob, Victor Kremenyuk, and I. William Zartman, eds. *The Sage Handbook of Conflict Resolution.* Thousand Oaks, CA: Sage Publications, 2009.

Blount, Sally, and Margaret Neale. "Reservation Prices, Resistance Points, and BATNAs: Determining the Parameters of Acceptable Negotiated Outcomes." *Negotiation Journal* 7 (4) (1991): 379–88.

Carnevale, Peter J., and Dean G. Pruitt. "Negotiation and Mediation." *Annual Review of Psychology* 43 (1992): 531–82.

Crocker, Chester A., Fen Osler Hampson, and Pamela Aall, eds. *Herding Cats: Multiparty Mediation in a Complex World.* Washington, DC: United States Institute of Peace Press, 1999.

———. *Taming Intractable Conflicts: Mediation in the Hardest Cases.* Washington, DC: United States Institute of Peace Press, 2002.

Fisher, Roger, and Daniel Shapiro. *Beyond Reason: Using Emotions as You Negotiate.* New York: Viking Press, 2005.

Fisher, Roger and William Ury. *Getting to Yes: Negotiating Agreement Without Giving In.* New York: Penguin Books, 1991.

Hopmann, P. Terrence. *The Negotiation Process and the Resolution of International Conflicts.* Columbia: University of South Carolina Press, 1996.

———. "Two Paradigms of Negotiation Bargaining and Problem Solving." *The Annals of the American Academy of Political and Social Science* 542 (1) (1995): 24–47.

Kremenyuk, Victor, ed. *International Negotiation: Analysis, Approaches, Issues.* San Francisco: Jossey-Bass, 2002.

Malhotra, Deepak, and Max H. Bazerman. *Negotiation Genius.* New York: Bantam, 2007.

Saunders, Harold. "We Need a Larger Theory of Negotiation: The Importance of Pre-Negotiating Phases." *Negotiation Journal* 1 (3) (1985): 249–62.

Watkins, Michael, and Susan Rosegrant. "Breakthrough International Negotiation: How Great Negotiators Transformed the World's Toughest Post-Cold War Conflicts." *International Journal of Conflict Management* 13 (1) (1993): 95–104.

Further Readings for Chapters 5 and 8

Attyas, Nimet Beriker. "Mediating Regional Conflicts and Negotiating Flexibility: Peace Efforts in Bosnia-Herzegovina." *The Annals of the American Academy of Political and Social Science* 542 (1) (1995): 185–201.

Brooks, Sean. "Enforcing a Turning Point and Imposing a Deal: An Analysis of the Darfur Abuja Negotiations of 2006." *International Negotiation* 13 (3) (2008): 413–40.

Caplan, Richard. "International Diplomacy and the Crisis in Kosovo." *International Affairs* 74 (4) (1998): 745–61.

Crocker, Chester A., Fen Osler Hampson, and Pamela Aall, eds. *Grasping the Nettle: Analyzing Cases of Intractable Conflict.* Washington, DC: United States Institute of Peace Press, 2005.

Curran, Daniel, James K. Sebenius, and Michael Watkins. "Two Paths to Peace: Contrasting George Mitchell in Northern Ireland with Richard Holbrooke in Bosnia-Herzegovina." *Negotiation Journal* 20 (4) (2004): 513–37.

Gaillard, Jean-Christophe, Elsa Clavé, and Ilan Kelman. "Wave of Peace? Tsunami Disaster Diplomacy in Aceh, Indonesia." *Geoforum* 39 (1) (2008): 511–26.

Ganguly, Rajat. "Sri Lanka's Ethnic Conflict: At a Crossroad Between Peace and War." *Third World Quarterly* 25 (5) (2004): 903–18.

Gibran, Daniel K. *The Falklands War: Britain Versus the Past in the South Atlantic.* Jefferson, NC: McFarland & Company, Inc., 1998.

Höglund, Kristine, and Isak Svensson. "The Peace Process in Sri Lanka." *Civil Wars* 5 (4) (2002): 103–18.

Holbrooke, Richard. *To End a War.* New York: Random House, 1998.

Jensen, Lloyd. "Negotiations and Power Asymmetries: The Cases of Bosnia, Northern Ireland and Sri Lanka." *International Negotiation* 2 (1) (1997): 21–41.

———. "Issue Flexibility in Negotiating Internal War." *The Annals of the American Academy of Political and Social Science* 542 (1) (1995): 116–30.

Kaufman, Stuart. "The Irresistible Force and the Imperceptible Object: The Yugoslav Breakup and Western Policy." *Security Studies* 4 (2) (1994): 281–329.

Leary, Kimberlyn. "Critical Moments as Relational Moments: The Centre for Humanitarian Dialogue and the Conflict in Aceh, Indonesia." *Negotiation Journal* 20 (2) (2004): 311–38.

Lieberfeld, Daniel. *Talking with the Enemy: Negotiation and Threat Perception in South Africa and Israel/Palestine.* Westport, CT: Praeger Publishers, 1999.

Mitchell, George. *Making Peace.* New York: Knopf, 1999.

Morfit, Michael. "The Road to Helsinki: The Aceh Agreement and Indonesia's Democratic Development." *International Negotiation* 12 (1) (2007): 111–43.

Saunders, Harold. *A Public Peace Process: Sustained Dialogue to Transform Racial and Ethnic Conflicts.* New York: St. Martin's Press, 1999.

———. "Sustained Dialogue in Managing Intractable Conflict." *Negotiation Journal* 19 (1) (2003): 85–95.

Schulze, Kirsten E. "From the Battlefield to the Negotiating Table: GAM and the Indonesian Government 1999–2005." *Asian Security* 3 (2) (2007): 80–98.

———. "The Struggle for an Independent Aceh: The Ideology, Capacity, and Strategy of GAM." *Studies in Conflict and Terrorism* 26 (4) (2003): 241–71.

Uyangoda, Jayadeva. "Ethnic Conflict, the State and the Tsunami Disaster in Sri Lanka." *Inter-Asia Cultural Studies* 6 (3) (2005): 341–52.

Weller, Marc. "The Rambouillet Conference on Kosovo." *International Affairs* 75 (2) (1999): 211–51.

Zartman, I. William. "The Timing of Peace Initiatives: Hurting Stalemates and Ripe Moments." *Ethnopolitics* 1 (1) (2001): 8–18.

———, ed. *Elusive Peace: Negotiating an End to Civil Wars.* Washington, DC: The Brookings Institution, 1995.

Further Readings for Chapter 6

Ansari, Ali M. *Confronting Iran: The Failure of American Foreign Policy and the Next Great Crisis in the Middle East.* New York: Basic Books, 2006.

Collins, Alan R. "GRIT, Gorbachev and the End of the Cold War." *Review of International Studies* 24 (2) (1998): 201–19.

Dobbins, James. "Negotiating with Iran: Testimony Presented Before the House Committee on Oversight and Government Reform, Subcommittee on National Security and Foreign Affairs on November 7, 2007." Santa Monica, CA: RAND Corporation, 2007. http://www.rand.org/pubs/testimonies/2007/RAND_CT293.pdf.

Druckman, Daniel, Jo L. Husbands, and Karin Johnston. "Turning Points in the INF Negotiations." *Negotiation Journal* 7 (1) (1991): 55–67.

Dueck, Colin, and Ray Takeyh. "Iran's Nuclear Challenge." *Political Science Quarterly* 122 (2) (2007): 189–205.

Garthoff, Raymond L. *The Great Transition: American-Soviet Relations at the End of the Cold War.* Washington, DC: The Brookings Institution, 1994.

Hutchings, Robert L. *American Diplomacy and the End of the Cold War: An Insider's Account of U.S. Policy in Europe, 1982–1992.* Baltimore: The Johns Hopkins University Press, 1997.

Limbert, John W. *Negotiating with Iran: Wrestling the Ghosts of History.* Washington DC: United States Institute of Peace Press, 2009.

Matlock, Jack F., Jr. *Reagan and Gorbachev: How the Cold War Ended.* New York: Random House, 2004.

Morris, Edmund. *Dutch: A Memoir of Ronald Reagan.* New York: Random House, 1999.

Reagan, Ronald. *An American Life.* New York: Simon and Schuster, 1990.

Risse-Kappen, Thomas. "Did 'Peace Through Strength' End the Cold War? Lessons from INF." *International Security* 16 (1) (1991): 162–88.

Savranskaya, Svetlana, and Thomas Blanton, eds. *The Reykjavik File: Previously Secret Documents from U.S. and Soviet Archives on the 1986 Reagan-Gorbachev Summit.* National Security Archive Briefing Book No. 203. Washington, DC: George Washington University, 2006. http://www.gwu.edu/~nsarchiv/NSAEBB/NSAEBB203/index.htm.

Shultz, George P. *Turmoil and Triumph: My Years as Secretary of State.* New York: Charles Scribner's Sons, 1993.

Sofaer, Abraham D. "A Legacy of Reykjavik: Negotiating with Enemies." In Sidney Drell and George Shultz, eds., *Implications of the Reykjavik Summit on its Twentieth Anniversary: Conference Report.* Stanford, CA: Hoover Institution Press, 2007.

Takeyh, Ray. *Hidden Iran: Paradox and Power in the Islamic Republic.* New York: Henry Holt and Company, 2007.

Further Readings for Chapter 7

Bapat, Navin A. "State Bargaining with Transnational Terrorist Groups." *International Studies Quarterly* 50 (1) (2006): 213–30.

Clutterbuck, Richard. "Negotiating with Terrorists." *Terrorism and Political Violence* 4 (4) (1992): 263–87.

Faure, Guy Olivier. "Negotiating with Terrorists: The Hostage Case." *International Negotiation* 8 (3) (2003): 469–94.

Faure, Guy Olivier, and I. William Zartman, eds. *Negotiating with Terrorists: Strategy, Tactics, and Politics.* London: Routledge, 2010.

Pruitt, Dean G. "Negotiation with Terrorists." *International Negotiation* 11 (2) (2006): 371–94.

Reiss, Mitchell B. *Negotiating with Evil: When to Talk to Terrorists.* Kindle edition. New York: Open Road, 2010.

Spector, Bertram I. "Negotiating with Villains Revisited: Research Note." *International Negotiation* 8 (3) (2003): 613–21.

Zartman, I. William, and Guy Olivier Faure, eds. *Engaging Extremists: Trade Offs, Timing, and Diplomacy.* Washington, DC: United States Institute of Peace Press, 2001.

Further Readings for Chapter 9

Brown, MacAlister, and Joseph Jeremiah Zasloff. *Cambodia Confounds the Peacemakers 1979–1999.* Ithaca, NY: Cornell University Press, 1998.

Choo, Jaewoo. "Is Institutionalization of the Six-Party Talks Possible?" *East Asia* 22 (4) (2005): 39–58.

Crocker, Chester A., Fen Osler Hampson, and Pamela Aall, eds. *Herding Cats: Multiparty Mediation in a Complex World.* Washington, DC: United States Institute of Peace Press, 1999.

———. "Ready for Prime Time: The When, Who, and Why of International Mediation." *Negotiation Journal* 19 (2) (2003): 151–67.

Koh, Tommy T. B. "The Paris Conference on Cambodia: A Multilateral Negotiation That 'Failed.'" *Negotiation Journal* 6 (1) (1990): 81–7.

Lee, Jung-hoon, and Chung-in Moon. "The North Korean Nuclear Crisis Revisited: The Case for a Negotiated Settlement." *Security Dialogue* 34 (2) (2003): 135–51.

Moltz, James Clay, and C. Kenneth Quinones. "Getting Serious About a Multilateral Approach to North Korea." *The Nonproliferation Review* 11 (1) (2004): 136–44.

O'Hanlon, Michael, and Mike Mochizuki. *Crisis on the Korean Peninsula: How to Deal with a Nuclear North Korea.* New York: McGraw-Hill, 2003.

———. "Toward a Grand Bargain with North Korea." *The Washington Quarterly* 26 (4) (2003): 5–18.

Park, John S. "Inside Multilateralism: The Six-Party Talks." *The Washington Quarterly* 28 (4) (2005): 73–91.

Pollack, Jonathan D. "The United States, North Korea, and the End of the Agreed Framework." *Naval War College Review* 56 (3) (2003): 11–49.

Poneman, Daniel, Joel S. Wit, and Robert L. Gallucci. *Going Critical: The First North Korean Nuclear Crisis.* Washington DC: Brookings Institution Press, 2004.

Pritchard, Charles L. *Failed Diplomacy: The Tragic Story of How North Korea Got the Bomb.* Washington, DC: Brookings Institution Press, 2007.

Ratner, Steven R. "The Cambodia Settlement Agreements." *American Journal of International Law* 87 (1) (1993): 1–41.

Ross, Robert S. "China and the Cambodian Peace Process: The Value of Coercive Diplomacy." *Asian Survey* 31 (12) (1991): 1170–85.

Rupp, Richard E. "Cooperation, International Organizations, and Multilateral

Interventions in the Post–Cold War Era: Lessons Learned from the Gulf War, the Balkans, Somalia, and Cambodia." *UCLA Journal of International Law and Foreign Affairs* 3 (1998): 183–222.

Sigal, Leon V. *Disarming Strangers: Nuclear Diplomacy with North Korea.* Princeton, NJ: Princeton University Press, 1998.

Snyder, Scott. *Negotiating on the Edge: North Korean Negotiating Behaviour.* Washington, DC: United States Institute of Peace Press, 1999.

Solomon, Richard H. *Exiting Cambodia: US Leadership of the Cambodia Settlement and Normalization with Vietnam.* Washington, DC: United States Institute of Peace Press, 2002.

Touval, Saadia. "Multilateral Negotiation: An Analytical Approach." *Negotiation Journal* 5 (2) (1989): 159–73.

Further Readings for Chapters 10 and 11

Byers, Michael. "Policing the High Seas: The Proliferation Security Initiative." *The American Journal of International Law* 98 (3) (2004): 526–45.

Hampson, Fen Osler. *Multilateral Negotiations: Lessons from Arms Control, Trade, and the Environment.* Baltimore and London: The Johns Hopkins University Press, 1995.

Kraska, James, and Brian Wilson. "Fighting Pirates: The Pen and the Sword." *World Policy Journal* 25 (4) (2008): 41–52.

Pinto, Ligia M., and Glenn W. Harrison. "Multilateral Negotiations over Climate Change Policy." *Journal of Policy Modeling* 25 (9) (2003): 911–30.

Sebenius, James K. "Designing Negotiations Toward a New Regime: The Case of Global Warming." *International Security* 15 (4) (1991): 110–48.

Whalley, John, and Sean Walsh. "Bringing the Copenhagen Global Climate Change Negotiations to Conclusion." *CESifo Economic Studies* 55 (2) (2009): 255–85.

Further Readings for Chapter 12

Friedberg, Aaron. *The Weary Titan: Britain and the Experience of Relative Decline, 1895–1905.* Princeton, NJ: Princeton University Press, 1989.

Kennedy, Paul. *The Rise and Fall of the Great Powers.* New York: Vintage, 1989.

Morrison, James V. "Historical Lessons in the Melian Episode," *Transactions of the American Philological Association* 130 (2000): 119–48.

Seaman, Michael G., "The Athenian Expedition to Melos in 416 B.C." *Historia: Zeitschrift für Alte Geschichte* 46 (4) (1997): 385–418.

Waelcgli, Heinz, and Dhavan Shah. "Crisis Negotiations Between Unequals: Lessons from a Classic Dialogue." *Negotiation Journal* 10 (2) (1992): 129–46.

Further General Readings

Art, Robert J., and Patrick M. Cronin, eds. *The United States and Coercive Diplomacy.* Washington, DC: The United States Institute of Peace Press, 2003.

Brett, Jeanne M., Wendi Adair, Alain Lempereur, Tetsushi Okumura, Peter Shikhirev,

Catherine Tinsley, and Anne Lytle. "Culture and Joint Gains in Negotiation." *Negotiation Journal* 14 (1) (1998): 61–86.

Jentleson, Bruce, ed. *Opportunities Missed, Opportunities Seized: Preventative Diplomacy in the Post–Cold War World.* Lanham, MD: Rowman & Littlefield Publishers, Inc., 2000.

Kissinger, Henry. *White House Years.* Boston: Little, Brown, 1979.

———. *Years of Renewal.* New York: Simon and Schuster, 1999.

———. *Years of Upheaval.* Boston: Little, Brown, 1982.

Nincic, Miroslav. "Getting What You Want: Positive Inducements in International Relations." *International Security* 35 (1) (2010): 138–83.

Rubin, Jeffrey Z., and I. William Zartman. "Asymmetrical Negotiations: Some Survey Results That May Surprise." *Negotiation Journal* 11 (4) (1995): 349–64.

Stein, Janice Gross. "Getting to the Table: Processes of International Prenegotiation." *International Journal* 44 (2) (1989): 231–36.

Zartman, I. William. *The Practical Negotiator.* New Haven: Yale University Press, 1982.

———. *Elusive Peace: Negotiating an End to Civil Wars.* Washington, DC: The Brookings Institution, 1995.

———. *Negotiation and Conflict Management: Essays on Theory and Practice.* London: Routledge, 2009.

———. *Cowardly Lions: Missed Opportunities to Prevent Deadly Conflict and State Collapse.* Boulder, CO: Lynne Rienner, 2005.

———. *Preventive Negotiation: Avoiding Conflict Escalation.* Lanham, MD: Rowman and Littlefield for the Carnegie Commission on Preventing Deadly Conflict, 2001.

———. *The 50% Solution.* New Haven: Yale University Press, 1976.

INDEX

About the Authors

Fen Osler Hampson is the Chancellor's Professor and Director of The Norman Paterson School of International Affairs (NPSIA), Carleton University, Ottawa, Canada. He holds a Ph.D. from Harvard University where he also received his A.M. degree. He also holds an MSc. (Econ.) degree (with distinction) from the London School of Economics and a B.A. (Hon.) from the University of Toronto. Dr. Hampson is the author/co-author of nine books and editor/co-editor of more than twenty-five other volumes. In addition, he is the author of almost 100 articles and book chapters on international affairs. His books include *Canada's International Policies* (co-authored with Brian Tomlin and Norman Hillmer) and *Taming Intractable Conflicts: Mediation in the Hardest Cases* (with Chester A. Crocker and Pamela Aall). Dr. Hampson is a frequent commentator and contributor to the national and international media. His articles have appeared in the *Washington Post,* the *National Post,* the *Globe and Mail, Foreign Policy Magazine,* the *Ottawa Citizen,* and elsewhere. He is a frequent commentator on the CBC, CTV, and Global news networks.

I. William Zartman is the Jacob Blaustein Professor Emeritus at the School of Advanced International Studies (SAIS) of The Johns Hopkins University in Washington, and member of the Steering Committee of the Processes of International Negotiation (PIN) Program at Clingendael. His doctorate is from Yale (1956) and his honorary doctorate from Louvain (1997), and he received a lifetime achievement award from the International Association for Conflict Management. He is author of a number of books, including *Negotiation and Conflict Management, The Practical Negotiator, Ripe for Resolution,* and *Cowardly Lions: Missed Opportunities to Prevent Deadly Conflict and State Collapse.* He is also president of the Tangier American Legation Institute for Moroccan Studies (TALIM), and was founding president of the American Institute for Maghrib Studies and past president of the Middle East Studies Association.